AF413424

I'M
A
LOT

I'M A LOT

Surviving Myself and All the People I've Been

ALISON LEIBY

The Dial Press
New York

The Dial Press
An imprint of Random House
A division of Penguin Random House LLC
1745 Broadway, New York, NY 10019
randomhousebooks.com
penguinrandomhouse.com

Hardcover ISBN 9780593731628
Ebook ISBN 9780593731635

Printed in the United States of America

1st Printing

First Edition

BOOK TEAM: Production editor: Annette Szlachta • Managing editor: Rebecca Berlant • Production manager: Sandra Sjursen • Copy editor: Hasan Altaf • Proofreaders: Dan Janeck, Hope Clarke, Diana D'Abruzzo

Book design by Alissa Rose Theodor

The authorized representative in the EU for product safety and compliance is Penguin Random House Ireland, Morrison Chambers, 32 Nassau Street, Dublin D02 YH68, Ireland. https://eu-contact.penguin.ie

For my parents. Thank you for all of your love and
support. I'm sure we'll have plenty to talk about
when you finish reading.

I still only travel by foot and by foot it's a slow climb
But I'm good at being uncomfortable so
I can't stop changing all the time
—Fiona Apple, "Extraordinary Machine"

"No, I mentioned the bisque."
—Elaine Benes

CONTENTS

INTRODUCTION

■ ■ ■

I was miserable at my grandfather's shiva.

It wasn't that I was overly devastated by his passing. Of course I loved him, but I was so young that I didn't exactly know him well enough to grieve. When he got sick, I was still riding a tricycle, and when he died, I was still begging my mom to let me wear lip gloss. So in my adolescent brain, this funeral was (like almost everything in my life) deeply about me.

I spent the entire time doing two of my favorite things: eating New Jersey's finest deli and talking to New Jersey's funniest old Jews. Good rye and good wry. Certainly death is sad, but this was more a celebration of life, and I should have been able to embrace that. It wasn't quite that easy, because every single person at that service opened our conversation with the same devastating sentence.

"You're the swimmer!"

The thing is, I *was* the swimmer. Swimming was the thing I spent the most time doing, talking about, and thinking about. It was the thing my grandmother bragged about at mah-jongg games, how I swam in national meets and won medals and practiced hard and traveled to exotic places like Princeton and Buffalo. But as of that month, I had made the gut-wrenching decision to walk away from my yearslong competitive swimming career (lol "career"). I was about to push off from the starting block for the last time and suddenly needed to find an entirely new identity, and every David, Shirley, and Saul in the tristate area was gripping my forearm too tight and calling me the thing I was about to no longer be.

What made that funeral so difficult—besides pacing myself on the rugelach and, of course, the actual death—was that I had built an entire identity around one thing (swimming), and then that thing (swimming) had to end and I was utterly lost (not swimming). The way I saw myself and the way I wanted others to see me was disappearing, so I had to find a new person to be in the world. Thankfully, not long after, I discovered the sport of rowing and quickly built my entire persona around that. But when my rowing career was cut short by a back injury, I had to find yet another person to be. And that is what I've done for most of my life, consciously or not, because I think that's what we all feel pressured to do on some level: define ourselves again and again.

I think about myself a lot. That doesn't mean I necessarily imagine I'm some kind of unicorn like Zoë Kravitz meets Martha Stewart meets a competition-winning borzoi (those dogs have *no* buccal fat). I just mean that I think about who I am to the world around me a lot. Sometimes I consciously do it, like when I'm posting about my seemingly glamorous career on Instagram or picking out the perfect jeans and sweater to wear while performing stand-up so I look easy-breezy and casual to the group of people who don't care about Khaite and look rich and cool as hell to the people who do. Sometimes I project who I am with less meticulous attention or careful concealment. The second anything even resembling conflict comes up, I cower and avoid in a way that screams to the world, "I am an only child and I do NOT know how to do this!!!!!"

And sometimes my identity is reflected right back at me to consider, like when I once saw a woman whom I refer to as Alison 2.0 in a coffee shop. She was exactly like me on paper but just 10 percent better in literally every way. She was a little thinner, her hair was a little shinier, her clothes were a little nicer. I hope she's dead now. JK! I'm sure she's living a slightly better life than I am in a two-bedroom apartment. But at least I hope we never run into each other again so I'm not face-to-face with my own shortcomings over an iced Americano.

I've spent most of my life loudly defining myself by whatever was happening to me currently—my job or my passion or my struggle of the moment. It's as if I have to grasp on to one defining thing and broadcast it as my identity to the world or I'll melt into a meaningless puddle. Until the next thing comes along.

Part of my obsession with how I think of myself comes from almost dying when I was nineteen and then being in and out of chronic pain for most of my life. The combination of cheating death and regularly masking your misery is the peanut butter and chocolate of needing to create a version of yourself for the rest of the world. I don't want you to feel burdened by my physical torture, so here's a fun personality costume. It's me, the person who always shows up to the party with the best natural wine, not your friend who has a hard time sitting in certain chairs!

Chronic pain takes up so much space in your mind, it touches every corner of who you are, inside and out. It has governed so much of my life that this book could easily have just been about that. But living in pain also forces you to find the other aspects of yourself that you can broadcast to the world, lest you be seen as someone "in pain" and thus a massive bummer.

Another reason for my obsession with how I see myself is that I'm a woman. Women spend so much of our lives needing to identify ourselves as a certain *kind* of woman. Are you a Carrie? A Charlotte? A Miranda? A Samantha? And if you're a Samantha, are you a sex-positive publicist who loves jewel-tone suits, or are you a Victorian child who wears bows and knee socks and is actually an overpriced doll?

Meredith Brooks wrote an entire song about this and used a litany of identifiers as lyrics before simply titling her song "Bitch." And I have to say, as some young people do, it still slaps. There is nothing more cathartic to scream-sing in a private-room karaoke after three gin martinis than Ms. Brooks's nineties anthem. And that song was not only a banger, but also a testament to the fact that women don't just have to claim their own identities: that we can have many of them, some that even feel opposites, all at the same time. I contain multitudes (and also lots of Diet Coke)!

I grew up taking quizzes in teen magazines, obsessively thinking about what I would do in hypothetical situations and hoping to learn what my prom style should be based on that (c'mon "sophisticated chic"!). My college years were dominated by the internet and tabloids, a brief period of looking out more than in when it came to my life. By my mid-twenties, I, like many of my peers, handed over the keys to my brain to social media, filtering everything I thought about myself through sepia tones and 140-character limits. In my thirties, I did the standard "adulthood" performance review, taking a look around me and seeing how my life was stacking up based on traditional markers: marriage, offspring. Now, in my forties, I am someone with no spouse or kids (complimentary) and a job that involves overthinking most things, and I find myself trying to make sense of who I was, who I am now, and who I still think I want to be.

I may not take teen-magazine quizzes anymore, but thanks to technology, I find myself searching for identities more than ever. Instagram and TikTok and whatever hellscape will follow force us to create, to *curate,* entire personalities for consumption. Sure, my Instagram feed is all stand-up shows and fancy meals, but my life offscreen is a lot of gray hairs and lying face down on the couch in the middle of the day. All those things are real, but I choose to be seen as a seafood tower and not a depression nap.

These days, I'm surprised to find that I'm claiming those "bad" identities and leaning into the parts of myself I spent a lot of time hiding. Those gray hairs and depression naps are part of who I am, just as my obsession with Bravo, my absolute disinterest in having children, and my debt-accumulating shopping problem that began with Loehmann's and has culminated with gathering quarters to buy seltzer at the bodega all are, too. I'm all those things, and I claim them now more loudly than I ever have. In embracing so many selves throughout my life, I've also suffered several identity crises, which include two instances of identity theft. When everyone was making banana bread and having Zoom hangs during the early-2020 Covid lockdowns, I was doing that, too, but while being on hold with Chase for eight hours a day so I could prove to them that I, shockingly, was not the person who spent all that money. Even my bank account has a sense of who it is.

So, for all of you, I have compiled a selection of all the mes. These are the people I have been, proudly or not, at different points in my life. They are the aspects of me that at times felt like the sum total of myself, some barely leaving breathing room for anything else. But they're all me, the good and the bad, the aspirational and the embarrassing, the productive and the inescapably debt-accruing (ahem, Loehmann's). They're all who I am.

I'M A LOT

I'M NOT DEAD

don't really celebrate my birthday.

It's not because I'm on some kind of high horse about being the center of attention (for one thing, I would *never* be on a horse). It's because my birthday is a few days before Christmas, and growing up, my birth got overshadowed by Jesus's. And I don't mean "the holidays," I mean Christmas specifically. Hanukkah has never overshadowed anything; in fact, it's the kind of holiday you can quickly celebrate when you get home from going out to dinner as long as someone stays awake for thirty-five minutes. But Christmas, with all its travel and family time, made it impossible for me to celebrate my own birthday. So instead, I throw an I'm Not Dead party.

Rather than celebrating the anniversary of my birth, I celebrate the anniversary of the time I didn't die. Technically, every day is that day, but I also have a more specific date that I honor every August. For many years, this entailed finding a bar in Lower Manhattan, hanging there with all my mismatched friends, and drinking way too many whiskey sodas with the occasional toasts to me not being dead. Sure, it's kind of macabre and depressing to some, but it's my party and I'll be a weird bummer if I want to!

I celebrate because when I was nineteen years old, I almost died from complications following my first back surgery. Different people use "almost died" in their own ways, but I want to be very clear: I was absolutely supposed to die, and it was only through a complete freak encounter that I was able to get treatment and survive. I know this not because I was super aware of the medical details of the ordeal, but because the few memories I do have are of doctors telling me I wasn't going to make it. And because in all my appointments after, I was talked to like a survivor. And not the Destiny's Child version of a survivor who's not gonna give up, who's gonna work harder. I was talked to like I had achieved something, somehow. Nurses would read my chart and say, "Wow, great job getting through that, you did it." Did what? I didn't save my own life. I didn't will my body to heal itself. "You've really been through something!" started to feel a bit like when a waiter tells you "Excellent choice" after you order a chicken Caesar salad. Complimentary but meaningless.

The summer after my freshman year at Cornell was set to be a great one for me. I'd had a stellar year on the rowing team as a recruit out of high school, I had a great group of friends I was eager to go back to, and I had landed on the incredibly lucrative major of English literature. Now I was back in my hometown and most of my high school friends were returning to Maryland for a few months to throw house parties and work outdoor jobs. Gone were my freewheeling nights of no curfews and ample keg beer with about as much carbonation as a pond. I was under my parents' roof, away from my college friends and dining hall of myriad brunch options. But I was excited to be home, see a few friends, train for the fall rowing season, and make a little bit of money that I could spend on a pair of Seven jeans with just the right wash to wear when I hit campus in August.

I was set up with the perfect summer gig: counselor for the U.S. Naval Academy girls' rowing camp. Four weeks with my best friend and high school coxswain making sure tween and teen girls didn't get in trouble on the campus of our country's most beautiful military college. Despite growing up minutes from the Naval Academy and rowing by it every day for four years, I've never been a fan. I grew up in a pretty liberal family with no military connection and spent my teens with zero interest in tucking in my shirt. Plus, I was grossed out when midshipmen* (Naval Academy students) were girls' dates at my prom. But I was willing to put my pacifism aside for free meals, a slumber party with my funniest friend, and basically getting paid to row for hours. My job was to do my favorite thing, and also to occasionally slip an embarrassed fourteen-year-old a tampon in the middle of lunch.

Rowing was all I wanted to do with my time. I loved it more than anything. Though it feels ridiculous to say I did anything for a "long" time before I turned fifteen, I had been swimming competitively for the majority of my life, and when I quit the team at the start of high school, I was in search of a new identity. While I loved the rhythm of it, swimming was an isolating endeavor, where I was alone amid the white noise of being underwater and in every win and every loss. Rowing, on the other (very calloused) hand, is a

---

* If you aren't familiar with midshipmen, just imagine a regular college sophomore who has a crew cut and a uniform, is possibly becoming a trained murderer for the state, and rarely sees girls. I'm not saying midshipmen are bad, but boy are they not the vibe you want when you're in a prom dress dancing to Nelly's "Hot in Herre."

team sport whose camaraderie transcends any group activity short of an orgy. The second I grabbed the gunwale of a fiberglass 8+, I was hooked.

Rowing in high school was one thing, but continuing in college was more than just a level up. I went from belonging to a rowing club outside of my high school to being handed hundreds of dollars of Cornell University Athletics merch to proudly wear on and off the water. We had trainers, we had nutritionists, we had more Big Red gear than Clifford. I was proud to wear my Cornell Rowing sweatshirt while I gently fell asleep in my medieval literature seminar. I loved "closing down" the dining hall with my teammates and best friends, on our fourth bowls of cereal after a full dinner while we scream-laughed to inside jokes that I couldn't explain even if I wanted to. Rowing was who I was on campus, and it was who I was when I returned home that summer.

But toward the end of the first month of camp, I started feeling pain in my back and legs. This wasn't new, really; back and leg pain is standard for a lot of rowers, along with having hands and heels that look like the inside of a nineties Coach bag. Rowing is tough on your back. Most people picture rowers just sitting in a boat facing forward, like you would in a kayak or a canoe, but you actually sit backward and have to strap your feet into shoes on a plank, and then you sit on a seat that moves back and forth on tracks. You use your legs, then your back, and then finally your arms to pull the oar back before you pop it out of the water and slowly glide back up to do it again thousands of times. So yes, my back had hurt before. I chalked this pain up to overdoing it with my all-day-every-day workout schedule, plus sleeping on a one-inch-thick foam mattress in a military dorm every night like a future nautical killing machine.

But the pain continued. Thank god my parents were still responsible for me (and I was still on their insurance). My mom insisted we make an appointment with an orthopedic doctor, which I was wary of but also looked forward to in a way. All of my medical experiences in life so far had involved a discrete problem with a clear solution. Until this point, if something was wrong with me medically, it got fixed. I broke my collarbone, they put me in a sling until it healed. I had trouble with my tonsils, they took them out and I was good to go. Wisdom teeth started coming in, we got those bad boys out of there and then I lost three pounds from not eating solids.

I assumed this time around would be no different. Maybe I'd get a shot or some high-level vitamins to take, and then I'd be pain-free. Plus, in my mind, my nineteen-year-old body was invincible. So I was expecting solutions, not major diagnoses, as my mom and I drove to the hospital in Annapolis, to the Sajak Pavilion. I learned a lot during this experience, but perhaps my greatest lesson was to be wary of doctors in medical complexes named after climate-change-denying game-show hosts. This was also my first time being in the waiting room of a doctor's office that wasn't geared toward me. Instead of the tween mags of my orthodontist or the *Highlights* and coloring books of my pediatrician, my new doctor favored issues of *Golf World*. There's an unsettling feeling about being not old enough to legally drink yet expected to entertain yourself with *AARP: The Magazine*.

My doctor looked at my MRI while I looked at his adult braces. It felt like we were both in the wrong era of our lives, medically speaking. He explained that I had a herniated disc between the L4 and L5 vertebrae in my lower back, and described how in between each of your bones there is a soft, cushiony disc of tissue that al-lows you to bend, as well as absorbs the shock of walking, running, biking, falling, basically any physical activity that causes impact. Over time, these discs can dry out, and can break or bulge, often ending up getting pushed back into your spinal column, the tube of nerves for your entire body. That was why I was feeling pain in my back that also radiated down through my legs, he told me. This typically happened with age, but I had degenerative disc disease, so my discs might herniate early and easily, and this one seemed to be the first to go.

He explained that surgery, a discectomy and laminectomy, was one way to alleviate this pain. I don't recall him providing any alternatives, but I didn't really want any. I wanted clear solutions. A piece of a disc isn't where it should be? Okay, go take it out so I can get on with my life. This isn't an onion-ring-in-your-fries-type fun surprise, this is a problem that needs solving. I wanted to be pain-free and back rowing for Cornell by September. Well, rowing, getting drunk with my friends, and finding the perfect C&C California T-shirts on sale as I bounced among my favorite online shopping websites. I barely thought twice and we scheduled the surgery for July 29, 2003.

Several times between scheduling the procedure and the day I showed up to the hospital, my surgery was referred to as "routine" or "not that bad." I am here to tell you that there is absolutely no such thing as back surgery that could be described as anything less than "an absolute nightmare recovery—and that doesn't even include the crisis of going to the bathroom." But when I arrived at the hospital, I had no idea about any of that yet. I wasn't even that scared, as I didn't really know what to be scared of. I trusted doctors because I was told to. Why wouldn't I?

On the way to my appointment, to kill time (i.e., help me ignore the fact that an afternoon surgery meant I had to fast all day like it was a Jewish holiday or a modeling shoot), my mom and I stopped by the other hospital in the area to see my cousin, who had just had her first baby. As we sat in her room, she told us about giving birth, and more important, the recovery she'd been suffering through, and then said, darkly, "The worst part is the stitches."

I was confused. What stitches? She hadn't had a C-section. What was she talking about? My mom and my cousin looked at each other. They knew. They knew what kind of stitches. That was the day I learned what an episiotomy is. When we finally headed to my hospital, all I could think was, *At least I'm not having* that.

My doctor and his braces were ready for surgery and so was I. My vibe was, *Let's get this show on the road.* I wanted to get in, get out, and get back to college. I had rowing races to win and college guys to let drunkenly finger me. Big things were happening and my herniated L4/L5 disc wasn't going to stand in my way.

Several hours later, I woke up screaming with giant metal staples holding my skin together, Frankenstein-style. (I know everyone's like you mean Frankenstein's *monster,* but honestly, for this description it could be either. The staples represent the visual style, or lewk, if you will, of the monster. But the decision to use staples is in the medical practice of Dr. Frankenstein. All that is to say, shut up and keep reading about my stupid back.) And then they just . . . sent me home.

My first week of recovery was a blur, and not for the reasons you'd expect (drugs). In fact, I was so terrified of serious pain pills that I think I took maybe one or two Percocet a day max because I didn't want to get addicted. I remember watching *Valley of the*

Dolls in a recliner in my parents' bedroom and then not being able to get out of the chair when I needed to barf. I remember it taking the length of a *Law & Order* episode to get in or out of bed in the morning, or when I had to pee in the middle of the night, all because no one from the hospital walked us through the delicate choreography of exiting and entering a bed while half your back is held together with office supplies.

But over the next two weeks my healing steadily progressed and I finally got to return to the doctor and have my staples removed. Once the metal was out of the way, I was told I could just continue on with the life of a normal nineteen-year-old. I could slowly start training to be on the water again. I could bend over to tie my shoes again (on the off chance I wasn't wearing flip-flops year-round). Everything was coming up Leiby.

That night, I was showering before my first solo venture out of the house. I hadn't driven since before my surgery, nor had I been anywhere unaccompanied by my parents. I was nineteen going on fourteen and ready to get behind the wheel and see my friends so I could talk about boys and drink without my mom or dad being in earshot. I patted down my legs with a towel, then stood up, only to experience the worst pain of my entire life shooting through my leg and hip. It was pain that made waking up screaming after surgery feel like a spa service at the Four Seasons. There is pain that you can clench your teeth through, use your heavy exhales to process. And then there is pain so deep, so piercing, so profound, that you don't even get a chance to choose how to react. You scream out in agony, making a sound you didn't know you were capable of making. I screamed and screamed in my bedroom as my leg turned darker and darker purple.

At first, my mom thought I was just joking around, which is a testament to what a nightmare child I was, so it took her a minute to recognize that the shrieks coming from upstairs were real. Then my parents saw what had happened: My left leg had turned dark purple from ankle to hip and swelled several centimeters and was so painful I could not move. I couldn't even touch it. My mom checked the binder the hospital had given us, detailing things for discharged patients to look out for in recovery, but nowhere in the literature did it mention one of your limbs turning into the eggplant emoji. She called my surgeon, who told us to just go right to the ER and he would meet us there.

We arrived at the ER, where they swiftly checked us in and sent me to a private room where excellent medical care was administered immediately and everything was covered by insurance. Lololol imagine! Yeah, no.

I sat in the waiting room with my purple leg for what felt like a week and a half while I wailed and wailed. At this point I was on zero pain medication, not even Advil. (Which is crazy, because these days when I show up at my parents' house, I usually take a small handful of Advil before even talking to them.) Finally, they admitted me and put me in a bed in the middle of a hallway since all the rooms were full. America! What a country! At least they started me on a morphine drip with a promise to fast-track me to a doctor. I still can't believe it took even that long for someone to take me seriously. I couldn't stop screaming. My left leg looked like Grimace and felt like it was going to kill me, which I assume is what Grimace would do if I ever encounter him in real life.

When I was finally admitted, the doctors on call determined I had a blood clot. Blood clots are apparently a very common complication post-surgery, and this one happened to be a bit more severe than the average one. It was technically a deep vein thrombosis.

You've probably heard the acronym DVT used in a pharmaceutical ad on TV that you can't fast-forward through, that's how common they are. Right up there with plaque psoriasis and thyroid eye disease. But I had never thought it was something that I would become intimately familiar with at age nineteen. Scary acronym aside, the doctors made it sound like I'd go home the next morning, which seemed impossible. Despite the steady stream of morphine and the extra oxy pills, I was still suffering the severe pain of whatever was happening to my left leg. In what world would I wake up tomorrow morning with this resolved? No one seemed to have a solution yet, and I couldn't believe the best plan was just waiting it out in a hospital by myself, without my parents. Waiting it out is how you treat a cold or period cramps or a bad haircut (if, like mine, your head is too large to chicly wear hats). I was scared and alone and facing a completely unknown medical situation.

Every hour that passed made clear that this wasn't a little blip in my recovery journey. The blood clot in my leg was eclipsing the fact that just weeks earlier, someone had sliced my back open and sanded down my bones. No amount of drugs was making this stop. The staff wanted me to start taking blood thinners, which is the traditional (aka only) treatment for blood clots. But you can't just start taking blood-thinning pills. That would be entirely too easy. No, you have to give yourself injections in your stomach of a drug called Lovenox, which sounds like a breakfast-spread-themed drag queen's name. I promise you Lovenox has none of the fun of smoked fish or reading someone to filth. They made me practice giving injections on an orange, which is maybe not the best one-to-one for human tissue. For starters, oranges don't scream. Also, I was nineteen, so my skin was nothing like that of an orange, it was smooth and supple and I miss it dearly. And I'd like to reiterate, I was on a colossal dose of opioids and basically still Lamaze-breathing through my pain. It was like trying to give an injection while also attempting sign language.

I stayed in that hospital room for four days. During that time I took a lot of drugs, and they did a lot of scans. The first one was the night I was admitted. The nurses loaded me onto a traveling hospital bed—don't worry, I screamed the whole time—to take me down to imaging. In attempting to raise the back of the bed so I could sit up more, the nurse accidentally released it entirely and the bed and my body swung to the floor like I was coming through the ceiling of a haunted house. It would have been hilarious if it wasn't outrageously painful for both my very delicate leg and my recently sliced-open back.

It turned out the clot in my veins extended farther than the range of the camera, so then it was time to go back down for a bigger imaging area of my thigh. Once again, the scan couldn't capture the full image of the clot, so the doctors had no idea how big it was, just that it was *really big*. Finally, several CT scans later, we learned I had a blood clot in my left leg that extended from my ankle all the way to a centimeter below my kidney. Between the size of the clot and the fact that thirteen Percocet and four oxys a day (and honestly, that's a low estimate) still weren't keeping my pain under control, the hospital sent me to the ICU.

This was when reality set in for everyone. The ICU is different. No one goes there when things are getting better. Back in the regular hospital room I had access to a variety of cable channels, including my beloved VH1 and Comedy Central. My mom was able to come in and out with snacks and treats, so I wouldn't have to suffer a horrific blood clot *and* eat hospital food. I even had friends stop by during visiting hours some evenings on their way to bars and parties so they could keep me company and watch me involuntarily pee in a bag that hung between us at the edge of the bed. In the ICU there weren't any sounds besides the beeping of the machines. There weren't any friends. There weren't any packages of Whole Foods pineapple and string cheese. There weren't any moments of lightness, and I spent every second down there thinking about how I was probably dying.

At nineteen years old I hadn't thought much about mortality. Death was reserved for grandparents and horrific diagnoses. I wasn't some sad story you see on *20/20* where Barbara Walters talks solemnly to the camera about a young girl with a whole life ahead of her and a tragic disease ravaging her body. I wasn't her because I couldn't be her. I couldn't wrap my brain around how I could go from the medal dock with my Cornell crew to a hospital bed this quickly. Sure, that happened to some unlucky people, but not me. *That can't happen to me,* I kept telling myself. *I can't die at nineteen from a back surgery complication.*

There is no real treatment for a blood clot. Clots are incredibly dangerous because if they break apart, the pieces will travel through your bloodstream and go directly to your heart, lungs, or brain and instantly kill you. So my future was bleak. The doctors projected that I'd spend at least six months on bed rest, but the clot probably wouldn't ever break up. At some point my left leg, without blood flow, would need to be amputated. Unfortunately, with the heavy dose of blood thinners in my body, I would bleed out and die from the surgery. The best-case scenario was that I would live in my parents' house as an immobile opioid addict until I died, which would not be long. Likely, the clot would break up and kill me sooner rather than later.

This wasn't a life I wanted. This wasn't even a life. I was on such a heavy dose of morphine and oxy that I didn't even really process what was happening, but my parents did. They had to sit in the hallway all day and night waiting for the impossible news that things had magically improved and I could leave the ICU, or that I had died. Those seemed to be the only two options.

But then a surprise third option presented itself. One night, my mom ran into the ICU attending, Dr. Peeler, who happened to be neighbors with Dr. Hofmann, an interventional radiologist at Johns Hopkins Hospital who had developed a new procedure that could actually cure a blood clot. Dr. Peeler told my mom he could get me an appointment. It was a moment filled with hope but also a hint of despair. Here was someone who might actually be able to fix this problem. But it was also scary to think that the only way out of this was a specialist at the greatest research hospital in the world. If he couldn't help, we were left with nothing.

At this point, my pain had *slightly* improved (in that I didn't scream every time someone touched my left side), and they sent me back upstairs to a regular room to try and get me out of the hospital. They said I needed to stand up, something I hadn't done in at least a week. If I could stand up, I could go home. And if I could go home, I could go see this doctor at Hopkins who might be my one shot at getting my life back.

With the assistance of two nurses, a handful of Percocet, and the railings of my hospital bed, I was able to get my recently operated-on spine upright on my completely purple and clotted left leg. It was a moment of triumph. It made the silver medal I won at the Eastern

Sprints Regatta just two months earlier seem like a stupid token. The nurses were thrilled, my parents were thrilled, I was thrilled. And then my mom shrieked out, "Oh my god, Alison!"

I was terrified. I had been lying on my back all this time. I had no idea what was going on back there. Was the wound wide open? Had it extended? Could you see bone?

"When did you get a tattoo???"

In the chaos of this crisis I had completely forgotten that I'd gotten a tattoo during the previous school year. Like most of my decisions, it wasn't particularly well thought out. My friend Katie and I were eighteen and we wanted tattoos, so we went and got them. We got our astrological signs, naturally. (Actually, not "naturally," because this was 2002 and it wasn't yet hip or chic to ascribe your entire personality and life trajectory to where the sun happened to be on a specific date. We were kind of ahead of our time.) So I got the sign for Capricorn* tattooed on the back of my right shoulder. And now in the midst of the physical victory of standing up for the first time in two weeks, my hospital gown had fallen down my shoulder and exposed this permanent teenage decision to my mother for the first time.

In a moment of what I assume was self-preservation, she chose to focus on my stupid teenage choice to get a tattoo that for some reason looks like the Philadelphia 76ers logo instead of the devastating reality we were trapped in. Thankfully, there were some bigger problems to deal with, and my dad was able to get her to stop caring about my bad body art and start caring about how they had to take me home because the hospital could no longer do anything

---

* Despite mocking "astrology girls," I guess I am very much one, as I have committed my sign to my body in permanent ink. Being so serious about something is *totally* a Capricorn move. I'm a Cap, baby!!!!

to help. Pills and bed rest could happen at home, they said, and that was the best place for me (to slowly die).

I wish I could articulate all of my thoughts during the time I was convalescing at home, facing the uncertainty of whether my body could survive this. I cannot. I was on so many pain pills that I couldn't tell what was happening. I was just trying to get from minute to minute without having the pain make me want to throw myself out the second-story window—which I couldn't even do because I wasn't able to go up and down stairs. Our classic eighties sunken family room became my carpeted prison.

At one point, I needed to pee, and what stood between me and the bathroom was just two steps. Even with the crutches and the handfuls of opioids, I couldn't do it; I couldn't make it up two steps. So my mother grabbed a bowl from the kitchen and I peed there, in the family room, in a bowl she held under me, while I cried. This isn't to illustrate how incredible my mom is (she is) or how stupid this architectural design choice is (very), but to show exactly how bad things were. I was a Division I athlete and I couldn't make it up two steps. I was the kind of teenager who just six weeks earlier was running three miles a day for fun *on top of* hours of rowing. Stairs weren't supposed to be a problem. Making it to the bathroom was only ever an issue when I was sprinting to throw up jungle juice at a frat party. I had spent my whole life being deeply in control of my body through sports. Now I had lost basic functions with no idea if I'd ever get them back, and I personally just didn't see much of a point in living. I was in a state of being awake and asleep and drugged and miserable, all at the same time, twenty-four hours a day.

Somehow, my parents got me out of the house and into a car to meet the specialist at Johns Hopkins who Dr. Peeler claimed could help me. At this point, anyone who promised me a life where I didn't have to sleep on a twin trundle bed between the piano and a glass coffee table in our first-floor living room seemed like a hero. Dr. Hofmann, who went by Rusty, was young and handsome and very easy to talk to. I also liked to call him Rusty because to me, Rusty is a golden retriever name, and imagining a golden retriever in scrubs performing this procedure makes the memory a bit easier for me to relive. He wasn't a surgeon testing out his experimental treatment on me, he was a friendly dog in a little green outfit walking around saving lives. No one needs to go to therapy to process *that* trauma.

Rusty didn't seem pompous, but he did seem confident. He had seen my charts and now he was seeing this crisis in real life. And to my relief, he was sure that his procedure could fix my clot. He would insert a catheter in the back of my left knee, which would pump strong systemic blood thinners into me to dissolve the clot. He would periodically check on the progress using CT scans until the clot disappeared, somewhere around twenty-four to thirty-six hours later. Then a mesh stent would be inserted into my left leg's largest vein so that it would stay open permanently and not collapse under the weight of the artery that crosses on top of it (a condition called May-Thurner syndrome that I wasn't aware I had until all this). So, like two days after checking in, I'd be walking out of there healed. Sounded good to me!

Obviously, this procedure was not without significant risks. Blood thinners on their own always present the risk of an aneurysm or a pulmonary embolism. Plus, these drugs are systemic, not targeted. We couldn't just start them and be like, "Okay, only go to the blood in the left leg to break up the clot." They were going to go everywhere, like when you spill a box of couscous on your kitchen floor. And that "everywhere" included my spine, where I had had surgery not three weeks earlier. If that wound opened up and started bleeding into my body, it could cause paralysis or even death. The procedure had also been done only about five hundred times. That's not a lot. They do 360,000 boob jobs a year. Five hundred is about how many *Law & Order* episodes there are.

After Rusty gave us his proposal, he encouraged us to talk to other doctors, get other opinions. But I could tell he knew his procedure could help. He didn't seem scared, or like he was trying to prove anything—he just projected the confidence that what he did would work. My parents and I left feeling encouraged. We left feeling optimistic. We left feeling like there was an actual way for me to not just survive this, but actually be able to return to something resembling my normal life. It was the first sign of hope we had since the clot developed. While every doctor at the hospital in Annapolis had said there was nothing they could do, here was someone who could do something.

Other doctors weren't so optimistic. In fact, every single one we talked to told us not to do the procedure. My spine surgeon said it was dangerous and that he couldn't support me going through with it. Our family friend, a doctor in the same field as Rusty, said if it were his daughter, he wouldn't do it, and that if you put a hundred doctors in a room, ninety-nine of them would say, "Don't do this procedure." But those doctors weren't sitting in the kitchen with me. They weren't staring at my left leg as it was literally dying in front of me. They weren't living in blinding, incomprehensible, excruciating pain all day, every day, which penetrated the wall of medications that was supposed to keep me from losing my mind.

My parents called Rusty and laid out the feedback we got. He was like, "Oh, your surgeon is worried? No problem, we'll bring in the head of orthopedic surgery." The head of orthopedic surgery. At Johns Hopkins. When my original surgeon heard that, he was on board. And throughout the back-and-forth, my parents always left the decision in my hands. If I wanted to do it, they were behind me. And if I didn't want to, they supported that, too.

I thought I had been in positions of grown-up responsibility before. I was the manager of a pool at eighteen. I applied to and got into Cornell. I had a car and had driven the five hours between Ithaca and Annapolis by myself several times. But never before did I have *this* kind of responsibility. There aren't many times we have agency as young people. We rarely get to ask our gut a question, because usually an adult has the answer. I'd listened to my gut a few times, and so far it had been largely trustworthy. It told me to go to Cornell, the most perfect place in the world. It told me to follow my passions for swimming and then rowing, which made me unimaginably happy. It told me to not dye my hair blond in high school (or ever) and nothing has ever been more right. The choice to do this procedure was mine, and I needed to listen to my gut. Sitting here on my laptop twenty years later, the choice is such an obvious one. And back then, sitting on the edge of a trundle bed by the kitchen just wanting to be able to walk again, it was an obvious choice, too. I never cared that it was risky. I never cared that it was dangerous. Yes, I might have ended up paralyzed or brain-dead or regular dead. But I also might walk out of there and be able to go back to college, back to rowing, back to my life. The alternative of sitting and waiting in my parents' house to—best-case scenario—survive having my left leg amputated while being addicted to opioids was never on the table. Not for me.

So we went to Hopkins. For the best hospital in the world, it didn't really stand out in the amenities department. At Anne Arundel Medical Center in Annapolis I'd had friends popping by on their way around town and sunny windows that kept my room from feeling like some kind of death casino. Granted, their solution was to just let me die with barely any intervention, so, not exactly five stars. But Hopkins was different. Sure, it had a stunning marble lobby to welcome the greatest doctors from around the world, but once you got upstairs where the magic happened, well, it wasn't the Ritz. The television in my room had only a handful of channels, so I spent most of my time watching ABC Family, which, I mean, wasn't I already suffering enough? And let me remind you, this was 2003, so my cellphone was a little Verizon flip phone that was sturdy enough to be dropped off the Empire State Building but offered nothing in the way of entertainment. Young people in hospitals these days just don't know how good they have it. I mean, I would have died to have TikTok then. Well, almost.

We began the procedure with the team bringing me down to imaging, a room I remember being very cold, with soft classic rock songs pumped in over the speakers, and lined in a blue tile that seemed clinical but would absolutely make a stunning bathroom now that I think about it. Rusty inserted the catheter in the back of my left knee and checked the screens to see that the clot was just where we left it the last time we looked, stretching from my ankle to my kidney.

The difficult thing about this procedure was that it was mostly just waiting for the blood thinners to break apart the clot under close observation. It's not even really a procedure so much as it is a treatment. For something that was supposedly so risky, most of my time was spent just lying still in bed being bored. Even the steady dose of painkillers couldn't make it interesting. At this point, morphine was about as thrilling to me as Advil.

While I lay in that bed staring at ABC Family sitcoms like I was in *A Clockwork Orange,* they monitored the drug levels by drawing my blood every two hours around the clock. At this point, I was about as afraid of needles as I am of bunny rabbits. (Actually, I might be less afraid of needles. Have you seen rabbit teeth? If they can bite through a carrot, they can bite through human skin.) Getting my blood drawn was no big deal, but on these intense blood thinners, just touching my skin left a mark, so of course putting a needle in a vein was next level. It wasn't even painful, just . . . colorful. By the first evening, my arms looked like I had full tattoo sleeves.

In addition to the poking and prodding, twice a day a horde of residents gathered around as support staff rolled me over like a log in the woods, all so they could see what systemic blood thinners being pumped into your body does to a recent spine surgery wound. Twenty-four long hours passed before they wheeled me back down to the freezing teal imaging room to see just how great this treatment was working. I'd been poked like a pincushion, flipped over like a pancake, and terrified to move for an entire day, so I was hoping this look inside would show good results.

I lay there on the cold, hard bed under cameras and was told the clot was still the same size. Nothing had broken up. Nothing had dissolved. Nothing had improved. I was out here risking my life for this wonder cure and it wasn't even working?

The hope of the last few days disappeared faster than the money in my checking account during wedding season. It hit me hard, and I knew it hit my parents harder. For every instant of terror and grief I felt through this process, my parents must have felt ten times that. I'm their only child. I wasn't even old enough to go to a bar, and now they had spent weeks watching me waste away in the ICU with no treatment options, moving beds to the living room since I couldn't even climb two stairs, and sleeping in the hallway of Johns Hopkins waiting for good news that wasn't coming.

But Rusty was undeterred. He told us that he knew this would work, it just might take longer, so he upped the dosage of blood thinners through the catheter in my leg and sent me back upstairs to keep waiting. We restarted the cycle. Nurses searched for a usable blood vessel on my now midnight-blue arms; a bunch of twenty-somethings stared at the one part of my body I couldn't see; and then I submitted to more poking and draining. All the while, no good snacks, no good TV, and no friends hanging out and updating me on who showed up to a house party with a new fake ID to buy beer. Maybe it sounds petty to focus on stuff like this when I was at the premier medical institution in the world being cared for by the top doctors in their fields. But I had no choice. I had to be annoyed that I couldn't watch *True Life: I'm Getting Calf Implants* on MTV because to think about the procedure was too much.

Fleeting contemplations of death on a regular day are terrifying enough, when you can shake yourself out of them and get back to grocery shopping or driving. To be trapped in the bed that might be your last, just counting the minutes until the next update, is an impossible mental task. It would be hard for anyone. But at that age, it was all I could do to not focus on the things I'd never get to experience. I wasn't going to return to college to keep studying and rowing and being with my friends. I certainly wasn't going to graduate. I wasn't going to move to New York or Paris or become an English professor or an advertising executive or a marine biolo-gist. I wasn't going to get to know my parents as an adult, nor would they see me in my adult life. I wasn't going to fall in love or get married or have kids. Every minute the odds of getting to do even one of those things grew slimmer. I was in pain and I was scared, but I was also angry. I had done everything right. I was a healthy athlete. I didn't fall off a cliff while rock climbing. The hardest drug I had done was shag weed smoked out of a poorly made apple bong. We went to the ER right away, I did the stomach injections, I was taking the medication, and here I was doing the big scary risky-but-going-to-work procedure and it wasn't working. It just wasn't fair. No one deserves this, but wasn't I included in the "no one"?

At forty-eight hours into the treatment, they brought me back down to imaging.

The clot was completely dissolved.

Blood was flowing, the blockage was gone from the blood vessels up my leg and hip and through my lower abdomen. My leg was traumatized, but recovering.

I was shocked. My parents were shocked. The family and friends who advised us against this route were shocked. But Rusty wasn't shocked. He knew he could save my life. He knew his treatment would work. And it did.

When I got back to my hospital room, I stood up. It was the first time in more than a week that I could actually stand on both my feet. I was weak, not exactly running up the halls of the hospital cheering and jumping up and down. But I could walk with no assistance from my bed to the chair across the room. I could get up and down from the chair on my own. I could get up to use the bathroom myself instead of peeing into a bag through a catheter, or into a mixing bowl held by my mother. When Rusty felt he no longer needed to monitor me, I was discharged. I walked out of Johns Hopkins.

And with that first step I began my journey to become the inspirational figure I am today. I awoke every morning grateful and centered. I abandoned my aimless college partying in order to dedicate my delicate life to helping others. I began a regimen of exclusively organic healthy foods and gentle movement exercise. I now end every day by screaming to the sky how lucky I am to be alive and I will never ever take for granted the preciousness of life!

No, I walked out of the hospital and immediately back to the life I knew and remembered. I ate grilled cheese and drank Diet Coke. I complained and gossiped to any- and everyone who would listen. When I did get back to Cornell a few weeks later, I immediately headed to a party at the men's crew house where I threw back warm cans of Natty Light and showed everyone the disgusting scar on my back that, thanks to the little detour into near-death-land, had actually opened up and healed not in a straight line but as more of an abstract art piece with a giant indented hole in the middle. I slept in. I regularly joked that I wished I was dead at even the slightest inconvenience. I didn't change.

People certainly knew my story and reacted to it all the time. Nurses would congratulate me on my huge "accomplishment" of not dying. My parents' friends threw on an extra set of kid gloves to talk to me because they knew the horrors my mom and dad had lived through. My friends didn't really know how to handle it, since most young people don't know how to talk about death. It was a mix of "Wow, I can't believe it!" with no understanding of what "it" was and trying to return to the normalcy I craved while also not quite acknowledging the big, nearly dead elephant in the room. I was different from them. Not because I was a survivor, but because I understood death in a way most of them didn't.

I grew up in the era of daytime talk shows, gripping memoirs, motivational speakers. Somehow, survival became one of our new favorite forms of entertainment. And the narrative of a survivor was simple: You become an entirely different and better person. Facing death in a real way should force you to reexamine all the ways you live your life wrong. And then you can magically just change all of them and spend the rest of your time on earth as the absolute perfect person. Because you survived.

I didn't find that to be the case at all. I was the same me as ever. I had stared into the face of death, spent weeks wondering when it would finally take me. And then I had beaten it. I didn't die. And I didn't change. But I did feel horrible for years. I felt like I was squandering this gift I was given.

I still hate birthdays. I still rush through important tasks so I can get back to my favorite activity, sitting and watching TV while looking at my phone. I still avoid virtually all confrontations. I still mentally mock adults with braces, like my spine surgeon in Annapolis, despite knowing good and well that I would never wear my retainer enough to settle into adulthood with the straight teeth my parents paid thousands of dollars for. I still roll my eyes at most sincerity and spend six days fixating on whether I should have bought a pair of jeans on sale that are nearly identical to ones I already own. I'm the same person I was before that blood clot.

And isn't that kind of what you hope? That these profound moments in our life don't completely alter us, but rather let us continue being who we always were. That's the solace we can take when we confront things like death or loss or pain. These monumental, earth-shifting tragedies do not change who we are. If anything, they can make us more ourselves than we even were before. I never celebrated my birthday when I was young because it was inconvenient. I never really celebrated my birthday after I survived because I found something else to celebrate: I'm not dead. I wouldn't say I'm a survivor or a medical miracle or a lucky lady. I'm just not dead. And that is more than enough to drink to.

I did get what I wanted when I walked out of Johns Hopkins. I went back to college and I even briefly trained to row again. I got to go back to my life. All of it—the nerve-racking, the depressing, the exciting. Hell, even the boring. I had never been more thrilled to be bored in my life.

I'M AN ONLY CHILD

When I was growing up, a lot of people thought my parents were separated. It wasn't because they got in public fights in parking lots or I started hyphenating my last name halfway through middle school. It's because my parents took separate vacations with me. Over January break, my dad would take me out to Colorado to ski. And then at spring break, it would be my mom's turn to take me down to the Bahamas or, at worst, Boca to lie on the beach all day and go to the movies at night. This arrangement was ideal for two parents who love each other very much but have wildly different interests. My mom isn't a huge fan of the cold, and my dad doesn't love to, as he says, "sit around in the dirt." So they took separate vacations. The beauty of being an only child is that I got to go on both. (I can't believe only children are stereotyped as spoiled.)

I never felt like I had a "normal" family. And I don't mean that the way someone says, "We're not a *normal* family" and then it's a straight couple with three kids who are like, "Sometimes we have breakfast . . . FOR DINNER!" Obviously, there is no such thing as a normal family, that's a myth from Christianity and capitalism to make people buy sectional couches and bulk toilet paper. But growing up, I couldn't help feeling like my family was different because I didn't have any siblings. My family can field a three-on-three basketball team, but only if none of us is injured, which is rarely the case. While a two-parent, only-child family isn't all that strange, that family structure is rarely reflected in our culture, and when it is, it's never positively.

Like most kids my age, I lived for TGIF on ABC, the block of family sitcoms that played every Friday night during my childhood and made me want fluffy bangs. There were so many different families portrayed on these shows, but the thing they had in common was there were always multiple children. Some shows had big families, some had blended families, but there weren't many shows depicting my home life: the sole child living with two adults. Maybe because that's not a fun show for kids to watch—it would mostly be about the adults opening mail while the kid reads alone in her room. It's not compelling television, but it was certainly a nice life.

In the heyday of BuzzFeed quizzes and millennial navel-gaze-y meme culture, I was bombarded with content about what birth order says about you. Certain personality traits, ways of moving through the world, preferences, and conflict styles were all neatly ascribed to whether you were an oldest, a middle, or a youngest child. When these memes occasionally included an only child, it was like, "Oh yeah, and these freaks have no idea how to fight." Our existence was an odd in-between place of not really being a kid, but also not an adult.

When people ask me if it was weird to be an only child, or assume *I'm* weird because I'm an only child, I tell them no, because I didn't know any other way. Having siblings was as foreign-seeming to me as having a pet iguana whose tail was always falling off and being found behind doors or between couch cushions, like my friend Sean had. I appreciated hanging out with my friends' siblings when I visited, but as soon as I got home, I was relieved to return to a home devoid of any other kids. Of course I had my own room, who else would I share it with? Of course all these toys and clothes are mine, who else's would they be? Of course I am terrible at handling conflict, who would I have fought with? My stuffed animals? They're all pacifists, even Walt the warthog.

Not only was I an only child, but I was the only kid in my extended family for most of my life. My cousin Brian, who's fifteen years older than me, was the next-youngest person in the family. (Eventually he and his wife, Cindy, had kids.) When I was growing up, the family around me was small: my parents and me, my aunt and uncle and cousins Brian and Stephen, and my maternal grandparents. The nine of us were close, though I do remember being both jealous of and confused by my friends who would go on family vacations and meet up with dozens of other kids they were related to and have massive dinners at long tables and play team sports against different branches of the family. My whole family could fit into one SUV.

Because I was the youngest person around by more than a decade, everything—activities, entertainment, topics of conversation—was geared toward adults. My options were to either participate or be by myself. I almost always opted to engage with the adult world even if I didn't appreciate or understand it, because I wanted to be able to hang with the big dogs (aka talk to my parents about what they liked). I listened to a lot of James Taylor before I got into MTV. I read John Grisham novels before I understood what law school was. I owned a shirt from Talbots before I needed a real bra. While my sibling-having friends were busy fighting over who was "it" in tag, I was laughing along to jokes I didn't understand on *Married . . . with Children.* And this shaped the way I related to adults other than my parents, too; my goal in life was to make older people like me and laugh at my jokes. I was absolutely the kid who had no problem befriending teachers, talking to them a bit more like a peer, because that's how I was treated at home. (I'm sure they loved that and weren't at all annoyed by a nine-year-old talking about what she saw on *60 Minutes.*) Things in our house weren't dumbed down; I had to reach up as close to the level of my parents as I could.

This always became the most apparent when I was hanging out with my family on our summer beach trips, which usually included my cousin and his wife and their friends, who were in their mid-twenties when I was in middle school. They would spend the day reading on the beach and swimming in the ocean with me, and then would go out at night to do adult activities like drinking Coors Light at bars. My options were hanging out with my parents (fine but not exactly thrilling), being by myself (acceptable but not quite a vacation to me), or spending time with Brian, Cindy, and Todd (adult, hip, cool, the height of excitement and maturity!).

While I couldn't join them at the bar as an eleven-year-old, I always tried way too hard to meet them at their level conversationally, which backfired from time to time. As a young kid I had a photographic memory exclusively for television and movie jokes. (Now my memory is useless. My podcast co-host, Halle, calls me "God's favorite Etch A Sketch" for a good reason.) If something tickled me, I needed to see it only once to instantly file it away in the recesses of my mind. And because my family has always loved comedy—for example, we often killed time by slinging quotes from Mel Brooks films, no line too obscure—I would watch the things I liked again and again to memorize them, even if most of the jokes made no sense to my prepubescent brain. I knew *SNL* commercial parodies better than I knew my times tables. I saw the movie *Airplane!* more times than *The Little Mermaid*.

One night, we were planning to order takeout for dinner. My mom asked us to go around the table and tell her what we wanted to order. When it was my turn, I knew I had a rapt audience because we were all super hungry after a day of mostly Pringles and seawater. And I knew I had the perfect joke to drop on them from my then (and current) favorite comedy, *Wayne's World*. So I confidently said, "I'll have the cream of sum yung gai."* I stood there proudly waiting for the waves of laughter and admiration to roll in, for everyone to say, *Wow, you are a VERY funny and smart child.*

My mom froze in a mixture of horror and amusement, trying desperately hard not to laugh as everyone else took the cue and bit their tongues to the point of bleeding, I'm sure. She asked me if I knew what that meant and I replied that it was from *Wayne's World*. Of course, I had absolutely no fucking clue that it was a cum joke wrapped in racism. I only knew that in the movie, Benjamin (Rob Lowe) was annoyed, Cassandra (Tia Carrere) laughed and rolled her eyes, and Wayne and Garth giggled at what was clearly a very funny line.

That wasn't some isolated occurrence, though. Throughout my

---

* Obviously this joke, like so many others of the nineties, has aged incredibly poorly. My deep apologies to the entire AAPI community for even including this, but you can see there is clearly no better example of a child saying something WILDLY inappropriate than this.

youth I said or did things that I only lightly understood because I was treated like one of the adults. And I loved the sense of inclusion with the adults that gave me. While many kids spend their youth trying to put as much distance as possible between themselves and adults, I was over here desperately trying to win them over, one movie quote at a time. Even if I had no idea what was going on, I was sitting at the same table. I wasn't a *kid* the way my friends were kids.

Growing up, I was rarely jealous of my friends who had siblings: The younger ones were like weird babies I didn't want to deal with, and the older ones all seemed like assholes who thought *we* were weird babies. Sure, sometimes it was nice to go to someone's house and there were enough people there to play capture the flag. But I mostly remember getting home, going up to my room and shutting the door, and lying on the bed in silence like a forty-four-year-old decompressing at the end of a long day at the office. And I knew the only person who might come bother me was my mom letting me know it was almost time for dinner—a dinner that I liked because you have more freedom to be a picky eater as an only child, when you're just one finicky palate to cook for. I never had to sit through a brother's soccer game or a sister's violin recital. When we planned activities and trips, it was around what *I* wanted to do, because there was no one else to factor in. In fact, on a lot of those trips I got to pick a FRIEND to come with me. It was the fucking best. I felt like Oprah giving away cars to a screaming audience. "You get a beach trip! And you get a beach trip!"

Looking back, beyond the chicken nugget dinners and alone time, I love that as an only child I got to have a real, individual relationship with each of my parents. I know lots of people with siblings also have robust relationships with each parent, and look, this isn't about you. This is about me, because I'm an only child and everything is about me. All I know is that the time I spent with each of my parents individually felt special because when we weren't together, they weren't parenting other kids. Neither of them ever seemed overextended when it came to taking care of me, at least from my perspective. I'm sure in real time they were both constantly ready to set the house on fire and go live alone in the woods, but to me, they were crushing it. I would go over to my sibling-having friends' houses and their parents seemed . . . stressed. Sure, it was probably partly my fault because there was suddenly yet another kid in the house, which meant another mouth to feed snacks to and an increased chance of injuries to deal with. But even as a kid, I could tell that my parents were both giving me real time, real attention, and their real selves.

While I had wonderfully close relationships with my parents, I discovered that certain things are better learned from a peer. New pop music, current slang for hot boys, the social suicide of visible athletic socks (remember, it's the nineties): These are all things that would have been more fun to learn from a fifteen-year-old than two people in their late forties. My parents may have treated me like one of them, but at the end of the day I wasn't. Sometimes I really did wish for a sibling: specifically, an older sister. Older sisters are, from what I can tell, the meanest human beings on the planet, but they are also the gatekeepers to becoming a woman. Moms are great and all, but there are limits to that relationship. And I don't have a "best friend" mom like some of the girls I grew up with did—you know, the kind of moms who come to high school parties and shop in the same stores as their teenage daughters. Those moms try to be young to relate to their daughters, while I was try-ing to be older to connect to my mother. But older sisters know everything. They know about tampons and foundation and fingering. They know about getting asked to dances and buying bras and that the cool girls in high school don't carry backpacks, they wear messenger bags. I lived and died by my stacks of teen magazines, but flipping the stark white pages of *Seventeen* is not the same as your sister coming in your room, pulling out a lip liner, and showing you how to apply it in the mirror, first on her and then on you. If you have an older sister, you don't have to use the metallic gunmetal-gray Lancôme eye shadow your mom gave you from a bonus gift at Nordstrom, apply it alone in your poorly lit bathroom, and then wear it to the Friday-night dance looking like you got a black eye from a robot.

Another problem with being an only child: While there is no one you have to share your things with, that includes blame. There is no one else to help carry the burden of fucking up. I wasn't perfect by any stretch of the imagination, but I wasn't a particularly wild child; I got good grades and basically obeyed my parents' relatively loose rules. This could be attributed to a variety of things, but I think ultimately, I just really like spending time alone, and it's kind of hard to get in trouble when your ideal night is spent with your computer and a stack of teen magazines. Growing up with no road map to getting in trouble and no one to get in trouble with, I think I became more likely to follow my parents' rules and stay home than some of my peers. Most of my experiences of underage drinking were sipping on two or three Yuenglings in my friend's room while we watched NCAA basketball. But the summer between my junior and senior years of high school, I did throw my one and only party, which is when a sibling would have come in handy.

Now, I am never one to victim-blame, but my parents were kind of asking for it. My dad often got to go on lavish incentive trips for work, and my mom wasn't missing the chance to go on a free luxury vacation, but kids weren't invited. So my parents just . . . went on the trip and left me home. It didn't even seem like they worried about whether it was a good idea to leave me there. Mind you, this was all before cellphones and social media—the era of brick-and-mortar parenting. But I was a fairly responsible kid and the neighbors were friends of ours and could check on things in a crisis, so what could go wrong?

Shockingly, not much. That week I went to rowing practice, then went to work as a pool manager, picked up something to eat on the way home, and watched TV or fucked around on AIM (AOL Instant Messenger for those who are either too old or too young to know) until slightly too late before going to bed and doing it all again. Honestly, it was freeing. Here and there I had a friend over to drink one or two beers, but mostly I was just kind of doing my thing, like Carrie Bradshaw, bopping around on my own, but in the suburbs and without the sex and all my clothes were from Abercrombie & Fitch. But toward the end of my meditation retreat at home, I decided to throw a party.

I'm sure if you asked my parents, they would imagine an out-of-control, teen-movie-style rager. The reality is, if they had seen this party they might have been bummed out by my low aspirations for rule breaking. Looking back, I'm not sure I would even call it a party. I had about ten friends over and we mostly just sat on the deck chatting with some beer and a few joints. At one point my friends Meg and Erin and I made daiquiris in the blender. Unskilled as bartenders at the time, we tried to break up the frozen parts with a wooden spoon while the blender was still running, which resulted in splinters of wood mixed throughout the frozen cocktails. We didn't tell anyone and served them anyway. And no one got hurt, except the spoon, which I tossed out in a panic, confident its absence would be my undoing when my parents came home. I couldn't decide which felt more incriminating, a missing wooden spoon or my parents discovering their wooden spoon looking like it had been gnawed on by several forest creatures.

The next day, I was meticulous as I cleaned up. I wiped down every surface, tossed every napkin, straightened every piece of pottery even though nothing had been touched. But the one thing I forgot to take care of was replacing the liquor we drank. My parents didn't keep a ton around, just a bottle of rum for frozen drinks and some beer and wine, but they always had a bottle of Grey Goose for my uncle, who enjoyed a vodka rocks before dinner. Obviously, we had drained all the liquor in the cabinet, and I decided to temporarily refill the bottles with water until I could get a lead on someone with a fake ID who could help me replace them. I didn't think it would be a problem, because my parents weren't big liquor drinkers (it was a Beringer white zin household), so it would be a while before anyone would know. Unless, of course, my family came over.

I was off at work guarding the lives of slightly younger teens in the pool when my parents got home and invited the rest of the family over for a welcome-back dinner—at which they discovered, via my uncle, that the vodka was just water. Instead of sitting around with their arms crossed waiting for me to get home so they could ground me, they decided to have more fun with it. These are the same people who went to Europe and left their teen daughter alone for seven days, so this wasn't going to be a standard talking-to. When I walked into the house, my mom and dad, my aunt and uncle, and my cousin and his wife were sitting around the table. I clocked the all-too-familiar Grey Goose bottle, half full of hydrating H_2O, sitting on the counter next to the flank steak and cut-up watermelon. I knew I was treading into dangerous waters, but I had to pretend like everything was normal and fine. My dad, overly jovial, welcomed me home from work and pulled out a chair for me to join everyone at the table. I tentatively sat down. No one in my family has any acting skills, so I could sense everyone's giddy nervousness just below the surface. But my dad has a master's in psychology and had spent the recent part of his career in sales and corporate America, so he could sell it, and he really wanted to.

He said, "Hey, it's summer, there's this great thing we used to do when I was younger where you soak watermelon in vodka."

I played along, telling him, "Oh that's cool, I think I've heard of that."

"Do you want to have some? It's totally okay with us, you can, you're in the house."*

I kept shaking my head and waving him off like, *No, no, I have practice tomorrow, I don't think I'll like vodka,* truly anything to end the game we both knew he was playing.

"C'mon, it's really good. I bet you'll like it," he insisted.

Now the rest of the table was starting to lose it. Everyone knew that this watermelon was soaked in water, not vodka. But I couldn't admit it, because that would mean I knew where the vodka went (into a pitcher of orange juice and down my and my friends' throats). After a few rounds back and forth like this, the truth came out. *No, I don't want any because I know that the vodka is just*

---

* I've always found the "in the house" rule a bit confusing. I mean, I had the party in the house, so shouldn't that have been within my rights as a burgeoning drinker?

water because I drank the vodka because I had a party because my parents flew to Europe and left me home alone like idiots.

This is exactly where a sibling would have come in handy. It would have been both our party, both our friends drinking wooden-spoon-laced daiquiris and stolen Grey Goose, both our failure to find someone with a fake ID to replace the nice vodka and the shitty rum. But it all fell to me. There was no one to fight with about throwing the party, but there was no one to blame when my parents caught me. When you're an only child, rule breaking and punishment are lonely experiences, like doing stand-up or being on a date with a narcissist. What's more, I had no one to complain to about how unfair this was once I was sentenced to not seeing my friends for a week (which I'm not even sure stuck beyond a few days). Having no inside-the-family sounding board and no ally against your parents is one of the biggest drawbacks to not having siblings.

What felt so jarring about my punishment (and the dinner-party mind games that preceded it) is that my parents felt more like my allies than my enemies most of the time. We were a unit! Not that they weren't authority figures when I inevitably fucked up—this wasn't some bizarre domestic communism where a fifty-one-year-old with a job and a sixteen-year-old with homework had the same rights and responsibilities. The hierarchy of families with multiple children felt so rigid in comparison to what amounted to me and my parents hanging out. We felt a lot closer to equals.

That equality was never more apparent than when I transitioned from only child to only adult. My whole life, I'd been kind of a permanent third wheel to my parents, so as I grew up, it wasn't a huge leap to go from being their kid to being another adult they know and talk to. During college and early adulthood, every time I came home to visit, I was a little older, a little different, a little more mature and capable of talking with them as peers. I'm sure my parents are reading this and are like, "What the fuck is our idiot child talking about, she's a young moron and doesn't know anything!!!!!!" But to me, my relationship with my parents seemed to make more sense as I became an adult.

As an adult, I see the ways that being an only child shaped how I move through the world. I tend to gravitate toward other only children. One of my best friends, Natasha, is an only child, and I think our friendship works well because we both understand that we each need a ton of alone time to do our own thing. People with siblings will never understand that need, the same way that only children will never understand conflict resolution or opening up emotionally.

Only-child stereotypes are obvious: You're selfish, you're closed off, you're bad at handling fights. I can't speak for all only children (they would all be super mad because we're incredibly individualistic and HATE being lumped into groups of any kind), but I can at least speak to these qualities in myself. I don't think I'm necessarily selfish. I'm sure like twenty to thirty people I grew up with would love to contest that, but thankfully books don't have comments sections, so too bad!! What other people might call selfishness, I think of as confidence. I'm not afraid to be very particular. I like my food, my apartment, my clothes, a certain way. The way I spend my time has only ever been about me, and after forty years, it's too late to shock the system with change. That's self-awareness. I know what I like and what I don't, and I know how important those things are to me because I've been figuring them out on my own my whole life. I don't think I'm emotionally closed off, but I've spent a lifetime working through a lot of my feelings internally or with a professional rather than sharing that part of myself with others. That's independence. Confidence, self-awareness, and independence? Those are good things. Those are words that sound like they'd be in a powerful Destiny's Child anthem. And I developed those skills because of the relationship I had with my parents as an only child.

What about being bad at handling conflict, you ask? Okay, that stereotype is very real, and I will own it. Every fight I've ever had has been because I had no idea what I was doing and waited until a small issue became a crisis because confrontation scares me. Blame my parents, this one is on them.

There is one element of being an adult only child that I think a lot of people with siblings see as positive. I believe people with siblings look at only-child families and are often jealous of the lack of confusion or fighting over the gnarly problems of aging parents and estates and wills and end-of-life decisions and everything else that comes with getting older. And it's true, there is no fighting for money or assets or jockeying for control in my family. You couldn't make *Succession* if there was only one Roy child. It would be one twenty-minute episode and everyone would be like, "Oh, obviously Alison gets the company and the money and the job and let's all go home." For better or for worse, when my parents die, it just leaves me. But this also means that their care, as they get older, falls solely to me. Managing where they live, being there for injuries and diagnoses, helping them move from a house to an apartment to a facility, being the decision-maker when they are no longer capable—that is all on my shoulders. I have no siblings to share the burden, to sympathize with me, to call crying when the idea of putting Mom in a home or saying no to a dangerous surgery for

Dad is overwhelming in every single possible way. The relation-ship with your parents as an only child is a two-way street, but it's a narrow one. No other cars are on the road. They help you and then you help them.

As my parents get older, I'm more aware every day of the job of being their sole caregiver. I'm scared. I am so, so, so unbelievably scared of what that is going to look like. Despite the fact that my mother is constantly talking to me about their plans and where she keeps all the account numbers and bank information as if they are planning a murder-suicide, I feel both wildly unprepared but also, strangely, ready for this impossible task. Living an entire life as a weird small adult prepared me to be an actual adult. I know that I can't just wait for someone else to take care of things because I spent my life having to take care of things myself—whether that was navigating playground friendships or failing to replace a bot-tle of Grey Goose. So when it comes to my parents' care, I've known the whole time I'll be on my own for that, too. And as they march on into old age, do I sometimes wish I had a brother or a sister to deal with the uncertainty of the future together? Sure. Would I trade my life as an only child with my parents to have that? No fucking chance.

My parents and I get to do things that so many people don't, such as spend quality time just the three of us. We always have, and we still do to this day because I'm not having kids and I don't currently (and might never) have a partner. The best example of this is our annual winter trip. Many years ago, we decided to go "no gifts" among the three of us, mostly because I finally had my own real money and no longer relied on gift opportunities to get my basic necessities like cashmere sweaters and Kiehl's products. Nothing on Christmas or Hanukkah, no Mother's Day or Father's

Day or anniversary expectations. Birthday presents only on the big ones (fives and tens, naturally). Instead, we put all the money we'd been throwing at gifts we might never use into one very nice vacation. Because my parents are retired and my career is flexible when it comes to travel, we go in January or February when the weather on the East Coast is awful and the weather in Aruba is, as it is every single day of the year, perfect.

It's my favorite week of the year. It's not exactly the most relaxing, because I have to prepare lots of topics to talk about with my parents (and, more important, ways to respond to the topics they decide to bring up, like which MSNBC anchor they like right now or who in the neighborhood recently died). We arrive separately and spend all day reading books and drinking near one another in the sun. And then we go have dinner at one of the many Italian restaurants in Aruba that exist for some reason. I love it because it's just us. It's the tropical version of what every day felt like growing up in our house. We're not forced to accommodate others. We don't have to dumb down anything we're doing or talking about. We all get time together and time to ourselves. We do the things we want when we want to and the way we want to. And my dad doesn't even mind reading his book "sitting in the dirt."

I'M A JOCK

· · ·

I cry at every sporting event. I sobbed watching a TikTok of a forty-six-year-old woman qualifying for the Olympic swim team. I wept my way through *The Boys in the Boat* when the Washington men's 8+ came from behind at IRCs to beat Cal and Harvard. I teared up at a New York Liberty game when Sabrina Ionescu hit a three at the half to tie things up. (This could also be because I was slightly hungover and for some reason the Barclays Center is a Pepsi facility, so there wasn't a Diet Coke in sight.) But fundamentally, sports make me emotional because I am, at my core, a jock.

I dedicated the first twenty years of my life to sports. The town where I grew up—Severna Park, Maryland—is known for big houses with green yards, docks full of boats, and the ability to get crab on just about anything, no matter the restaurant. *Chicken sandwich? What do you want on that: lettuce, tomato, crab?* And it's also known for being a town of jocks. When you get to first grade, they hand you a lacrosse or field hockey stick and you've got the next twelve years pretty locked up. Most kids play a different sport every season for a few years, and then you pick which of the "good" ones you want to dedicate your life to. I think I went to the only high school in the country where being on the cheerleading squad was actually social suicide.

In Severna Park, popularity was directly tied to both athletic prowess and your relationship with Jesus Christ. It kind of makes sense when you think about the fact that the same school obsessed with a legacy of lacrosse championships also worshipped a dude with shredded abs who wore sandals year-round. Oddly enough, he seemed to be the only Jew any of my classmates liked. Unfortunately for my own social standing, I wasn't a lacrosse star and I didn't care about Jesus. I was zero for two in being accepted by the Kaitlins and Ryans of the school.

I joined my summer swim team when I was six and instantly loved everything about it: The brightly colored racing suits and caps and goggles. The fact that every day I got to go to the pool, my favorite place on the planet (at a time where I only knew, like, five places total). Hanging out with older kids on the team and possibly one day befriending them. Jumping in the water and being jolted by the cold, shocked into movement because to sit still in the pool in June would be to freeze to death in a swimsicle situation. The white noise of being underwater, broken occasionally when you came up to take a breath. The pop of screams and cheers encouraging you to keep going before you're plunged back into the meditative waves of nothing below the surface.

I also loved swimming because I was good at it. Whatever gene makes you good at running, I don't have it. I do have whatever gene makes you good at swimming, which I assume is some kind of fish-hybrid DNA that we haven't discovered yet because we don't research it, kind of like a cure for endometriosis. It was exciting to me that success in swimming was individual. Sure, I swam in relays and celebrated when our team beat another team. But I alone won my event. I got ribbons for winning my heats, ribbons for winning events, ribbons just for hitting personal bests almost every time I got in the water. I was stacking ribbons the way mobsters stack cash in movies. I had so many ribbons I had to keep them in the big box that I got my American Girl doll in. You know, the $82 doll who came with a whitewashed backstory and made you read a book. Well, obviously I got one for Hanukkah when I was nine, and obviously I kept the box she came in because it looked fancy,* and I filled it with proof that I was a good swimmer.

In fourth grade, I made it official with swimming. I said no to fall field hockey, I called my spring lacrosse coach to quit before the season even started. I eschewed any other athletic possibility and poured everything I had and everything I thought I could be into swimming year-round. I joined my local team, which was called SPY (short for Severna Park YMCA), and I instantly drank the Kool-Aid. Well, the Gatorade. The Glacier Freeze Gatorade to be exact, because while I don't know what the Arctic region is supposed to taste like, I loved the pale blue color. So I drank a lot of actual Gatorade, and I threw myself headfirst into swimming. I forced my parents to buy *all* the blue-and-white team gear. In addition to my racing suit and cap, I had T-shirts, sweatshirts, even a branded duffel bag that I dragged to and from practice. They could have sold a cyanide pill in cerulean with the SPY Swimming logo

---

* I believe that American Girl dolls are where the millennial obsession with keeping the box something came in started.

and I would have begged my mom to buy it so I could swallow it immediately.

The thing about making one activity your entire identity is that then you actually have to do it. I spent all my time submerged in water, alone with my thoughts. I went to practice a minimum of six days a week. My skin was dry, and I reeked of chlorine at every hour of the day no matter how many times I showered. And swimming itself was *hard*. These days, I roll my eyes at the intense workout classes/cults people buy into. And while I'm sure I'd fail miserably at Barry's Bootcamp, I also know that the people in those classes wouldn't survive one swim practice for thirteen-year-olds. I spent two and a half hours in the pool every day, some days adding an extra swim in the morning before school started, and some days an hour for dry-land strength and flexibility training. And this wasn't gliding up and down the pool in a smooth freestyle; I was fighting wake in a lane with eight other swimmers while trying to beat them and the clock over and over again, for thousands of meters a day. We had one drill where we strapped on belts that had long ropes attached to big white plastic paint buckets and then swam laps while the resistance dragged us back. You're basically swimming in place as an item from Home Depot slowly tries to drown you.

Grueling physical activity aside, I loved every part of swimming in those first few years. I would see my friends at practice and we'd laugh until we couldn't breathe in between sets, doing bits underwater and using our gear as Carrot Top–style props. Nothing compared to the thrill of seeing the dot matrix printer pages that heralded official meet results. I'd rush to the bulletin board and trace my finger from my name to my time and placement. Never in my life had I felt more important than when I walked into an aquatics center wearing my bright blue parka, knowing I was part of something special, a part of this team where we all did this thing that the Katies and Ashleys of my school just couldn't understand as they ran around a field in pleated skirts carrying glorified butterfly nets.

Being good at something when you're young is a double-edged sword. Because you've experienced so little in life, the thing you're good at swells up and takes over your identity, like adding roasted red peppers to literally any dish—they become the whole thing. It's human nature to want to be comfortable. We like staying in our own lane (pun absolutely intended). And being good at something is comfortable. So why wouldn't a teenager still over a decade away from a fully developed frontal lobe lean in hard and make swimming her whole life?

As I got deeper into the sport, I took swimming more seriously than Daniel Day-Lewis took acting. My preparation for meets made his *Lincoln* methodology look like a corporate improv workshop. I'd play intense music on my Walkman while refusing to look up at anyone, head down under the hood of my parka as if I were minutes away from a heavyweight championship fight or posing for an Eminem album cover. Every race played out like a movie in my mind. I could hear dramatic music (usually the score of *The Cutting Edge*) playing as I approached the pool. This was it. *I am a focused aquatic machine and this race is the most important race ever and I'm out here fighting for my life against the fiercest competitors and everyone is locked in to see who among us will shatter records and win Olympic gold and defy physics and have the kind of swim that they will one day recount in an interview in* Swimming World *magazine while showing off a Kay Jewelers' worth of medals.*

In reality, I was a fourteen-year-old girl in a pool with seven other fourteen-year-old girls, swimming four lengths of breaststroke at a pretty average pace at an aquatics center in Laurel, Maryland, while most of the people in the stands were just waiting to see their kid make an appearance so they could get out of there and go to Friendly's on the way home. As for my competitors, most of them would swim for maybe a few more years, then trade *Swimming World* for *Cosmo.*

Despite my outsize fantasies, I actually did well. I was no star of my year-round team, though I fantasized that magically overnight I would be faster than my friend Sarah, who stood a solid four inches taller than me with half the body fat. But I was in the mix. I qualified for nationals, I placed at big meets, I swam in the fast lane.

And then I didn't. Here's the thing about young athletes: You're on borrowed time. At fourteen, I was tall and lean. I stood a towering five feet six and was outrageously fit thanks to three hours of working out a day. I had abs. What a waste, abs on a fourteen-year-old. It's like putting caviar on a Pop-Tart. And suddenly I turned fifteen and my body started to change from a ripped child's to a normal young adult's. I think I was one of the only young cis girls on the planet who was kind of pissed to have boobs. Top-ranked swimmers didn't have boobs. They also didn't have hips or periods or social lives or healthy relationships with food and exercise, but I wasn't concerned about those things then. One day I had a perfect body for swimming, the next day I did not.

I spent a year fighting this uphill battle. While my other fast friends were moved up to the team's elite practice group, I stayed with the kids who were a little younger and a little slower. I didn't leave meets with the giant ribbons I was used to. I no longer qualified for nationals. But I was determined to hold on to swimming. I even made my parents pay for a weekend workshop called Total Immersion, which was supposed to change the way you swim by teaching you the secrets that only the Olympians know. (From what I can tell, the secret is paying some guy in Florida a few hundred bucks to say, "Swim taller.")

But the things I loved about swimming kept evaporating before my eyes. Instead of goofing off with my best friends after practice, I found myself silently carpooling with near strangers. Excitement turned to dread as I pored over meet results and saw how far I was falling, like getting on the scale on January 2. At the pool, everyone else's mailbox was stuffed with a rainbow of shiny ribbons, which they'd quickly shove into their bags like they were on the receiving end of a drug deal, while mine held only a small slip of paper reminding us that parking lot construction started on Tuesday and to please plan drop-off and pickup accordingly. My fantasy of talking about my early SPY days to a *Sports Illustrated* reporter on the eve of my fifth Olympics gave way to nightmares of reading that same interview from my rival as I chain-smoked Virginia Slims in the back of a bowling alley. The once meditative silence of the water was now an echo chamber of self-hate, broken up only by the sound of the pace clock on the wall beeping to remind me I was once again behind.

During my last regionals, I swam the two-hundred-meter breaststroke, an event that nobody likes because it's long and slow and thus not that exciting or competitive. It was my last chance to qualify for nationals that year, and I told myself that if I did it, things could continue. I could still be a swimmer. I could still be a

"nationally ranked" swimmer. I could still be the person I'd identi-
fied as for ten years.

I can't tell you what the actual race was like because I don't remember the specifics of any one event. They all blend together like
a chlorine-scented acid trip. I do remember flinging myself off the
starting block, breathing heavily, and alternating between looking
at the dark line of tile below me and the wall that I was desperate
to reach as my head went in and out of the water. And I remember
slamming my hands into the touchpad when I finished, whipping
my head around, and ripping my goggles off to squint at the big
screen that displayed everyone's time. I didn't care if I beat the girl
next to me or the girl in lane 7 or 2 or 6. I only cared if my time read
under 2.26.00, the qualifier for nationals. But it didn't. And while
my body bobbed there, my heart sank.

I went through the motions of cooling down, then stopped after
a few laps. My mom came over, wondering how long it would be
before we could leave this hellish dome of chlorine I had forced her
to sit in for hours just so I could swim for less than three minutes.
I remember looking up at her and finally admitting, "I don't know
if I want to do this anymore." I knew it was finally time. I was
done.

Swimming broke my heart. After that, I forced my mom to drag
me once or twice to the pool in Annapolis so I could glide up and
down the same twenty-five meters trying to figure out who I was,
as if the bottom of that pool would somehow spell out the next
seventy years of my life. Was it too painful to swim without the
structure and rewards of a team? Did I love swimming enough to
do it for fun and exercise despite the ego-death of no longer being
considered good? Could I really continue a life of dry skin and hair
if it didn't come with ribbons and trophies and praise?

The answer was, I couldn't. What I loved about swimming was the identity it gave me, the way it let me ignore the social hierarchies of school and feel different and special but still be part of a group. I could come home and look at my ribbons and think, *I did that; that was me out there being fast*. That's what I loved and craved so much at that time: I needed to feel special but included, a standout who had accomplished something concrete, but still a cherished member of a team. During adolescence, you're figuring out who you are and who you're going to be, and fitting in and standing out need to happen in tandem somehow. When you're young you're just pumped to have friends. If you're anything like me, when you get older you want everyone to leave you alone. But your teen years simultaneously require inclusion and exceptionalism. Swimming gave that to me. A race time is a race time. My success was my success. And without those, I was just going back and forth in the pool without a purpose. The problem with making one thing your entire world is when that one thing falls apart, your entire world goes with it.

I quit swimming cold turkey. But suddenly, I had no idea what to do with myself. I had dozens of hours a week, an unyielding sense of competition, and a metabolic level that demanded I find another athletic outlet soon. My dad, sensing my desperation and also my apathy for lacrosse and field hockey, found a rowing club that had a youth program. I didn't know the first thing about rowing, but I loved boats and the water. I had already spent a decade below the surface, so the natural progression was to be on top of it.

Rowing, or crew depending on whom you're talking to, can be a tricky sport to explain to people. Everyone thinks it's like kayaking or canoeing, but the only thing it has in common with those activities is they all take place on boats. Sometimes when I tell people I rowed, they hear it as "rode" and think I rode horses. I would never *ever* ride a horse. Horses are the opposite of boats. The easiest reference for most people I meet is to say, "Like in the movie *The Skulls*." Or, for people with a passion for cryptocurrency, "Like the Winklevoss twins."

I immediately felt the same way about rowing as I did the first time I jumped into a pool: I was obsessed. Moving through water made sense to me. It's about being long, about gliding as far as you can, creating the least wake, always moving forward (well, if you're rowing, technically backward). I loved being out on the water in the sun, the Severn River lapping against the sides of the boat. I loved hearing the coxswain yell phrases like "ready all," "weigh enough," "power ten in two, that's one . . . two . . . on this one." I loved that the jargon felt like speaking a second language: the catch, the drive, the finish, the slide. I loved that to be a rower, you were part of every step of the experience. You'd carry the shell (boat) out of the boathouse and onto the dock, where you'd put it in the water, grab your oars, and screw them into the oarlocks. Then you'd get in and slip your socked feet into the always-too-big shoes nailed to a piece of wood known as the foot stretcher. Once you'd shoved off the dock, you and the rest of your boat would move as one. If this all sounds like a foreign language and you glazed over reading it, you know exactly what was so appealing to me about rowing.

My love of rowing included my teammates, too. Just like swimming, my rowing team existed outside the school sports program. So there on the dock, kids from different high schools gathered; kids who, like me, wanted something outside their social ecosystem, who wanted to try something other than the field sports our peers valued so much.

I was good at rowing almost immediately. It felt natural to me, like something I had always been destined to do. It must have been like when Gwyneth Paltrow first put on a pair of white jeans. She must have been like, "This. This is it." I always thought my years of swimming and its smooth, rhythmic back and forth gave me an ideal stroke for rowing. And the beauty of everyone finding this sport as a teenager—it's not something you can really do until you're big enough to carry a giant fiberglass boat around—was that we were all starting from zero together. Joining a rowing team in ninth grade meant I wasn't competing with athletes who had been doing it since elementary school, I wasn't trying to assimilate into an established group of friends and teammates.

Unlike swimming, rowing had a unique social cachet that felt special and even more appealing to my teenage self. Crew has a history of prestige and elitism, and at the time was also newly cool again. In the 2000s, crossed oars and the words BOAT CLUB and CREW adorned hundreds of graphic T-shirts and sweatshirts from Abercrombie & Fitch, American Eagle, and basically every souvenir shop up and down the East Coast. The crew shirts I owned were from real races that I actually rowed in. My culture was, quite literally, everyone's costume.

Where swimming was an almost entirely individual sport, rowing has a bizarre team element unmatched by anything else. Swimming is like *American Idol,* where you're competing against everyone else, so your only job is to be the best and ultimately win the show, but your best also helps the show be a huge success.* When Katie Ledecky wins a gold medal, we're all like, "Hell yeah, U.S.A.!" (which feels like the only time I'll ever feel that sentiment

* I personally think that Kelly Clarkson made *American Idol* and not the other way around. They found the best singer in the country on the first try.

again). But mostly we're thinking, *Holy shit, she is an outrageously fast swimmer.* Rowing isn't like that. Rowing is like Real Housewives. You all have to work together to be the best cast so people say, "What an incredible season of *RHONY,* a perfect combination of batshit personalities." While you compete to get into that boat, and you jockey around for who is in which seat, ultimately you have to all work together. Bethenny and Ramona need to get along (or have a topless screaming match in the pool while floating on noodles) to make the Mexico trip work. Similarly, stroke seat and bow need to be paced exactly the same to achieve real speed. And when you are working together, there's really nothing like it.

When everyone is rowing in sync, you can feel something called swing: the momentum when everyone gets their oar to hit the water at the exact same time, then drives through the water at the same power and speed, and finally pops their oar out and gently glides back to do it all again at the same controlled rate. It can take years for a boat of strangers to find that swing. And it can take even longer to hear the bubbles. When everything is perfect—when a crew is working together and the boat is really moving—it literally lifts out of the water and glides forward, and you can hear bubbles under the fiberglass hull of the boat in the bow. It feels as if you're being lifted out of a foamy sea like Venus herself, in a literal shell (hers scallop, ours racing). In my entire life I have never felt anything as thrilling as the bubbles.

During my junior and senior years, our club's elite boats consisted of four rowers and a coxswain. We had a magical combination that worked. My friend Caroline was in bow (the front seat). She, like me, was a clinical overachiever with too many extracurriculars but enough anxiety about success to match her overloaded schedule. She had bouncy blond hair and loved country music, chicken tenders at TGI Fridays, and being the best. In front of her, in two seat, was Sara. She was one of the only Jewish friends I had growing up, so I always felt we had a special bond. She joined our team after moving down from Nyack, New York, and I felt deferential to her just because she had rowed anywhere else besides Annapolis. In three seat was Stella. She was younger than the rest of us, but seemed like sixteen going on twenty-eight because she was tall and threw parties and wore tube tops. She also knew how to push herself. I was stroke seat, setting the pace for everyone behind me, and then, seated in front of me, directly facing me for several hours every day, was my best friend Meg, our coxswain. She was intense, driven, and also out of her mind and the funniest person I knew. I remember the first time I was assigned to the stroke seat, when I climbed into the boat, I looked at Meg and saw she was trying desperately hard to not burst into laughter just at the sight of me because every inside joke we had was bubbling to the surface between us. I stared at her through my Oakleys and we both swallowed our giggles and got to work.

We were friends who all went to different schools and got to come together every day and be good at something. Our morning practices started at four forty-five, and I would drive my car down B&A Boulevard in the pitch dark with the windows down, blasting a Guster CD because I was genuinely so excited to get to the boathouse. I loved showing up to school when everyone else in my first period had just woken up and I'd already had two hours on the water. I had massive open blisters and thick yellowed calluses all over my hands from feathering and pulling. I had bruises and scrapes on the backs of my calves from slamming my legs down on the drive and catching the edge of the slide. I had red, bleeding wounds on my ankles from the shoes on my foot stretcher being sized for a six-foot-four man and not a five-foot-six teenage girl. We were banged up and bloodied the way ballerinas are, but without any of the sex appeal.

When the high school crew glory days ended, I was recruited to Cornell. That may sound like my athletic prowess had anything to do with my acceptance or perhaps even got me a scholarship. Nope! I don't think there is a lower-priority sport, even in the Ivy League, than women's rowing. The club curling team had more pull with the university than anything we were doing down on Lake Cayuga. But this did mean that I showed up on campus part of a group. I didn't have to go out of my way to befriend everyone on my dorm floor or in my 101 classes, because as a student-athlete I had a built-in identity and set of friends waiting for me. Freshman college crew teams are a mix of experienced, often recruited athletes and people who have never seen a racing shell in their lives. At Cornell, this kind of walk-on recruiting was done at the mandatory freshman swim test. For some reason the university makes every single incoming freshman student on campus complete a very basic swim test, and if you don't pass, you have to take cursory swim lessons, so that even if you leave college with $200,000 in debt, at least you learned how to swim. The rowing teams would send people to watch the swim test, and if anyone seemed like a decent swimmer or athlete, they were plucked out of the water and asked if they wanted to try crew. It's honestly not a bad plan from a safety perspective, and it confirmed my suspicion that being good at swimming means you're probably going to be good at rowing.

Fall was chaos at the boathouse. Imagine a dozen or so eighteen-year-olds wearing spandex and speaking in rowing jargon clashing with another few dozen who are walking around a dock for the first time. But it was also the most fun. The recruited girls (and a few extra-tall walk-ons) made up powerful 8+'s that competed in head races—several miles of gliding down the water in warm-but-crisp fall weather—up and down the East Coast. The freshman men's and women's teams traveled together in the fall, so there was a fun sense of community across the gender divide. My friend Natasha and I forced a busload of freshmen on the way to Princeton for the Head of the Carnegie to watch a VHS of *Sister Act 2: Back in the Habit*. The men's team resisted, demanding we (once again) watch Arnold Schwarzenegger's *Pumping Iron,* but on this trip we finally won. They all acted pissed, but by the time Lauryn Hill was singing her solo, they were extremely into it, too.

By the end of the fall, the team had been pared down a ton and it was time to enter winter training. We sprinted, lifted, and erged our way toward spring, and the vibe went from communal to competitive as we jockeyed for position between the first and second boats. There were a handful of super-tall, experienced girls who were destined for the first boat. There were also some good but not as powerful girls who would definitely be in the second boat. And then there were a few of us whose future was up in the air. I was one of those athletes, fighting for my life every practice so I could get into the first boat. In the spring, though, a hip injury left me sitting out a race against Dartmouth, and I figured that was it, I would have to be in the second boat. I flashed back to the end of my swimming days, but this was different. Plenty of my friends were in the second boat. The deep talent of our team meant that most of us were pretty close in skill and strength, so boat assignments were almost arbitrary at times.

I will admit, though, that my ego, and the piece of me that always, since I first jumped in a pool thirteen years earlier, needed to be the best, was bruised. I struggled with those feelings, but I also knew how to take them in stride. This wasn't the first time I'd had to swallow my pride* and get back to work. The decline of my swimming career had prepared me for this. When I stepped onto the docks at Cornell for the first time, I had four years of experience and a natural ability that put me at the top of the freshman team throughout the fall. But now this was the first true test of my will: Could I hack it when I wasn't the best?

I took stroking the second boat of the women's team seriously and we entered the league championship regatta extremely confident. Our second boat was faster than some schools' first boats, so we breezed into first place in our heat, securing a place in the finals. Unlike with so many of my swimming events, drowned out by the silence of the water, I remember every stroke, every breath, every call from our coxswain. In the final, we were pitted against the second boat from Wisconsin, whose rowers all had several inches on us height-wise. They pulled ahead at the thousand-meter mark and stayed there, but we fought hard to put everyone else behind us. Our boat had swing. Our boat had bubbles. I was in stroke seat, and every ten strokes in that final five hundred meters I heard, "Up two in two, that's one . . . two" from our coxswain, telling me to lift the rate a bit, with light hands at the catch, and finish with an even stronger drive. We crossed the finish line many seconds ahead of the next boat, earning a silver medal.

That was my last race ever. I'm glad it stuck in my mind, but maybe that's because nothing came after it. It remains this gleam-

---

* "Choke on the rinds, but the lack thereof would leave me empty inside." Sorry, I just had to finish that thought thanks to Eve 6.

ing achievement because from there my rowing career disappeared. I spent that summer having fun and fucking around as summers are meant for. And then my disc herniated. And then I had surgery. And then I almost died.

I clearly survived because you already read that essay, and also you're reading this book, so spoiler alert: I'm Alive (Celine Dion voice). But I obviously did not get back on the water that fall when I returned to Cornell. While the rest of the team headed to the lake, I spent my time doing physical therapy, riding a stationary bike on dry land, or "running sprints" in the pool while wearing a flotation belt so I could regain the cardiovascular strength I lost in those weeks in the hospital where I didn't stand up. When cuts had to be made to the varsity team, it was no surprise that I was part of that group. I was still building back up to my full strength, and no one knew if I could even really row again.

I was devastated by the rejection, and though I could drink through it because I wasn't beholden to early-morning erg sessions anymore, I was once again left with a giant hole in my life and my heart. It was even more difficult than quitting swimming, because I didn't feel like I had a choice. My body had betrayed me.

I had no idea where to put the energy I had poured into sports over the last fifteen years. My personality was "athlete." I had to find something. But almost every team on campus was made up of people who had been training for their sport since they could walk or hold a stick. I couldn't just show up on the softball field like, "Hi, put me in at second base, I was a rower." Natasha had also been cut and was in the same boat. Well, we both weren't in any boats, and that was the problem. Lifelong athletes with nothing to do, we turned to club sports. She joined the rugby team and I, ironically, joined the lacrosse team.* But while it was fun to run around with a lacrosse stick, it didn't excite me enough to stay.

After a season of lacrosse, I got really into running for a few months, and would spend an hour every single day on the treadmill. Then I learned about Bikram yoga from a trip down to the Ithaca Commons and started attending classes regularly, which I continued to do after I graduated and moved to New York. Anything that was outrageously difficult and required intense dedication was up my alley. I wanted something to take over my life. I wanted to define myself by a physical activity that not everyone could handle. After spending hours a day training in highly competitive environments, I still could not wrap my head around doing a twenty-minute jog. What was the point? If you weren't going to put in two or more hours of cardio and weights, why even bother getting off the couch to do anything at all? My life after sports, just like my life in sports, was all-or-nothing. It's as if I never learned how to casually exercise the way people without competitive sports backgrounds do. I was either completely removed from physical activity or I was sneaking to the gym between open mics to run six miles. But still, nothing could fill the hole left in me from my days of being an athlete.

That changed when I moved to L.A., of all places. As you read on in this book, you'll notice that I'm not the biggest fan of the City of Angels. That's mostly because I don't love driving everywhere and was living there during a rather dark period of my career, so I associate L.A. with crying in my leased Honda Civic on

---

* This is what happens when you're from my hometown—even if you haven't held a stick in a decade and you resent the social structures that come with it, you will always know how to play lacrosse. It's in the water.

the 101. At that point in my life, I felt lost and directionless, the same way I had been twice before.

Then one day my friend Erin took me to the pool.

Like me, Erin was a comic in New York who had moved to L.A., but unlike me, she had figured it all out. She introduced me to the things in L.A. I still genuinely love, like Dave's Gourmet Korean at the farmers' market and the Glendale Nordstrom Rack. When she took me to the Glassell Park pool, we were planning to just sit in the sun and talk shit about every person we had ever met, which was the foundation of our friendship along with comedy and vegetable-heavy snack plates. But after we'd run through our agenda of gossip, we decided to leave our lounge chairs to hop into the lap lanes.

At this point, I hadn't swum laps in fifteen years. At most I had kicked around in the ocean on a few beach days. I think Erin and I did all of twelve laps in total, half of those using kickboards so the comedy scene gossip didn't have to end because our heads were underwater. It felt amazing. Really fucking amazing. Something in my brain clicked that day. Maybe I could start swimming again. Maybe this could be the key to my happiness, the refreshing splash of water in the desert of my life in L.A. and its even drier desert of comedy opportunities.

A few days later I bought a new black Speedo and a silicone cap and goggles and drove to an indoor pool in El Sereno. There were a few other patrons scattered around in the water, mostly families with young children using the lane as a landing spot for attempted dives that became belly flops and the impressive "kicking with your head just far enough above water to continuously shriek" that many children perfect their first time in a pool.

I picked an empty lane and jumped in. While my physical fitness level was nowhere near what it had been in my competitive years, my technique came back immediately. I couldn't swim for two and a half hours and keep pace, but I could swim all of the strokes and whip through flip turns just like I used to for as long as my heart and lungs could handle. When I finally finished what was probably a hundredth of my former self's workouts, I propelled myself out of the water with the grunting moan of a U.S. Open tennis player meets a breaching whale meets the orgasm you give yourself when you're sad and don't have any drugs and think, *Maybe this will do it.* As I sat on the side catching my breath, the young lifeguard walked by and said, "You're a good swimmer."

I was floored. Not that I needed external validation, but—fuck, who am I kidding, I *desperately needed* that validation. I was drowning without it. I had been in L.A. for months and couldn't figure out how to get validation for parking, let alone myself.

From that day on, I started swimming again. Not because an eighteen-year-old said I was a good swimmer (though not *not* because of that), but because it was the first time I truly felt good, felt like myself since moving to Los Angeles. I swam at all the pools I could find, the indoor facility at Echo Park in the winter, the Rose Bowl on Mondays when the public pools were closed, and back to Glassell Park in the summer to sear a giant white X from my practice suit onto my tanned back. I bought fins and borrowed hand paddles for drills. I downloaded recommended practices from USA Swimming. I slowly evolved from struggling through a five-hundred-meter session of freestyle to timing sets and sprinting butterfly back and forth under the East L.A. sun.

In all the shame and loss that came with the end of my youthful swimming career, I had forgotten why I ever swam in the first place—I love swimming! I love the jolt of energy you get jumping in the pool the first time. I love feeling weightless and gliding up and down a lane, as opposed to the rest of my life, where it seems like everything is an uphill slog and there's nothing but crushing resistance. I love the complete quiet of being below the surface, no phone calls, no intense music or annoying podcasts, no jackass talking at you in a coffee shop about how *he* has been really struggling in the comedy industry because no one wants to hire straight white guys anymore. All of that is gone, and it's just me, in the water, doing something I love.

As a younger person, I loved sports because I loved being competitive. I loved being special and part of a team. When I stopped being an athlete, I struggled to know who I was. Yes, I had been "a swimmer" and "a rower" for years, but what I really *was* was competitive and intense. And I am still competitive and intense. (Just ask the other shoppers at Union Market when there is only one container of bright green half-sour pickles left.) That part of me has evolved. It's expressed itself in professional endeavors and also mellowed out significantly. But it's still there. I still catch glimpses of that part of me in the pool. When I'm upside down in a flip turn at the wall, my brain sometimes transports back to that simpler time when swimming was my whole world and the next lap was the only thing I had to think about. But then I push off the wall and kick toward the surface, and I have a new feeling. I feel lucky to do something I love so much and for it to bring me only joy. The agony of losing is gone. What's left is just me getting to do something I love, that I've always loved.

When I moved back to New York a year later, I kept swimming. I'll never row again, and I know that. I have made my peace with the fact that my spine can no longer handle lifting boats over my head or an hour of steady-state rowing. I miss it, but I get to fondly remember that my final race ended in big smiles on the medal dock at one of the most prestigious collegiate races in America.

In the years between my elite athletic career ending and returning to the pool, I've been through a lot. Comedy is competitive, and I walked in knowing that. When I think about the entertainment industry and its vicious cycle of intensely emotional ups and downs, I'm grateful that I came into this industry an athlete. I arrived in this world ready for devastation, with an understanding of failure and the capability to work hard but also move on.

I love sports. I think I'll never be competitive in them again (lol, "think," as if at forty-two I'm going to change beach volleyball forever), but I love that I spent fifteen years as an athlete. I know I wouldn't trade those years for anything. And I know that tomorrow at noon, when I show up to the YMCA to swim my two-thousand-meter practice in my worn-out navy-blue Speedo, I'll still be a swimmer. And whether he knows it or not, I'm racing the guy in the lane next to me. Just for fun, of course.

I
HAD
AN
ABORTION

don't remember when or how I learned what an abortion is. I do remember when I didn't quite know yet: Crazy Hat Day in third grade.

When School Spirit Week rolled around that year, I needed to come up with a "crazy hat" to wear, even though I had no clue what that had to do with school spirit, not to mention it sent a mixed message about indoor hat wearing at school. My mom suggested that I cover a regular baseball cap with lots of "crazy" pins from a collection she'd amassed over the last few decades. (In retrospect this was probably so she could avoid spending $15 on something stupid I'd wear once—the same logic she passed down to me, and the reason why I would never buy a wedding dress, since you wear it once and then leave it in a closet forever. I'd rather have a camel-hair coat for that price.) We sat on the floor of my parents' bedroom and riffled through the box together. I selected a lot of the usual suspects, like my beloved Book It! pin (of course covered in stickers because I *was* a reader as a child and I *still* reward myself with pizza for finishing a book). But then I reached for a black pin with a pink triangle on it that said CHOICE. I didn't know what it meant, but I liked it. It kind of had *Jem and the Holograms* vibes, as if you could touch it and magically change back into Jerrica. My mom noticed and grabbed it, saying, "Not that one."

At eight years old, I didn't even have a real working knowledge of what sex was. My mom didn't take time out of our arts-and-crafts project to walk me through the concept of terminating a pregnancy, let alone why that was something that would need a pin and a slogan and an entire political movement. I think I learned about it a few years later, either through fearmongering in health class or in a rumor whispered in the swim team locker room about someone's older sister and her even older boyfriend.

While I may not remember the specifics of how I learned about abortion, I absolutely remember the tenor of every mention of it throughout my entire life: It was the biggest thing that could happen to a woman, a shameful and horrific consequence of sex. It got half a class period's worth of time and was mostly described as "a horrible situation," "a great tragedy," and, all too often, "poor decision-making." Kids in my rather conservative Maryland town could barely utter the word because it felt so scary. It was bigger even than becoming a mother. Giving birth (an actual big thing) was glossed over as a stepping stone on your journey to having a family.

In TV shows and movies, abortion was often "a very special episode," usually about a young girl who finds herself in trouble. It was saved for scary dramas, featured "bad" characters, and was played out as a wildly painful trauma to endure. In *Dirty Dancing,* it's a nearly fatal experience in a back alley. Or abortion was something that didn't happen because the character would opt to continue her pregnancy and avoid the horrors of the procedure. She would either pivot to happily becoming a mother (I see you, Miranda Hobbes) or be written off the show to raise a baby somewhere. So every mention of abortion when I was growing up, in real life and in fiction,* was traumatic and too overwhelming to actually address.

As a young person with little understanding of the world outside our lacrosse- and golden-retriever-loving enclave, I understood abortion was a big deal, but not for the same reasons as my friends who whispered about it at swim practice. Without saying much, my mother had always instilled that it was very important—important enough to defend with a commemorative pin. She had gone to march on Washington in 1992, where she'd gotten the pin and a matching T-shirt that read PRO-CHILD PRO-FAMILY PRO-CHOICE.† I'd seen the shirt throughout my childhood and never thought twice that it might be something others wouldn't agree with. If this "choice" is in the same bucket as "family" and "child," then surely it's a good and important thing and not a moral abomination. It wasn't a massive life ruiner as our community believed; it was an important right, a right women should fight for.

Once I was a teenager, my mom walked me through her politics,

---

* There was one program I saw when I was younger that DID depict a girl deciding to have an abortion and then actually staying on the show. It was *Degrassi: The Next Generation* and my college friends and I watched it in our living room hungover every weekend. Way to go, Canada!

† This shirt is now in my possession. If she couldn't save a nineties Coach bag for me, at least I have this.

telling me about the march in Washington and that she was an active donor to NARAL. She didn't need to spend too much time explaining why, since supporting abortion access certainly aligned with my family's liberal politics, which weren't the norm in blond-haired, blue-eyed, Jesus-loving Severna Park. There was one provider in town, and anti-abortion activists regularly parked outside with the graphic signs that we've all come to know and love: tiny hands, bloody fetuses, threats of an eternity burning in hell. It was a super chill and not at all upsetting sight to see as I shuttled between school and sports practice every day.

But while I spent my childhood learning that abortion was the biggest deal, I never thought about sex the same way. I saw how the Christian girls I grew up with feared sex, how they wanted to wait for their husband and save sex for creating a family. None of that matched up with the politics in my home, or the fact that my parents were both divorced before they were married to each other. There was no way sex could be the big deal everyone said it was. And it wasn't, really. When I lost my virginity as a teenager, it wasn't to my first great love, he was barely a first great like. (No shade! Nice guy! Just not exactly *Romeo and Juliet* over here.) I had a very wild and free twenties and thirties living in New York and meeting guys I was interested in enough to bring back to my apartment. I've never been a "third date before sex" person. Honestly, I've rarely been a "first date before sex" person. More often than not, I've been a "two beer/shot combos before sex" person. It's not that I haven't taken the idea of sex seriously, but I never put it on a higher pedestal than "Will this be fun and relatively safe?" If the answer is yes, then sure, why not?

I've also played it fast and loose with birth control for most of my adult life. In the early 2000s, my drug of choice was Yaz. It was really popular at the time, like MTV's *TRL* and Abercrombie & Fitch* (the first time around). But after my near-fatal blood clot, I went off hormonal birth control, and I know that many women who took the same pill also developed blood clots. These days the vibe around it isn't so much "Yazzzz qween!" as it is "Yaz is the subject of several class action medical lawsuits." After I got off the pill, my birth control plan was a patchwork of condoms, the pullout method, and the occasional Plan B that I purchased at the Wegmans pharmacy in a panic. I kept kicking the idea of a more reliable birth control method down the road, always assuming I'd figure it out when I was in a "serious relationship." But a series of flings and one-night stands usually meant condoms anyway, so I figured I'd be fine.

Starting in my late twenties, I found myself in a long-term casual relationship with a guy I'd known for a while. He was objectively hot, funny, and flirty in a way that felt like he was saying lines written for television. The way he would talk to me (and other women) would feel just as acceptable in an episode of *Sex and the City* as it did in the basement of a bar in Queens. We got along, we had great sexual chemistry, and we had no interest in elevating our relationship beyond this in any way. It was like a New York fairy tale for a busy lady with too many jobs and not enough time. We knew each other both very well and nearly not at all. When we would bump into each other around town, half the time we would hook up, and the other half we would text each other later to make lukewarm plans to hook up soon.

---

* Abercrombie & Fitch had its heyday when tiny polos and low-rise jeans were wiping out the bank account of every teenager in America. Then its graphic tees got lightly canceled and fashion culture moved on from the mall. It is now popular again and I have to fix my face whenever I compliment a woman in her forties on some jeans or a sundress and she's like, "Get this, it's from *Abercrombie*!"

Seven years into this on-and-off arrangement, I was on a career trajectory that felt legitimately thrilling. All the hard work and slogging through open mics and bad shows and failed interviews and writing packets had paid off and I was finally getting the exciting opportunities I'd always wanted. I was in the back half of my first season writing for *The Marvelous Mrs. Maisel* and I was asked to go on tour opening for Ilana Glazer and to be an executive producer on her first stand-up special. It was the most high-profile work I had ever done in my career, and I was elated. One day I was sitting in my *Maisel* office in Brooklyn drinking the free mini cans of Diet Coke, the next week I was jetting off to exotic places like Milwaukee and Tucson, where I'd treat myself to the green room Diet Cokes. This was the glamorous comedian life I had always dreamed of: free soda in different cities.

It was complicated, but I made both jobs work. *Maisel* gave us a few weeks off at the beginning of the summer while they were in production, so I wrapped up my time in the writers' room, then did the two-week tour with Ilana and crew, only to fly back the morning after the special taped to attend a table read for a *Maisel* episode, and then two days later I was on a flight to Miami for a week to work on location. There was barely time in that schedule for me to carve out meals and sleep, but it was totally worth it. A few years earlier, balancing a tricky schedule had involved taking a red-eye flight from a comedy festival where I lost money after paying for my own travel, then immediately heading to my day job doing data entry at *USA Today*. Now I was flying business class and sitting in rooms of celebrities reading my jokes. It felt surreal. It felt like a mix of "I can't believe this is happening!" and "Of course this is happening, this is what was always supposed to happen!"

In the panicked weeks leading up to all that travel, I had a few mind-clearing appointments with my casual sex friend. Different stresses have different remedies. Sometimes you want a massage, sometimes you want a nap, sometimes you want to meditate, and sometimes you want a guy you know to show up at your apartment at nine P.M., make you cum three times, and then leave so you can sleep peacefully alone in the middle of your bed.

Days before I headed off to start the tour, my good friend Kris came over to eat snacks and work on the pilot we were writing together. We had done this once a week for months and ended up with a solid script, an encyclopedic knowledge of *The Comeback,* and an undying love for a seltzer brand (Fiz) that has since disappeared off the face of the earth. At our last writing-and-snacking session before I went on tour, Kris was about seven months pregnant. She had been unimpressed with the whole experience. She would show up in bike shorts and an oversize band T-shirt and point to her growing belly every week, saying, "Isn't this *so* weird?" To be fair, it was weird. No matter how many people I know have children, it is always weird to see someone you know go from not pregnant to pregnant to a parent in less than a year. Kris was reclining on my couch eating the last of some feta dip when I went into the bathroom and noticed what seemed like spotting. I yelled from the bathroom, "Ugh, I think my period is about to come. RIGHT for the beginning of tour, this is the worst."

Most women have a sense of their menstrual cycle, either by intuitively understanding their body or by relinquishing all control to their phone via a tracking app. I'm a mix of both. I'm a longtime user of Clue to keep track of my period and its ever-changing nightmare of symptoms. But I also feel in tune with my body. Nearly three decades into menstruation, I have a pretty good handle on the warning signs of an impending period. Irritability, irregular digestion, swollen breasts, crying during a commercial for Dawn soap when they remind us their products are used to clean off ducks and seals after oil spills. I was checking all the period boxes and already dreading being on a cross-country flight with cramps, bloating, and the kind of fatigue that often leaves me thinking, *If I stopped and took a nap on this bench, would someone kill me or just rob me, and how much cash do I have on me right now?*

A few days later my period still hadn't shown up, but that didn't quite worry me. Given the adrenaline, stress, and irregular sleep and eating patterns, I figured my cycle was going to get thrown off with all the travel. We had started in Tucson, then went on to Phoenix, then to Nashville. By the time we got to St. Louis, I was extremely tired and nauseous, but my period was still nowhere to be seen. And when I opened my period-tracker app to see how bad it was, Clue was like, "Girl, what the hell is going on over there?" (Okay it didn't say that exactly, but that was the tone.) I was well over a week late, something that had never happened to me before, and I felt like shit, with no period in sight. I knew what I needed to do: buy a pregnancy test.

I felt scared as I headed to CVS, which was new for me since it's usually a joyful occasion.* I love drugstores. I love any store where you can plan to stop in for a box of tissues and leave with two kinds of M&M's, nail polish, gummy vitamins, Diet Coke, a sparkly birthday card, and the latest in advanced Swiffer technology. But on this trip, I was on a mission. A mission in a red state during a moment of radically conservative anti-abortion lawmaking. It was June 2019, and Missouri, Texas, and a few other states had proposed eight-week or total abortion bans. I was accustomed to my

---

* This was before every drugstore became a Plexiglas prison for deodorant and Advil.

liberal New York CVS stores, the ones with ample seltzer offerings and the belief in a person's right to their own bodily autonomy. I figured a CVS in Missouri would have the shelves of the fertility aisle lined with crucifixes and topped with a wooden sign that said BLESS THIS MESS in that "Live, Laugh, Love" font.

Thankfully this was a normal CVS, as I presume they all actually are, so I grabbed my pregnancy test (okay, and a Diet Coke),* and headed back to my hotel room. I had never taken a pregnancy test before, so I went into the bathroom, sat down on the toilet, and unfolded the instructions. After several Covid waves I'm now almost too comfortable with home diagnostic testing, but in 2019 it was all new to me. I imagined that just like everything else, taking a pregnancy test in real life would be exactly as I'd seen on TV. A woman sits down on the toilet, sticks her hand with the test into the bowl between her legs, and does her best to aim her stream of pee onto the stick. Then she leaves it on the back of the toilet and the wrong person finds it and—uh-oh! Confusion ensues! I was the only person in this hotel room, so at least that part felt unlikely. But I read the instructions for this test and learned that instead I should pee into a cup, and then put the stick in a cup. The diagram made it look less like a medical device and more like the swizzle stick in a cocktail that is about to ruin your life.

Of course, this hotel room had no disposable cups anywhere to be found, just those crystal scotch tumblers that are inexplicably in hotel bathrooms. What kind of *Mad Men* fantasy do they think I'm living out in a Courtyard by Marriott? But I didn't have a choice.

---

* This is easily the fourth or fifth Diet Coke reference in this chapter and I just want to recognize that I am aware of this, but it is my personal belief that Diet Coke and reproductive freedoms are inextricably linked, and so while this is an essay about abortion, it is also, as are likely many essays in this book, about soda.

So I peed right in the glass and dropped the test in. It didn't even make me wait; it barely broke the surface before instantly turning blue. I'd been agonizing over taking this test for a few days and it barely took a few seconds to give me the answer.

I was pregnant. I was pregnant and didn't want to be pregnant. I was pregnant and didn't want to be pregnant and I was in Missouri. For a lot of people, that's a horror movie. It's a life ruiner. It's the scariest thing that can happen to a person. I was extremely lucky at that moment because I was in Missouri only for another twelve hours.

I did what any responsible person would do when they found out they were pregnant: I texted one of my best friends, Divya, "lol i'm pregnant." I didn't tell anyone else. At the time I thought about sending that same text to all my other friends, at least those in the best-friend tier. For a second I was like, "Should I tell my mom?," and then I laughed out loud at the idea of sharing this with her. Not a chance.

In this moment, I knew I did not want to be pregnant. This was not the time, not because I was so busy with my career or that this wasn't the right guy, but because there was never a time I wanted to be pregnant. I didn't want this baby because I don't want any baby. My disinterest in motherhood crystallized in this moment: I do not want to be a mother. Not now, not ever. So, unlike some people, I didn't have a phase of decision-making to sort through. I wasn't weighing pros and cons or evaluating if this moment was the one. I knew what I was doing, and now I had to do it.

When I got to my new hotel room on our next tour stop, in Milwaukee, I called Planned Parenthood of Greater New York.

I explained to the nice woman on the phone that I needed an . . . [whispered] *abortion.* Even on the phone with Planned Parenthood, I couldn't say that word in a normal tone of voice. It could have been because I was sitting on the Milwaukee RiverWalk next to a seagull the size of a royal corgi and I didn't want it to judge me. But I whispered it mostly because regardless of how much agency I had or how long I had been an advocate for reproductive rights or how understanding the person on the other end of the phone was, it still felt too big to say. We have burdened the word *abortion* with so much cultural and political baggage that simply mentioning it polarizes a conversation.

The first thing the receptionist asked me after my whispered confession was "Are you pregnant?," which was not a question I was expecting. Of course I was pregnant. Who is calling to make an abortion appointment without knowing whether they're pregnant or not? People must be out here sleeping with a guy and then thinking, *I have* got *to get ahead of this, whatever happens.* (Actually, I understand that move.) But I told her yes, I was very much pregnant.

I was in the last week of the tour at this point, but I had only one day to squeeze in a quick abortion before I had to be on location in Miami for work. Thankfully, Planned Parenthood was open and performed abortions on Saturdays. My lucky day! Next, I had to decide if I wanted "the pill or the procedure." I haven't been so stumped by a question since the last time a waiter asked me, "Fries or salad?" I knew there were two options, but I had no idea which one I should choose. Pill certainly sounded easier. For any other medical situation if they were like, "You can take a pill to deal with this or you can have minor surgery," you'd always choose the pill. But then I remembered one time I took Plan B in college and it felt like having twelve periods at once, so maybe the procedure was the answer. I kept begging the receptionist to just choose for me, which for a variety of extremely valid reasons she could not and would not do. When she informed me that they put you under for the procedure, I was like, "Okay, then that's definitely the answer, isn't it?" I mean, it was going to be a Saturday after all, I should be doing at least *some* drugs.

While my body was seemingly rejecting the idea of being pregnant, my mind was barely registering what was happening. I was far more stressed out by the logistics of scheduling and traveling and working than by my upcoming abortion. Despite years of conditioning that abortion was a "big deal," this was turning out to be a "big deal" the way that scheduling a meeting during a holiday week is a "big deal": mostly just annoying and tedious. I didn't spend a single day staring out the window wondering about my future. Not once did I curl up in bed crying over the difficult decision I was making. I've learned throughout my life that things that actually happen are rarely like what we've been taught to expect, but this felt extra strange. Surely I had to feel SOME way about this, but I didn't. I wanted to get it all over with so I could go back to my "regular" life. But at the same time, I was relieved I didn't see that pregnancy test and collapse in grief and despair.

Finally, I landed back home in New York after a very fun and nauseating week wrapping up the tour. That Saturday, my alarm went off at seven A.M.: It was time to do this.

When you have a procedure abortion at Planned Parenthood, they make you commit to a four-hour window for the experience. (If you thought movies were getting too long, wait until you have an abortion.) I met Divya near the subway in SoHo and we walked over to the clinic to get this show on the road. I wasn't really nervous, but I also had no idea what exactly was going to happen. My nerves weren't around my decision, or my new life as a woman who had an abortion. I was mostly anxious about how it would feel physically, and where it would rank on my leaderboard of surgeries. I crossed my fingers it would hover around the bottom, somewhere below my root canals. It was a hot and sunny June morning, the perfect kind of morning to be holding a big iced coffee while walking around. Instead, I couldn't have anything to eat or drink because I would be under light anesthesia. I guess if I had to give up my morning caffeine ritual at least it was for a good reason: getting knocked out so that I was no longer knocked up.

I had walked by this Planned Parenthood hundreds of times because it was across the street from a venue where I hosted a comedy show. Something that didn't register until this particular walk down Bleecker was that it's also directly across the street from a luxury maternity store called Hatch, which at the time had a linen jumpsuit in the window that cost $400 and a stupid straw hat that I assume would have set me back a month's rent. Can't that store exist in the quiet corners of upper Madison Avenue or tucked away in Park Slope? Does a storefront that poses the question, "Haven't you always imagined yourself a mommy influencer with dozens of photos of yourself looking ethereal in a field?" need to be in eyeshot of the entrance to one of the very few places you can get an abortion in this city??

Once inside, I discovered the Planned Parenthood office was kind of a labyrinth of different types of waiting rooms. The first one, right inside the entrance, was the biggest. At eight it wasn't particularly crowded, and the people sitting there were mostly guys in athletic shorts and sandals hunched over their phones, miserable from the excruciating task of sitting in a chair for a few hours. I assumed they were the husbands, boyfriends, and maybe the one-night stands of the people who had made it through to the other rooms beyond the front desk. Divya came with me to be my chaperone home (apparently after light anesthesia you're incapable of sitting in an Uber on your own), but once I was escorted back, she left to play tennis and buy us pastries for after.

It wasn't until the next waiting room that the reality of this situation landed on me a bit more. The room was noticeably smaller and exclusively for patients. Maybe we had all ended up there in different ways or had different emotions around what was about to happen, but every person in that waiting room was about to have an abortion. I wondered how many of them felt the same way I did. I wondered if they were eager to get the procedure done because it was an annoying speed bump in their lives. Or perhaps they wanted it to be over because it was a tragedy they weren't ready to process yet. Maybe some were not so eager to be out of here and were savoring these moments for emotional reasons. Looking around that room, I found myself thinking, *Should we all go out together later? Like a happy hour or something?* It would have been nice to share with one another how we got there and what the hell we were supposed to feel next.

This was the moment that all the TV shows and movies had taught me was going to be so fraught and scary. So far, finding out I was pregnant and making my abortion appointment had mostly involved reading printed instructions and speaking with a medical scheduler, which are both unpleasant but not exactly life-changing. Presumably, the abortion itself would be the same level of administratively annoying and unemotional. But thanks to television and film, I had expected teary eyes, crumpled tissues, whispers of "It's all going to be okay." I thought maybe after leaving our friends and family in the first waiting room, we'd all be there for one another, that this weird sorority would support its own in the face of one of life's most tragic moments. I knew that this decision was permanent and occasionally fatal. I knew that people—my mother included—had spent their lives fighting for my right to be here, in this waiting room. I had imagined that this would be a bigger moment in my life than my spine surgeries, graduating from college, dropping out of grad school,* and finally wearing through my favorite jeans to a point of disrepair combined. That I was about to become a different person. That on the other side of the waiting room I would be something new: a woman who had an abortion, like a scarlet *A* I'd wear around for the rest of my life—a devastating future, since red kind of clashes with my complexion. And then I sat down and realized we were all just women on our phones trying to get through the day. I was relieved to find yet another step in this process just as mundane as the rest. I was scrolling through Twitter. The woman a few chairs down took two phone calls during our time together and neither one was a sobfest about what she was about to endure. One of them was just some fairly juicy-sounding gossip about someone else.

When the nurse finally called me back, she ran through the standard physical exam stuff: blood pressure, temperature, weighing me for some reason. I've never ignored a number faster in my entire life. I wasn't very far along, but still, I told myself this was obviously a meaningless temporary weight. I even joked with the nurse, saying, "Well, for now!" when she read out the number on

---

* So after I didn't get into any of my literature PhD programs, I did briefly enroll in a master's program in media studies at NYU before I started doing comedy. I quit after a year and was blown away to learn I still had to pay back those loans. Seems unfair.

the scale. My lifetime defense mechanism has been inappropriate jokes when I'm nervous, and she totally rolled with it, laughing as she wrote down a number that I refused to recognize.

Then I was sent back to the waiting room for another half hour before another nurse came and brought me back to another exam room, this time for a sonogram, which felt like the weakest, wettest massage I've ever received. It all seemed pretty standard until she started asking me questions that took me out of the "this isn't that bad" haze I was in.

"Do you want to know if there's a heartbeat?" she asked.

I was caught off guard. It was a question that I had assumed they only asked when you were in one of those clinics that pretend they perform abortions but are really run by religious extremists who think they can trick a woman into having a baby. I debated for a minute. Did I want this information? What good would knowing that possibly do? It wasn't like there was anything that could change my mind. They could roll that gooed-up wand over my abdomen and say, "It turns out you're about to give birth to a quadruple threat who will sing like Donna Summer, dance like Channing Tatum, act like Meryl Streep, and be the only person in the world who can develop a real cure for seasonal allergies," and I would still do exactly what I came there to do. I didn't want to be pregnant, I didn't want to give birth, and I didn't want to be a mother, full stop.

I declined to know whether there was a heartbeat. I already had one heartbeat to focus on, and that felt like enough.

Nothing could have prepared me for her next question, though: "Do you want to know if it's twins?"

I was speechless. I'm never speechless. I always have a joke or a response or at least something to say. I must have stared at her blankly for twenty seconds. I couldn't stop wondering whom this question was for. Who shows up to have an abortion and then finds out it's twins and is like, "Oh, two? Never mind, I'm good, thanks! I'll just keep 'em!"? I again declined the information, not because it would change my decision, but because even though it was my body, it kind of didn't feel like my business. (A day later, in a true George Costanza "jerk store" moment, I thought of the response, "Is it going to cost more if it is twins?")

There was a little more waiting after the sonogram and then it was finally time to have my abortion. I changed into a hospital gown and put my T-shirt and boat shoes in the little locker they provided me. Everyone was nice, which should be obvious, but it didn't feel put-on or purposeful, like they were pitying me or kid-glove-handling my experience because I was a fragile woman in a tragic scenario who needs extreme gentleness so she doesn't shatter into a billion sad pieces. They were all just friendly professionals trying to make this as painless as possible. A nurse brought me back into the procedure room, which was bright white and very cold. The doctor explained that I would be awake and conscious, but wouldn't remember anything from the procedure, which would in total be around fifteen minutes long. Then a technician started an IV in my arm while trying to make small talk by asking what I did for work.

I panicked and said, "I'm a comedian." I almost never tell strangers what I do for work, mostly to protect myself from having to go down a long dark road of talking about comedy and which famous comedians I know and how I "come up with my jokes." There is no real answer to that question. If you're reading this and ever meet a comedian, don't ask this. None of us can answer it.

I wish I could remember what came next in that conversation, but the next thing I knew I was sitting in a chair in the recovery area drinking a ginger ale and talking to a different nurse. I came to mid-sentence, saying, "It's crazy, I'm not even nauseous anymore."

The nurse responded, "I know, you said that."

Confused, I asked, "What do you mean you know? When did I say that?"

"Oh, you talked the whole time."

The. Whole. Time. I talked the whole time. I talked through the entirety of my abortion. I said I'm never speechless and I guess this is proof. Even an abortion won't stop me from talking, and more specifically, from complaining.

I finished my ginger ale and cookie, stood up, got my clothes from my locker, and left. That was it. The big thing was over. And it . . . didn't feel big. Just a few weeks earlier I'd had two root canals and that experience was harder in every conceivable way: physically, emotionally, financially. A lifetime of expecting this to be tragic and traumatic and overwhelming was wrong.

I met Divya in the waiting room, where she was now sitting, post-tennis and with a big bag of cookies, among the boyfriends. We grabbed an Uber, got home, and pulled out all the treats and spread them across my coffee table. Kris came over to hang, not because I needed support in the traumatic event I just endured, but because we hadn't seen each other in three weeks and we had a lot of gossip to catch up on. She sat next to me on the couch, she eight months pregnant now, I about two hours un-pregnant. But nothing had changed. I wasn't a different person, huddled among my friends in need of love and care. It was like every other Saturday I've had, except that I was wearing a pad. Twenty-four hours later I would be sitting in a business-class seat having a late-morning gin and tonic on my way to a week of work in Miami. Life kept going.

Having an abortion didn't even come up very much in conversation. It was easy to tell my close friends, whom I just filled in when I next saw them.

"How was the tour?"

"It was great, honestly. It's wild to play to such big crowds every single night. We spent a lot of time in a sprinter van. I saw Caroline in Dallas, since she lives there now. Also, I had an abortion when I got back. Oh! And the Miami shoot was nuts, they had this massive wrap party at the end at a Michelin-starred place!"

I passed it off as nothing. No one had a big reaction. A few friends wished I had told them sooner, more just to have the information than to do anything, since there just wasn't much to do. I could read on some people that they wanted me to feel more, just because I think they thought it was supposed to be a big deal, too. It was like we all were learning in real time how not a big deal this was (for me at least!), and moving on in conversation felt both right and weird.

Then my mother visited. She had just retired from forty years of teaching, so as a treat I got her train tickets and a hotel room to spend time with me in New York. My parents visit a lot, but they are always coming up together, which isn't ideal, since my mom absolutely loves New York (she grew up just over the George Washington Bridge) and my dad would probably rather sit alone on a bench in the woods than walk fifteen blocks to another crowded restaurant. My treat to her was some one-on-one time in the city she always wants to be in. And we really did live it up. We went to the Whitney, we walked along the High Line, we browsed through a Madewell without getting into a fight. It was one of our best days together, ever. Not once did my mom hold up a shirt in that store and loudly say, "Who would buy this?"

Lunch was where things took a turn, though. We both settled into our seats at a stylish farm-to-table restaurant with our Diet Cokes and started talking about what was happening in the news, specifically politics, now that we were in the twilight years of the first Trump administration. I'm incredibly lucky that I rarely have to worry about talking politics with my parents. Sure, there are some newer progressive viewpoints they don't know about, but they're always open to them as lifelong liberals. I mean, they're still boomers, but they're liberal boomers and I'll take that as a win. And when it comes to abstract discussions of reproductive rights, talking to my mom has always been more like talking to a friend than to a parent from a different generation. We talked about how deeply afraid we both were about the abortion bans that were being passed that summer, and that this concerted effort to strip away abortion rights might actually work.

Then my mom said, "I don't think I've ever told you this, but I had an abortion before *Roe,* and the Mafia did it."

What.

What.

Like WHAT are you talking about? You DON'T KNOW if you've EVER TOLD ME that you had a MOB ABORTION????????? I feel like we'd remember that conversation. Something tells me both of us would file that away as a pretty big moment in our mother-daughter relationship.

When she was in college, my mom got pregnant and needed an abortion. Bravely, she told her parents. I'd always known my grand-parents to be more liberal than conservative: I'm pretty sure they always voted Democrat, and they weren't the type of relatives I had to steel myself against every Thanksgiving because who knows what kind of slurs or rants about who deserves housing would come out of their mouths. And as a Jewish family, our dogma is not anti-abortion like many Christian denominations'. But this was the late sixties and their daughter was pregnant, so I have no idea the strength it took for my mom to tell her parents. Hell, my mom is pro–abortion rights and very liberal, and at age thirty-five I was still terrified to tell her.

She explained that at the time, my grandmother worked for a law firm that helped the Mob. (I tried to stop the story there to be like, "I'm sorry, what was Grandma up to?" but we kind of just breezed by it and I still don't have any answers on that whole deal.) She then explained that the guy who set it up assured them it would be safe, telling her, "Don't worry, we do all the Rockettes," which might be the most New Jersey thing that's ever been said.

The fear I always felt about abortion aligned with the experience my mom had. Hers was the tale that terrifies young people: My grandfather dropped her off in a parking lot, where she and another girl were picked up in a town car, blindfolded, and driven all over New Jersey, possibly in circles, for what seemed like hours. They eventually got out at a house my mom had never seen before and were taken to an apartment above the garage. Upstairs, a woman administered a medical douche and then gave my mom a tea to drink, which is one of the pre-*Roe* versions of today's abortion pill. My mom was there all night. She couldn't talk to anyone; she couldn't call her friends or her parents. And then twenty-four hours later my grandfather had to show up at that parking lot and hope they brought her back.

My mom didn't tell me this harrowing story because she wanted to have the world's most intense girl-talk session. She told me this story because she knows what America looked like without *Roe*, how scary it was when people didn't have access to abortion. She brought it up when it mattered, when the actually big, genuinely traumatic experience of her abortion might become the reality for many, many people. Hearing that an upper-middle-class white woman had this terrifying journey to accessing abortion before *Roe* is a reminder that for the last sixty years, people of color, queer and trans people, disabled people, and poor people have been facing the same difficulties while the rest of the country has pretended that access has been protected. For them, it never was.

My mom's lunch-hour story time highlighted for me how silent we still are about abortion and how important it is to talk about it. I'd been afraid to tell my liberal mother about mine. Hell, I whispered the word *abortion* to an actual abortion provider. And here my mom had been sitting on this secret for half a century. Of COURSE we think of abortion as a huge, big deal, we can't even talk about it! I never knew about my mom's abortion, and if I had, perhaps I would have spent my life being less afraid of it, knowing that people do it and even the most harrowing stories can still have the happy ending of a life that continues where you left off. And maybe if I talk more about my abortion, other people facing the same experience will feel less like it's an abstract horror and realize it's a medical procedure you can have and still be yourself.

I always thought that being a "person who had an abortion" was a life sentence, like it was the defining quality you have, that you're a tragic cautionary tale who lives in shame and fear. But now I know that being a "person who had an abortion" is just that, being a *person* who happened to have an abortion. That's what I am. I'm also a person who has stupid tattoos. I'm also a person who has been nominated for writing awards. I'm also a person who briefly got really into hot yoga. I'm also a person who wrote a complaint letter to a salad chain (Chopt, stay on your toes). I'm all of those things, and my abortion is a small part of a really big life. That's how I see it, and I hope that's how others see it and perhaps see their own lives. Abortion doesn't define me any more than any other thing in my life defines me. It's just a thing I have done. And I'm glad I did.

I'M A
LOEHMANN'S
INSIDER

■ ■ ■

I still have a receipt from Loehmann's for a Chloé wool skirt I bought almost fifteen years ago. I can't say for sure where my birth certificate is right now, but I know exactly where this receipt is stored: safely in an unmarked envelope in my desk drawer next to my weed gummies. This receipt should be hanging on a wall in a gilded frame next to my degree from Cornell, since it represents an honestly more impressive feat than finishing four years at an Ivy League institution.

I first saw the skirt, in the winter of 2008, when I was swanning around New York with my first corporate job, and I immediately recognized it from its runway début in a fall/winter collection a few years earlier. It was a brushed-wool and cashmere suiting skirt that was light to the touch but looked like wearing it would make you feel powerful, like if an Avenger were an executive. It had a high waist and A-line cut, as opposed to the ubiquitous pencil skirts seen everywhere from Dior to J.Crew. Even before I tried it on, I knew that despite my entry-level salary and purse full of bagel-shop napkins, it would make me feel like a professional, but not stuffy and conservative. The color was a noncolor, which is my favorite kind of color. A little green, a little gray, a little brown. It was like the chicest mud on earth. The waistline was smooth, no belt loops or visible closure, just an invisible zipper that kept all the lines clean. It had pockets (feminism!), but not the way you'd have anticipated. What looked like a normal seam at the hip actually disguised slim pockets that you could drop some cash or a phone into, though you wouldn't want to actually disrupt the simplicity of the silhouette by doing that.

The skirt retailed for more than $2,000. It hung on the Loehmann's clearance rack for weeks, where it was then discounted to $500. I saw it every Tuesday and Friday when I went in, stalking it from afar while I browsed the Joe's Jeans rack and the other more appropriate (aka cheap and casual) fixtures for my early-twenties self. Eventually the skirt got a light-blue sticker, which meant it was a further 20 percent off, but still wildly out of reach on my entry-level book-publishing salary. Each week I checked on the skirt, confident that someone with great style and more money than me would scoop it up. I visited it like it was a grandparent in a nursing home: checking in, making sure it was still there, then leaving and going on with my day knowing it wasn't really a part of my life. Then one Friday I popped in on my walk home up Broadway and the racks were re-stickered. The skirt was jammed between a pastel-pink Malo sweater and a pair of no-name cotton pants. And there it was, the coveted red sticker, signaling an additional 75 percent discount. The skirt was $125, still steep when you're barely making rent, but attainable luxury indeed. I grabbed it and hustled to check out like I was getting away with a crime. With my Diamond-level Loehmann's Insider Club membership (sorry to brag!), I received another 10 percent off the price. I paid and looked at the receipt for my favorite part, the money I "saved" off the original retail price. There, in giant gray letters at the bottom, it said, "You saved $1,982.50 off retail!" That's more than my rent was at the time. That's more money than I had in my checking account for years. That's more than I had probably spent there to earn my Diamond Insider status that I proudly flashed the sales associate every time I made a purchase like I was an FBI agent arriving to a scene. This was it, the greatest achievement of my life.

I don't have the skirt anymore, even though I do still have the receipt. I no longer go to an office and I also no longer live on just hummus like I did at twenty-four, so the skirt doesn't fit in my life or on my hips anymore. But I still remember feeling so special knowing that not only was I wearing an outrageously expensive Chloé item, but I got it without generational wealth or marrying a hedge fund manager whom I hate. I remember it like I remember so many purchases from the now defunct Loehmann's on Seventy-third and Broadway, which I scoured twice a week on my walk home from my office at Columbus Circle to my apartment on the Upper West Side.

Loehmann's was my meditation. It was where I practiced mindfulness. It was my Zen garden where the rest of the world washed away. It was how I kept myself calm and sane. These days, I just rage-scream into my bathroom mirror every morning to the dismay of my cat and neighbors. Maybe it seems odd to consider a discount department store a way of feeling complete oneness with the universe, but I think it's perfect. Loehmann's was the most chaotic place on earth, aside from LaGuardia airport at Thanksgiving. Filled-to-the-brim racks with very little rhyme or reason to them; every surface covered in merchandise; loud signage hovering over every fixture; announcements and music playing over the sounds of avid shoppers aggressively shoving hanger after hanger down an ungreased metal rack that squeaked with every swipe. But sometimes you need a ton of noise for things to feel silent. The more chaos around you, the easier you can focus on the task at hand and tune the rest out. I went to Loehmann's to dissociate.

New shipments of clothes, shoes, and accessories arrived every Tuesday and Friday, so on those days I would walk in for my hour-long meditation. I'd take off my headphones and stow them with my phone in my big Marc Jacobs purse so I could focus. It was far less of a feat to ignore your phone back then because it was just a small plastic brick that didn't do anything besides call. When the store doors closed behind me, I was in my element. Top 40 radio softly played over the speakers, scoring my shopping experience with Jason Mraz and Kelly Clarkson. The temperature was always perfect, neither hot nor cold, just reasonable and noninvasive. Then I would begin my practice.

The street level was chock-full of contemporary designers that either faded in relevance or stopped existing around the final Obama years. Elizabeth and James, Vena Cava, LaRok, James Perse, racks and racks of Theory suiting and neutral Vince sweaters. Here was where you would find stacks of jeans from every currently hip brand, each sporting their own unique style of stitching on the back pocket. You could easily spend twenty-five minutes sifting through denim, spotting Seven's signature squiggles, Paige's leather tab and diagonal stitches, and Hudson's Union Jack patch. Then you'd take the escalator downstairs, where, under the low ceilings and fluorescent lighting, the real work began. This cavern was the home of the designer racks, the maze of floor-to-ceiling shelves of shoes, a lingerie section that was boudoir meets medical supply store, and, of course, the coveted clearance section. There was an area for purses and wallets, and the staple of every Loehmann's from 2008 until it closed: the display of Missoni scarves in their bright orange boxes that were priced at $79.99 for half a decade. Everyone had these scarves. You couldn't throw a day-old bagel in Manhattan during the mid-aughts without hitting a woman wearing this scarf.

I would go to every single rack and look at every single item. The beauty of Loehmann's was the disorganization. Sure, there were signs, but you might easily find sleek Helmut Lang trousers mistakenly nestled among a row of mature flowy linens from Eileen Fisher. The clearance section was its own separate experience. It was so jam-packed that I could spend a whole thirty minutes on one rack, each item deserving scrutiny and inspection. You could find a size 8 socializing with the size 2s. You could find a runway item hobnobbing with occasion dresses. Sometimes those racks contained only deeply discounted activewear, and sometimes they felt like an entire country of their own, populated by the most expensive items from last season priced the same as Old Navy. Just seeing the freshly filled fixtures (that's a known tongue twister for compulsive shoppers), I felt like a lawyer diving into a mountain of evidence. I'd roll up my sleeves and think, *Time to get to work*.

The hunting is what made it so meditative. My brain was focused on one tiny thing at a time. When I was shopping at Loehmann's, I was thinking only about what was right in front of me. I was wondering if an Akris wool skirt would work with sweaters I already owned (yes, thank god for neutrals), and if a discount from $850 to $129 was a good enough deal (not necessarily!). What I wasn't thinking about was how I had no idea what I wanted to do with my life. I wasn't thinking about how my job had seemed great but turned out to be boring. I wasn't thinking about my college friends morphing into unrecognizable caricatures of adults, absent from my life save for occasional wedding photos popping up on Facebook. I wasn't thinking about how I missed rowing but knew I could never do it again, and how I missed the ease of living at home even though I never wanted to do it again. I wasn't thinking about the loser guys I was sleeping with after nights running around the Lower East Side and how I wanted them to call but also didn't. I wasn't thinking about the future or the past. All I was thinking about was this wool skirt. And when I was done thinking about this skirt, I was thinking about the next skirt.

I don't remember *every* item and *every* purchase from my Loehmann's days—I don't have the resources of the Library of Congress for that kind of archiving—but I do remember a lot of them. There were my teal suede KORS Michael Kors ballet flats with the perfect oval toe bed. The sand-colored, super-tall suede wedge heels, also from KORS, the bridge line between the ubiquitous and affordable MICHAEL Michael Kors and the rich and luxurious Michael Kors Collection only ever found on runways and in boardrooms. (Yes, those classifications mattered as much to me as what the Big Ten versus the SEC means to someone in a bar on a fall Saturday afternoon.)

I think fondly of two Marc Jacobs silk origami-style camisoles that I bought, one in black and one in a nonmetallic bronze color, with delicate spaghetti straps and pleating and seams that made them look like unfolded paper cranes that you could wear. Those were both priced like they were undergarments, but I knew they would be my version of the going-out top. I found a strapless gray wool See by Chloé cocktail dress that I wore to a few parties before swapping it with my dear fellow Loehmann's lover Divya in exchange for a pair of black Chloé ballet flats. The Loehmann's economy existed outside the stores and extended to a best-friend barter system in which prices and values were inherently understood by two extremely advanced shoppers.

And then there was my Dolce & Gabbana cocktail dress, made in the same fabric—a black background printed with flowers in bold primary colors—as the evening gown Carrie Bradshaw was supposed to wear when she was walking the runway in season 4, episode 2, of *Sex and the City*, "The Real Me." The dress wasn't even my style; it had a flowy knee-length skirt, a banded waist, and a slightly gathered scoop neck with angel-hair-thin straps, and was clearly meant to be worn to a garden party or a museum reception honoring someone who had donated to the new Impressionist wing. I wore it to my friend's wedding back home in Maryland with red Sergio Rossi pointed-toe flats I had bought in Paris during college, also at a deep, deep discount. I sat at the country club among the blondes I went to high school with, who were all wearing boring jewel-tone jersey dresses, and I smiled with the secret knowledge that I was wearing all designer. While they were in Lilly Pulitzer and White House Black Market looks, I was matching *the* style icon of the 2000s, wearing head-to-toe Italian luxury like the big-city twenty-four-year-old I was. I lived in Manhattan and worked in the fancy book-publishing industry like the lead in a romantic comedy. I had made it.

I absolutely cherished every item I bought from Loehmann's. And while I loved looking in my shallow excuse for a closet to see Marc Jacobs skirts and Marni cardigans, I loved that meditative experience of shopping in that store more than anything I bought.

And I loved not only being alone with my thoughts, but also getting to participate in that grand Loehmann's tradition of the communal dressing room.

I know so many people loathed it, but oh, I loved the communal dressing room. Maybe it was a lifetime of playing sports and being in and out of locker rooms with a bunch of friends and strangers, but I never once saw it as intimidating. To me, it was camaraderie. You walked into a room that was lined with mirrors at 360 degrees, with racks and hooks hung every few feet to mark your little corner of this reflective kingdom. A low bench lined the walls so you could avoid putting your purse and other clothes on the (probably never cleaned) carpet. It was a house of mirrors at a carnival, it was an all-ages locker room, it was a fashion show at a sleepover, it was the physical manifestation of womanhood. It was capitalism, it was fashion as art, it was body-image hell, it was everything.

Like every single person on the planet, I have an erratic relationship with my body image that goes up and down more than the stock market. Everything I know about the stock market I know from *The Big Short* and quarterly phone calls with my investing guy where I basically black out from confusion and start scrolling Instagram. But I do know that like my body image, the stock market is volatile, often ends up in a crisis, and is shockingly tied to emerging technology. I could be innocently flipping through magazines and suddenly hate the way every part of my body looked. My arms were too large; my stomach wasn't flat enough; my calves were too wide to ever look good in a sandal with an ankle strap. (Mind you these feelings all rushed over me at the time when my body was VERY in line with what the culture deems attractive, more so than it ever had been or likely will be again.)

I'd be moving through the world disconnected from and hating everything about my body. And then I would go into Loehmann's and somehow seeing my body among others made me feel better. Not in a "Wow, okay, I'm in much better shape than all of these people!" way, but more like, "Oh, we're all human and we're all just getting through the day." In a regular dressing room, you just see your own perceived failure to fit into or look good in an item of clothing. In Loehmann's, you could see a woman with a "perfect" body put on a dress that just made her look kind of frumpy, and then turn around and see someone with a less "perfect" body slip into a pair of jeans that made her look unbelievable. It's where I learned the idea that you don't need your body to fit into clothes, you just need clothes that fit your body. It's when I started realizing sizing didn't have to control so much of my self-worth, because it was all arbitrary.

Once, when I was down in the bowels of Loehmann's, a bunch of items on hangers heavily draped over my arm, I found myself in the dressing room next to an older woman pawing through her collection of St. John clearance items. I had stripped down to my Calvin Klein T-shirt bra and Hanky Panky thong, and she was wearing roughly the same amount of clothing, except she had giant tinted sunglasses on, too. We nodded to each other as I dipped in and out of some J Brand jeans and 3.1 Phillip Lim silk tops. Then I stepped into a gunmetal-gray Narciso Rodriguez cocktail dress.

It had a scoop neckline but wide enough straps to wear a bra, fitted to my body but not too tight like the Hervé Léger bandage dresses that were all the rage back then and showed every morsel of food you ate that week. It had tiers and layers of silk and chiffon with tiny pops of magenta. Normally tiers and layers make my body look like one of those paper party decorations that lie flat and then you open it up and it's a 3D pineapple. But this dress made me look statuesque. I felt like Christy Turlington on a red carpet.

As I struggled to reach the zipper up the back, my neighbor kindly offered to help. She secured the dress, and when I took a look in the mirror, she told me, "Oh, you have to get it. Look at your figure!"

Figure is a word used almost exclusively by the silent generation to say a woman's body is, as we millennials would put it, smokin' hot. She was right, though. It was a fantastic dress. It was marked down from thousands to $249, still a big purchase for me.

"Get it," she urged.

I replied, "Oh, I don't really have anywhere to wear it."

"You'll find a reason."

I took her words to heart before asking her to help me unzip the top so I could climb out of this dress that, at retail, cost twice my rent. I tried on the rest of my items. Nothing else had worked out that day, so I took the dress with me as I kept walking around the store. I held it while I browsed the bags and wallets. I hung it up on a shelf while I slid into a pair of too-tight patent leather pumps. I swung it over my shoulder as I breezed through lingerie, examining the Natori bras I would stock up on only when my previous ones had disintegrated. Finally, I put the dress back on the clearance rack for someone else to discover and I left empty-handed. While that woman in the dressing room was right that I'd find a reason to wear it, she also didn't know that I was so broke I had stolen toilet paper from a bar two nights earlier. I was in no place to get a "you'll find a reason" Narciso Rodriguez dress.

I've always thought about that moment with sadness. Not that I didn't get the dress—though obviously I wish I had gotten the dress—but I miss the sense of community that the Loehmann's dressing room provided. In a regular dressing room, during any moment of crisis, you have to ask for help. You'll be squished into a too-small halter gown, sweating more than you do at a Bikram yoga class, about to dislocate your shoulder just so you can keep breathing despite the bodice boning,* and you'll have to yell out, "Actually, Crystal, everything's *not* okay back here." And then a tiny twenty-two-year-old comes and jaws-of-lifes you out of a bridal-shower dress you didn't even like to begin with. That embarrassment disappeared in the Loehmann's communal dressing room. As long as there was one other shopper in that house of mirrors, you had a comrade in arms, someone with whom to share the joys and the indignities of trying on clothes because they were doing exactly the same thing. You were never alone.

Shopping at Loehmann's is not for everyone. In fact, it's not for most people. I just happen to have the very specific taste, experience, and skills required for it to become not just a preferred store, but a lifestyle. Simply liking clothes or liking shopping isn't enough to make a Loehmann's shopper. Wanting to get a deal isn't enough to make a Loehmann's shopper. You need to know what you're looking for and care enough about those specifics to stay on a vigilant, perhaps monthslong, hunt to find it. There's a reason other department stores are well organized, with labeled racks and employees to help you. I understand that, I respect that. But that isn't me.

Personally, I knew what I was looking for, in the physical sense at least. I was looking for designer clothing at bargain-basement prices because that was the only way I could afford anything nice, anything that made me feel like the adult I was supposed to be. I was living in Manhattan in a dark apartment, in an even darker

---

* I will never understand why dresses need boning. I have bones! I don't need more bones!

room within it. I was eating canned soup and free cheese cubes from after-work events, and I was drinking fifty-cent beers on Wednesday nights at a horrifyingly college-y bar in my neighborhood that hung bras on the ceiling. I was walking everywhere and rarely taking cabs. I needed luxury I could hold on to. I needed something that telegraphed to people that I was somebody, that I belonged here. That I was never leaving. The right clothes were my ticket to acceptance, and I actually knew how to acquire them. It didn't matter that I got my Delman flats on a deep discount because size 10s are an oasis of inventory in every store, we all wore them to walk down the streets in New York City (Band-Aids and all).

The height of my Loehmann's habit lasted from when I was twenty-four to when I was twenty-seven. It's a pivotal time in most people's lives. I wasn't a girl, I wasn't really a woman yet—though I was still very connected to Britney Spears. I was trying on different adulthoods, figuring out who I was. What did I actually want out of my career? Who were my friends in New York? What did a partnership really look like? What kind of woman was I? Loehmann's let me have different looks for different parts of my life and try on who I was in an elevated way without committing thousands of dollars to one coat that I'd soon regret. Even the Narciso Rodriguez cocktail dress could have signaled a new version of me, if I'd found a reason to wear it.

Once, crammed into a clearance rack, I found the softest sweater I had ever touched. It was Monique Lhuillier, plush cashmere in bubble-gum pink with little pearls in place of regular buttons. A gorgeous item but deeply not my style. But it also worked because I didn't have a style. I imagined wearing it with ripped jeans, taking something girlie and making it seem edgy and cool by juxtaposition, the way the Olsen twins or Nicole Richie would. So I splurged and spent $100 on it.

I wore it only once, to one of the weirdest dinners of my life. The rising popularity of the original TV show *Gossip Girl* coincided with a downturn in the fortunes of one fancy restaurant on the Upper East Side, whose name changed with the season. Park Avenue Spring (at the time) ran a promotion that my friends and I discovered on one of the many websites dedicated to cheap ways to eat and drink your way through the city: If you came in dressed like you were on *Gossip Girl,* you got a free appetizer, entrée, side, and dessert *per person.* Mind you, this was a fine-dining restaurant with $30 entrées and a wine list that read like a European-history textbook. I still remember my outfit: a pleated Marc Jacobs skirt, a white Theory tank top, and Michael Kors Collection snakeskin pumps, topped off with my pink and pearl cardigan—the perfect look for this very strange event. I sat there in my head-to-toe designer with six girlfriends dressed exactly the same, drinking Italian white wine and eating Chilean sea bass, and when the bill came, sure enough, it was $0. It made no sense to us why they would do this. Until we looked around and saw groups of over-tanned men with pinkie rings and expense accounts surveying the twentysomething women doing their best schoolgirl cosplay. This was at least a decade before Me Too, obviously.

But I was glad I had my perfect Upper East Side cardigan in that moment, the same way I was glad I had my D&G garden-party dress for my friend's country club wedding and the way I had my Theory suiting pants for work and my dark blue Habitual jeans for bars. I had tiny Botkier bags for nights out when the only things I needed were a credit card, a driver's license, and my small brick of a cellphone, and I had my massive putty-colored Marc Jacobs leather bag with eight pounds of hardware on it for my day-to-day schleps to work with a book, two half-read *New Yorker*s, bodega snacks, three tinted lip balms, and at least two stolen cans of Diet Coke from an office fridge. (Carrying the contents and the bag itself qualified as a CrossFit class.) I had my ladylike DKNY and Cole Haan coats for when I was Mary Tyler Moore–ing my way up and down Columbus Avenue in the New York winters and my cool-girl Andrew Marc funnel-neck leather jacket that I wore over gray American Apparel T-shirts to smoke weed outside bars off Bedford Avenue in Williamsburg. I had no idea who I was and what I wanted, but I didn't need to, because Loehmann's let me try it all on. I was a powerful career woman, a downtown cool girl, a chic lady who lunches. I had boho and corporate and girlie and sporty all ripped from the runways and hanging in my closet to grab at a moment's notice. In an era now defined by personal style and capsule wardrobes, I had my own mini department store in my mini bedroom.

Loehmann's was a huge part of my life when the rest of it felt rather empty. I was lost in my twenties. I had a ton of fun and people I loved, but, like many of us, I spent a chunk of that decade trying to sort out who I might be, and often running into walls in the process. I both didn't know what I wanted from a career and wasn't particularly skilled at the things I was doing. I was a bad assistant. I wasn't great in a corporate setting, and I was just as bad a fit in the nonprofit world I went to next. I was creatively unfulfilled and felt like I could not find any professional wins. As friends of mine met and partnered with and broke up with boyfriends, my romantic life seemed to go nowhere, with dates that got canceled and one-night stands that never saw a next day. I wasn't saving money, I wasn't feeling great, physically. I was lost. But I would stop in Loehmann's and find a cloud-gray cashmere Helmut Lang blazer marked down from $650 to $75.98 and feel like I actually achieved something.

Maybe all this brand naming and style explaining feels materialistic. Maybe this is a disgusting chapter of this book and my life and you're reading this being like, "Truly who cares if you wear expensive jeans???!! Read the news and go to therapy!!!!" And I get that! But I'm a woman, and I be shopping. And shopping is not frivolous and clothes are not meaningless, despite what our male-run culture tries to drill into our heads. For a lot of modern history, shopping for clothes was the only way women could even really participate in the capitalist economy.*

Men, on the other hand, are allowed to buy things for the sake of "experience" or "passion" or "interest." That doesn't make it better or worse, but it does make it harder to tabulate and criticize than my closet full of cute tops and chic jeans. A woman who spends money on clothes is frivolous, superficial, materialistic. A man who spends a lot of money on expensive whiskey or nine different ESPN packages† has a hobby. A woman who spends a lot of money on shoes has a shopping problem. I'm not here advocating for shoes to be more socially valuable than alcohol (I would never), but it's true that buying clothes and caring about them is maligned for seemingly no reason except that mostly women do it. And the worst part is that we almost *have* to care about clothes. We're told

---

* I hate capitalism and resent needing to participate in it, let alone making participation in it feel remotely like feminism, and I would burn the whole thing down if I had the energy! Anyway, thanks for buying this book!!!!!!!!!!!

† Okay, neither of these things is necessarily "male" and is also a very specific type of man, but when you describe people who spend money on whiskey and sports channels, most people think, *Oh, men!*

we have to be appealing to men both to attract one (if that's something you want) and to move through our very patriarchal, heteronormative culture. That often means dressing on trend, something that changes very rapidly for women, now more than ever. We have to buy the clothes and shoes and bags that tell society what kind of woman we are so they know what to do with us. We have to shop because we're told we have to look good, and then when we start to actually enjoy that and have a little agency in it, we're considered materialistic bitches.

The world makes me want to shop. I don't actually love spending money, and in my forties I'm less thrilled with the options for my constantly changing (for some reason) body. I'm incredibly aware of the human rights crisis that the fashion industry has created and the environmental disaster that results from every major manufacturing operation. I'm also comfortable in my style and rarely stray from the things I like to wear and want to buy. At this point in my life, I very much know who I am. I may still be exploring things like how my body processes gluten, but the externally changing parts of my life feel set. Now that I know these things, I want to present that person to the world through my appearance. I've settled into a look (in a good way) and know how to shop for high-quality, long-lasting pieces because I don't see that look changing, mostly because I don't see that person changing. And yet I still love to shop.

Loehmann's sadly closed its store doors for good in 2014. Embarrassingly, I cried. Crying when a store you don't own closes feels like a symptom in the *DSM-5* of having lost all touch with reality and needing to be treated for acute consumer syndrome. But I felt like I lost a part of my life that I loved. In the years since, I've had more stress in my life. Part of that is just aging and the anxieties and responsibilities that come with it. Part of that has been the trajectory of my life and having a career in the volatile and deeply destabilized entertainment industry. Part of that is the even more terrifying state of the world. These are the times when I feel like the only thing that will help me get through the day is a one-hour trip to my favorite meditative space where I can literally shut off every part of my brain—except the one that quickly recognizes a rare Dries Van Noten print when it sees one.

I'M UNEMPLOYED

• • •

The summer of 2020, I feared for my life. We were only a few months into the Covid-19 pandemic and nowhere near understanding the virus killing thousands. There were police assaulting protesters in the streets of cities across America. But in addition, I had a more specific threat to my existence that July: A golden retriever named Austin tried to drown me.

I was at Jacob Riis beach with my friend Natasha. We had been chatting on our towels while we watched a woman training her dog along the shoreline, yelling, "Austin!" as he galloped toward her to touch her hand. Once we got hot and sweaty, we went in the water. I'd swum out in the ocean beyond where I could stand, and while treading water, I saw Austin's silly face above the surface as he came paddling up to me. As he approached I thought, *Oh, this is great, I'm in the ocean AND I get to pet a dog!* He kept getting closer. When he was within arm's reach, I expected him to pause for me to scratch his head and then move on. Instead, he took his big paws and put them on both my shoulders, slowly sending me under the surface. After a few seconds he stopped, and then moved on to Natasha, who was swimming near me, and briefly shoved her deeper into the water before swimming off to terrorize someone else. He was an adorable monster.

Aside from near death by golden retriever, Natasha's and my midweek beach trips that summer were always pretty similar, though they still felt like a novelty, or like I was playing hooky. Never before in my adult life in New York could I wake up one morning and decide it was a beach day—at least not without lying to some bosses or canceling shows. I spent my days in writers' rooms, my nights at clubs and bars doing stand-up, and any free time in between writing everything from pilot scripts to humor essays, refining jokes, and appearing on podcasts. But when Covid shut down all the work I had, suddenly the beach on a Wednesday was a weekly occurrence. Natasha was in a similar situation as a celebrated pastry chef who ran desserts for two of the city's greatest restaurants in addition to organizing charity bake sales and volunteering with food banks. We both went from working outrageously hard all day and generally defining ourselves by our very cool jobs to sitting alone in our apartments as the industries we mortgaged our young adult lives for seemed poised to never return from lockdown. No one was eating in restaurants. No one was sitting in comedy clubs. The pastry chef and the comedian were both now just two women in their thirties with a lot of time on their hands. We finally had the leisurely schedule that working hard for decades usually earns, but we had it against our will and without a mountain of money. It was painful how loose my days were, how free I was to do whatever I wanted, because there was nearly nothing to actually do and barely anyone to do it with. So we went to the beach.

I would borrow my friend Sam's car and pack up all our beach essentials. I loaded deli containers of crunchy grapes and watermelon, a few Diet Cokes, and a bottle of natural wine into my cooler bag. Then I'd grab a can of Pringles, which I consider to be the ultimate beach chips because of the closable lid that protects them from the ocean's moisture and also thieving seagulls. Then I'd drive up to Greenpoint and pick up Natasha, who'd prepared our signature "friendship sandwich": a thin layer of high-quality turkey, some rough-cut cheddar cheese, and then a mountain of sprouts, cucumbers, romaine, and any other green things she could find at the market, all smashed between some excellent bread. We'd lug our stuff all the way to where Riis nearly becomes Fort Tilden and set up camp among the other midweek beachgoers who I always assumed also lived alone and were going absolutely stir-crazy during lockdown.

When we sat there looking out at the water, occasionally trying to play cards but realizing it was too windy and we didn't actually know any games, we would talk a lot about what we were going to do with ourselves. Television writing jobs were slowly starting to return with Zoom rooms, and I'd be back working on *Maisel* again by the end of the summer. But stand-up, like Natasha's career in dining, was the Wild West. I didn't want to do outdoor shows, rolling up to Prospect Park at three P.M. to stand in a field like a cow, my rusty jokes competing with a child's birthday party, a game of slam ball, dozens of picnics, and screaming birds. I had no interest in scaling a fire escape four floors up to do a rooftop show while the JMZ lines rumbled by next door. But stand-up was what I loved. It was what I had spent most of my nights over the last decade doing, and suddenly there was nothing to do.

The sun would set, and it would feel odd to be in my apartment.

I should have been lingering in the back of Union Hall looking at my illegible notes about online shopping and being in my thirties. I should have been hustling to the train or walking through the East Village after a set, listening to my own voice in my headphones to see if that new tag worked as well as I thought it would. But instead, I was sitting in my apartment drinking wine alone and rewatching the tape of what became *Oh God, A Show About Abortion*. I had known I really had something there, but I first performed the show on March 2, 2020—ten days before the world shut down.

The disappearance of stand-up during the pandemic was hard not just because I liked being out at night, getting attention, and seeing my comedy friends. In the years since I'd started doing comedy, stand-up became how I defined myself: I wasn't a person who did stand-up; I *was* a stand-up. For better or worse, my worth was tied up in my work. Learning none of the lessons I should have in my athlete days, I lived and breathed comedy from sunup to so far after sunset that sometimes it was sunup again. I always defined myself by the work that I did, and I came to comedy after years of toiling away in the wrong kinds of jobs and industries. Even when I was in wildly different "wrong" lines of work, I found myself trying to force an identity out of what I was doing. And when I realized those jobs were wrong or I was in a job that was more for treading water than existential and creative fulfillment, I felt adrift in the world, not only unsure of what to do, but of who I was. Then I finally found the thing I wanted to be. It was exhilarating! After years of searching, of trying on different personalities like they were a mountain of jeans in a Loehmann's dressing room, of failing and giving up at different things, this made sense. I was ready to put in the work because I loved the work. And just like that (cue Che Diaz quitting stand-up after not selling their pilot), it was gone.

I didn't always know I wanted to be a comedian or a writer. I loved watching comedy of all kinds when I was growing up. I stayed up to watch Janeane Garofalo's half-hour special and can still quote my favorite jokes from it more than two decades later. My friend Siobhan and I would watch *Upright Citizens Brigade* and *Strangers with Candy* from our own bedrooms that were barely a block away from each other, each of us with our eyes glued to the screen and cordless phone pressed against our ear so we could laugh at the absurd jokes together but apart. Our family Hanukkah parties would always end with everyone sitting in the living room to watch tapes we had made of the best *Saturday Night Live* holiday sketches and commercial parodies, everyone red in the face and teary-eyed at our favorites, which we'd already been quoting all night in anticipation.

Despite loving comedy since I understood what it was, I never thought I could actually do it. I don't know who I thought decided who got to be in comedy, but in my mind there was no way any random person could just start doing it, especially a person like me, who had no performance background and no idea how show business worked. I knew that doctors went to medical school, lawyers went to law school, but I didn't understand how comedians became comedians. I'm not from a family in the entertainment industry. I didn't grow up in New York or L.A., where so many people end up in show business after being surrounded by it their whole lives. I had zero performing arts background except for years of playing the piano, which was mostly messing around with my mom's Billy Joel songbooks. On top of that, most of the famous people in comedy, especially stand-up comedy, were men. Whenever I did see a woman on Comedy Central's showcases, she became my instant favorite, but she was always the exception to the very male rule. Comedy felt like a strange fantasy I was lucky to enjoy as a bystander, not a career path I could choose to follow. I figured if you wanted to do a creative job like comedy or writing, a famous person shows up at your door and says, "You! Get to Hollywood NOW!" So as I navigated my own professional endeavors, comedy never felt like it was on the table. But I've since learned that the path to doing comedy is long and confusing, like a Christopher Nolan movie, because my bizarre résumé is something that led, however circuitously, to my comedy career.

Lifeguard, American Pools
2000–2002

Annapolis, Md.

Lifeguarding was probably my horniest job—picture a bunch of people at their physical peak walking around in bathing suits all day getting sun damage. A lifetime spent as a swimmer made this the obvious first job for me. Not obvious was the fact that the company I worked for let me straight-up be the pool manager when I was seventeen, which is entirely too young to be in charge of a folding table, let alone an entire community facility. Lifeguarding was easy and fun for me. So easy and fun that when the Writers Guild of America went on strike in 2023, I debated returning to my watery roots to lifeguard for the summer for some extra cash (and to kill time). I sadly do not qualify to be a public pool lifeguard in New York City because I don't have good enough vision (something that was decidedly *not* a problem for American Pools in 2000). Another dream deferred.

Associate, Sunglass Hut
2002–2003
Annapolis, Md.

I am a firm believer that everyone should work in retail or service at some point in their life. Sunglass Hut was my first of many retail jobs. I didn't work there because of a passion for eyewear (though working there *did* give me an addiction to expensive sunglasses I have never been able to kick). I took this job because the storefront was on the water in downtown Annapolis, where all the exciting bars and restaurants and shopping were located. My best friends, Meg and Erin, worked at Karma Creations (a store that sold home accessories imported from Mexico) and Hats in the Belfry (hats, naturally) respectively, so we'd count the hours until we could close up shop and sneak beers from the historic downtown fixture Middleton Tavern.

Librarian, Olin Library, Cornell University
2004–2006
Ithaca, N.Y.

Over the three years I worked at my college library, I think I cumulatively made like $39. Olin Library was one of the main research libraries at Cornell, where almost every student came to get books, write papers, or at least sit in the coffee shop drinking lattes their parents paid for. I worked at the desk, mostly on night shifts when there was less traffic and more undergrads aggressively banging on computer keyboards to churn out papers that would be due in nine hours. Librarian fit with the whole English major/book lover/creative vibe I had finally landed on in college. I would listen to a Shins album on my first-generation iPod and just shelve books. It was therapeutic. The greatest day of my time there was one particular nine P.M. shift when I was pretty stoned and in the back scanning a stack of books. My manager said that the other student employee was out sick, so they were sending over one of the students who worked at the library next door. To my surprise, in walked one of my friends, Gigi. She was also stoned and we flipped the absolute fuck out over the fact that we were getting paid to be stoned together.

Sales Associate, Nordstrom
2006–2007

Annapolis, Md.

When I graduated from college, I had one real goal: to become an English professor. It was my dream to get paid to read, write, and talk about arts and culture. In fact, that's literally what my job is now, but it's arguably more lucrative and stable than working in academia. Back then, I didn't realize that I could have the career of a professor without suffering through six years of a PhD program. I was an Ivy League–educated book lover (who'd worked in the library after all!), so I had to get an advanced degree and spend my days in good blazers rambling on about Virginia Woolf. While I completed the rigorous application process,

I lived with my parents and worked at Nordstrom part-time to save up some money. Of course, I saved up absolutely no money at all because I worked in the Savvy* department, which was designer jeans as far as the eye could see. Every dollar I made went directly back into the department so I could collect over-priced James Perse T-shirts and True Religion jeans with a microscopic rise, which I would then wear out to the bars to get blackout drunk every night with my manager, Lauren, who looked like a Barbie doll. I was severely depressed because I was twenty-three and felt stuck and unfulfilled, my one goal slipping away as I got weekly rejection letters from PhD programs. I also wasn't good at sales, unless someone who loved clothes as much as I did breezed into the department and was ready to throw down a few hundred bucks.

Editorial Intern, *Baltimore* Magazine
2006–2007
Baltimore, Md.

While folding Rock & Republic jeans at Nordstrom, I also got a postcollege internship at the city magazine for Baltimore. My job mostly entailed writing and editing event blurbs and getting something with crab on it for lunch every day. This was my first job that was, like, a possible career. I grew up on nineties and early-aughts rom-coms, so "magazine writer" was absolutely a de-

---

* The best thing Nordstrom did, besides a good return policy and the best tomato soup in the game, was give the departments enigmatic, vibes-based names rather than clear labels. Savvy was contemporary designer, women's workwear was Individualist. The plus-size women's department was called Encore, which . . . they do not do anymore for very obvious-seeming reasons.

sirable occupation and personality for me to have, but it was nothing like the movies. I worked in a windowless office of almost exclusively women. I never once wore a slingback heel to work. And whenever I dropped a stack of folders and papers, *I* had to pick them up myself without the help of a cute stranger!!!

Fashion Publicity Intern, Yigal Azrouël
2007
New York, N.Y.

Once all my grad school rejection letters came in and I resigned myself to the fact that becoming an English professor was not in my future, I packed up and moved to New York to live with one of my best friends from college. If I couldn't be parked in a modernist literature seminar at Yale, then I wanted to be in the city. After scouring Craigslist for jobs, I landed an unpaid internship with Yigal Azrouël, a fashion designer I loved. My Nordstrom jeans-and-T-shirt vibes weren't quite on par with downtown-chic fashion insiders, but I just loved being around the clothes. However, after a day and a half I realized that messengering a leather handbag to Byrdie Bell's Tribeca apartment was cool, but wasn't necessarily the kind of dues-paying job I wanted to have. I learned there was a difference between loving clothes and actually wanting to work in fashion. I spent my short time there huddled in an office with our showroom model, a stunningly tall and thin young woman named Tinamarie. I wanted to hate her so badly for her otherworldly beauty, but I couldn't because she was cool and fun and kind. Two weeks into the internship I quit to do something else, and though we texted a bit, I lost touch with Tinamarie. She ended up marrying one of Russell Simmons's business partners and now is a life coach in Miami with a few kids, so it all worked out for her.

Editorial Intern, *The Onion* A.V. Club
2007–2008
New York, N.Y.

After realizing that fashion was not for me, I landed what seemed to be a dream gig. I continued looking for writing jobs while I spent my two weeks in fashion, and thankfully I got a job as a (once again unpaid) intern at *The Onion,* specifically working for the A.V. Club, which was the section of the paper devoted to non-satire coverage of arts, culture, and goings-on around New York. It was heaven. I worked right in SoHo next to Dean & DeLuca, where I would pick up a scone and a latte once a week with my parents' money as a little treat. Then I'd get to hang out with all kinds of funny people writing little blurbs and then go out to comedy shows and book parties. Being in the world of comedy and writing felt right. To me, it was the first time any of my jobs made sense. I still didn't quite know what anything was or how to do most tasks, but the culture was right for my personality. Everyone wore jeans to the office. Knowing about the world by scouring all corners of the internet wasn't just accepted, it was encouraged. People had side projects. There were jokes and Bloody Marys and Rollerblades. It was heaven. When I met people out in the city and told them I worked for *The Onion,* it felt amazing. That was in part because it was "cool" and I was desperately chasing "cool" at that point in my life. But it also meant that when someone did appreciate how exciting that was, we could connect over a thing I actually loved: comedy.

Sales Associate, Bloomingdale's, SoHo
2007–2008
New York, N.Y.

Obviously I could not live in New York with just an unpaid internship, no matter how cheap the rent in Greenpoint was at the time. I stuck with what I knew and got a part-time job at Bloomingdale's, mostly because at the time New York did not have a Nordstrom. I was just as bad at sales here as I was the last time I worked in retail—arguably worse, since this job felt even more like it was just filling in the financial cracks in my life. Everyone else on the floor took it way more seriously, especially my department manager. I cried there almost every day.

Sales Marketing Assistant, Random House
2008–2010
New York, N.Y.

When my internship at *The Onion* ended, my editor sat me down and was like, "Yeah, we don't have any money to actually hire you or anyone, so, this is it." Maybe not those words, but that was the gist. From there I spent months and months trying to get a job, any job. I applied to magazines, newspapers, media companies, PR firms, advertising agencies, truly any- and everywhere that would hire an idiot in her twenties with an English degree and a few unpaid internships under her belt. I think it was harder to get a job because I still didn't understand what my passion was. I knew I liked comedy and writing, but I didn't know what kind of comedy and writing I wanted to do, or how to do it, or, even more important, where you could get paid for that kind of thing. I know for many people their job is not their passion, and I'm deeply envious of them. I thought that I needed to find the thing that made me feel whole, the thing that told the world who I was, but I felt so defeated because I wasn't sure what that could be. A lot of my friends did: They were in law school or starting careers in design or human rights. I was still treading water to stay afloat financially (aka calling my parents in tears begging for rent money) and trying to figure out why I could not get hired. Looking back, it was obvious: I was a lost twenty-three-year-old who didn't know the first thing about anything. Thankfully, after a long and brutal year of applying and interviewing and absorbing rejection after rejection, I got a job in the sales marketing department of Random House (yes, THE Random House that published this book you're currently reading!!!!). I reported to two absolutely wonderful people who were good managers and taught me things. Sure, I seethed with jealousy when new authors were published because I thought I should be writing books, but I wasn't actually writing books so I couldn't be that jealous. I amassed so many books that every time I moved apartments it was less a chore and more an Olympic event. But the financial crisis of 2008 hit during my first year working there, and of course everything got terrible. Publishing was struggling in the rapidly digitizing world, and my job got eliminated. I was lucky enough to stay with the company and move over to a department that was much less inspiring to me, with a manager who didn't seem to understand me as well as my previous bosses had. I spent a year stapling together presentations on romance novels for Target before I knew it was time for me to go.

Communications, Museum of the City of New York
2010

New York, N.Y.

If you don't know MCNY, it is a horribly mismanaged but excellent museum up at the top of Central Park. More important, it's next to El Museo del Barrio, which has the best museum cafeteria I've ever been to. Every Thursday my co-workers and I would go get mango salsa with plantain chips and chicken tinga tacos and gossip about how bad everything was at our museum. I made some lifelong friends there whom I still see and drink lots of wine with, but I was not made for that world. Museums in general don't have a great sense of humor, and mine did not fit there. Shockingly, I wasn't even fired for being bad at my job. I was laid off thanks to a budget restructuring, which I discovered when I showed up to work and my desk chair was gone. They invited me to work the rest of the week, to which I simply said no.

Ad Sales Temp, Brides.com
2010–2011

New York, N.Y.

I have no idea what I did at this job. I had just dipped my toe into comedy as I was exiting my museum job, and I knew I just needed a way to make money while I figured out how to do stand-up. So I went to a temp agency and they sent me to the Condé Nast satellite office, where I worked with some very nice people doing a job I surely was fucking up constantly. To this day I don't fully know what CMS is and I do *not* want to know. That is none of my business. My biggest memory from this job was that one of my co-workers would get a Big Mac and a Filet-O-Fish from McDonald's for lunch every day and alternate bites from each of them. He once told me he used LinkedIn to meet women. I still wonder what happened to him.

Ad Sales Associate, *USA Today*
2011–2012
New York, N.Y.

Temp jobs don't provide health insurance, so I had to find something full-time and low stakes to keep my comedy habit going at night. Somehow, I got hired to work in the ad sales department of the weekend insert of *USA Today*. No, I will not follow up with any information about what that means or what I did. I know I did a terrible job there. They told me. I spent all day on Gchat and Twitter, and called out sick during my second week simply because I didn't want to go in. My boss thankfully kind of figured out my deal. (Why he let me do that I'll never know.) He was from Jamaica, and I would later learn he was also an internationally touring reggaeton DJ by night. The bulletin board at his desk in our shared cubicle had two pictures on it: one of his house on Long Island and one that I could only describe as a color printout of a pile of snakes. I made no friends, not a ton of money, and still to this day have no idea what my daily responsibilities actually were. Zero stars.

This ad sales job was my last "day job" that didn't have a connection to comedy. During my time at Random House and the museum, I had started realizing what my actual passion was. Working at *The Onion* showed me the kind of professional environment I wanted to be in, and every job I did after it paled in comparison to working in that SoHo loft. And as I moved through other jobs, I spent a lot of time goofing around on the internet. I got deep in sites that covered the comedy industry and followed blogs of people pursuing the same thing I wanted to. I started to see a road map for what I wanted. I'd been out seeing comedy shows and dreaming of being up there. I could do it. I knew I wanted to create. I wanted to write. I wanted to make things that were funny.

I had started doing a little online writing through blogging and submitting to some websites, and I listened to *The Moth* and *Risk!* podcasts weekly to get inspiration. I was working at my various day jobs and coming home to write blogs and read and watch everything I felt could be vaguely educational for my future as a "creative." My job, twenty-four hours a day at this point, was figuring out how to chase my passion.

I understood that the first step toward writing comedy was to lean into what you know, so I decided to tell the story of how I almost died when I was nineteen. It felt like a perfect fit for the storytelling shows and podcasts I liked, which were as popular as pencil skirts.* I took a storytelling class at the Peoples Improv The-

---

* These things were popular at the time.

ater, taught by the brilliant Kevin Allison,* where I learned about structuring stories, zeroing in on details, and the art of performing, how to draw people in and let them know who you are. When it was time for our class show in a small black box theater, I found out that what I loved most about telling a story onstage was getting laughs from the jokes peppered throughout my harrowing tale. Sure, it was fun to let the audience into my horrors, to keep them in suspense (even though my basic presence kind of gives away the central question of whether I died). It was exciting to be up there alone, the success or failure of the performance entirely on me, not unlike the swim meets I remember all too clearly. But man, when I'd hit a punch line or pause before the reveal of my mom being upset about my back tattoo, nothing in my life had ever felt better. And then I realized, *Wait, that's stand-up.* So I did the only thing my overachieving, rule-following, academics-obsessed brain could handle: I signed up for a stand-up comedy class at the same theater.

Everyone in comedy seems to have an opinion about what "real" comedy is and the "right" way to do it. The answer is, of course: my way. No, I'm kidding, there is no "right" way. Anything that gets you doing it is the right way. Comedy isn't the kind of thing you can really learn from a class, but the class got me hooked. Our instructor, comedian Tom Shillue, would guide us to locate the humor in our totally unfinished jokes. When the course ended, I realized I was absolutely head-over-heels obsessed with stand-up comedy. After years of bouncing around industries that circled entertainment, I had found where I was supposed to be. I was twenty-six and felt so old to be realizing what my great passion was, but looking back on

---

* Kevin was also a cast member of my favorite MTV sketch comedy show, *The State,* and it took me two full classes not to be freaking out inside my head that I was in the presence of an icon. He is wonderful.

it now, it feels so unbelievably young to have figured out something of this magnitude. To find your *life's passion*? And barely be old enough to rent a car? I didn't want to waste any more time, so I asked Tom what I should do next. He said, "Go do as many open mics as you can, every night." And that was it. I never looked back.

The first open mic I did—after googling "where to go to open mics"—was at five P.M. on a Monday at New York Comedy Club on Second Avenue. I walked in nervously with my notebook, paid the host, ordered my obligatory drink* (a bottle of Bud Light), and sat down. I looked around and saw a sea of mostly white men staring at their phones or scribbling on paper. I remember locking eyes with the one other woman in the room, the hilarious Katie Hannigan, who was also just starting out at the time. We bonded instantly, our eyes silently saying to each other, *This is unsafe, right? If something happens, I got you.* But it was fine. They didn't exactly laugh at our jokes, but they didn't try and kill us, and that's a win. It felt invigorating to have done it. I'd performed in the comfort of classes or in front of friends. Everyone there was going to laugh, even when you aren't funny (and at least the first hundred times you do stand-up, you aren't). Despite my nerves, I felt this sense of accomplishment not just at getting up and doing my jokes, but at the fact that my years of feeling directionless might be over.

Every day, I showed up to my desk job at eight A.M., and the second the clock struck five, I was out the door, crisscrossing the city to get to open mics, from a club in Gramercy to the back of a bar on the outskirts of Williamsburg and then back into Manhat-

---

* At the comedy clubs in the city when I was coming up, you had to pay $5 and/ or buy a drink from the bar to get your five minutes. Part of me thinks it's a scam that preys on young broke people pursuing a dream. Part of me yearns for the day I could get a Bud Light for $5 in Manhattan.

tan for the eleven P.M. improv-theater open mic where you got two minutes of stage time. I loved every second of it. Chatting with other new comics in the back of the room, sustaining myself on Sabra hummus-and-pretzel cups from the bodega and venue-mandated cheap light beers. On the subway rides I would listen to my sets, analyzing setups and punch lines while also constantly observing the world around me to see if something was funny or odd or scary enough to talk about onstage at my next open mic. I'd get home somewhere in the midnight-to-one range, collapse into bed in my shared apartment on the Upper West Side, sleep for a few hours, then get up and do it all again.

This part of my life was a beautiful mix of hard and fun. I was so invigorated by the prospect of what came next that I didn't really care about how punishing the lifestyle was. Schlepping to Bushwick to bomb in front of twelve strangers was my version of messengering a purse to a socialite: the dues-paying I was absolutely up for. The work I put into pursuing comedy showed me I hadn't really put in effort to get something professionally before. In my previous jobs, I wasn't *working hard,* I was just working. Now I was, as the fitness influencers and crypto bros say, grinding. I poured every ounce of myself into comedy. Trying to make it in entertainment was like playing high-stakes poker, but I absolutely had to try. I leveraged every ounce of my life against this career. I lost friends in dramatic blowups, and also in the slow erosion of no longer being able to make time for them in my life. I pushed pause on saving money because every dollar I made at my day jobs, I put right back into comedy by buying podcast equipment or paying for transportation to festivals. My romantic relationships were limited to hooking up with the people around me in comedy, because I would never waste a precious night—or even an hour—that I could spend at an open mic or at a show or writing. And if I wasn't doing one of those things, I wanted to be asleep.

And it started to work. My schedule shifted from three open mics a night to one open mic and one or two bar shows. Eventually I was booked on bigger and cooler shows. Instead of paying $5, I was getting paid upwards of $10 to perform. My hustling had paid off. I was getting recognition, I was finding my voice. I was hired to write for different websites, recapping *Top Chef* for Eater and even publishing a parody book with my best friend and writing partner Alyssa Wolff. I was booked on lineups with huge names like Zach Galifianakis and my idol Janeane Garofalo.* I ran two successful shows at UCB for years. I was making it. I was a comedian!

Then the successes started really paying off: I started getting television writing jobs. Stand-up was not a means to an end, but a piece of a larger career puzzle that in my mind always included TV writing. I started out on a short-lived pop culture show out in L.A. for E! before it became an all-Kardashian network. Off the heels of that I was getting sent more and more submission packets for other shows, most of which would exist beyond a four-episode run. I got a dream job writing for one of my comedy heroes, Robert Smigel, for a Triumph the Insult Comic Dog special for Hulu. I was primed for my next great success, assuming that fame and fortune and continuous employment were just around the corner.

I had wrongly assumed that progress is linear. That eating shit was for your twenties, and once you were in your thirties and knew what you wanted, one success would lead to another until you

---

* To this day it is hard for me not to quote her own jokes from the nineties back to her because they are still such a foundational part of my love of stand-up.

died rich. I had always imagined my career like a cartoonish corporate board meeting, where a suit-wearing CEO points to a graph with a bold red arrow pointing up and he says, "Well, another year of record profits for us, men!" But an entire year of applying to and getting rejected from television writing jobs taught me that your career trajectory is not a straight line up; it's full of peaks and valleys, dancing up and down. It's a constantly beeping EKG, the highs and lows proving you're alive and human. But when you're in one of the downturns and swimming in rejection, it's hard to not connect it to your worth, especially when you've spent years gluing your worth to your professional success.

I had moved to L.A. in hopes of changing my luck after hitting a ceiling of success in New York at the time. Flying across the country to basically start over in a new comedy scene, shockingly, didn't catapult me to new levels of fame and stardom. It was more the opposite. I slogged through my miserable year in L.A., driving up and down the 101 scream-crying in my car after every email from my agents saying, "They're going in another direction." I dragged myself to open mics, even though I considered my comedy career long beyond the "sign up to show up" lifestyle, thinking I should be booked to headline, not arguing with an open-mic host at a restaurant in Sherman Oaks. And then finally it came through—I got a job. I was hired as a staff writer on Comedy Central's *The President Show,* which to date is still one of my favorite jobs I have ever had with my favorite people I have ever worked with. Even better, it was back in New York. I packed up my very few belongings and headed home to the East Coast.

I was more than a decade into my pursuit of comedy and finally felt like it was working out. I was having the absolute time of my life doing what I loved. I hosted two shows at UCB, one on Sundays with my comedy brother for life, Robert Dean, and the other a monthly showcase for traditional stand-ups to try telling a long story onstage to a full crowd, an ode to my storytelling roots in the comedy world. Eventually, I was writing for *The Marvelous Mrs. Maisel* and felt like I had the cushiest job in the business, eating shellfish at crew lunch and ordering rugs from West Elm to furnish an office that was larger than my first apartment. I was comfortable in my skin, in my voice, in my path.

And then it all ended.

When Covid shut everything down in 2020, I felt like I was cut off at the knees. Before, I could say, "I'm a comedian. I'm a television writer." Now I was nothing. There was no stand-up, no making television; there was just sitting at home and wondering if leveraging so many other aspects of my life to make this one work had really been worth it. There in my little one-bedroom apartment on Atlantic Avenue, I wondered if dedicating the last decade-plus of my life to one thing was not the best use of my time on this earth. Why bother pouring everything you have into one passion if that passion could disappear and leave you alone and empty? Sure, no one could have known that a pandemic would shut down public life, but I could have at least picked up some hobbies or a partner along the way so the abrupt end wouldn't be so fucking boring and lonely.

Being trapped at home with no opportunities in sight, I was forced to reckon with who I was without work, with what might happen if my entire existence didn't hinge on my professional success. Since I had started doing open mics, I hadn't spent more than two evenings in a row in my apartment . . . probably ever. Now, all alone at home, I learned a lot about myself because I had to. My long cooking sessions listening to Faye Webster albums and my stoned solitaire games to force my eyes away from the screens that controlled my life made me look inward. When my regular beach trips with Natasha faded into Zoom writers' rooms and the post-vaccine return of stand-up, my life looked different than it had before. I had been through something, and my life had changed.

I emerged from lockdown understanding that my career should not be the only thing I care about. I learned that just because your passion is your job, it isn't your entire personality. When your work is creative, career and passion get twisted together like the wonky friendship bracelets Natasha and I both tried to make during our arts-and-crafts era of lockdown. The days and nights can feel longer, the transition from work to fun is fuzzier. Covid lockdowns forced me not only to disentangle my personality from my career, but also to let go of a lifetime of societal conditioning that this is just how creative work is. Apparently, it doesn't have to be. I strangely felt more in control of my career after learning I can't actually control it at all. All I can do is try and make the things I want to make as well as I possibly can. Maybe that's jokes, maybe that's scripts, maybe it's who knows what comedy could become (probably branded video content where I'm hawking a supplement that's mostly made of birdseed with a filter that makes me look twenty-four). And when I finally relaxed for the first time in my comedy lifetime, I started making things that were really meaningful. I got back onstage and I got back to working on my stand-up hour, *Oh God, A Show About Abortion*. It was mounted at Cherry Lane Theatre in spring 2022. Now, 2019 me would have tried to be doing the show while also working in a writers' room or performing at other late-at-night spots around town after each performance. But instead, I focused solely on this project. I just wanted it to be good and people to like it.

In May, only two weeks into performances, the *Dobbs* opinion leaked, and we all knew that the Supreme Court would overturn *Roe v. Wade* by the end of June. I remember finding out during a dinner with my manager Chris Burns at Via Carota (thank god for expense accounts) after my eighth performance of the show. I had decided to put my phone fully away during our meal so that I could be focused, since in the hours after the show I always got a barrage of tagged Instagram stories or texts from acquaintances who were in the crowd. After two Negronis and a lot of expensive pasta and salad, we both pulled out our phones. I had fifty-two missed texts. I was devastated and scared and weirdly a little galvanized by the news of *Roe* ending. This was a terrible thing for humanity, but I had to acknowledge to myself that the show could be a positive in this moment.

It sucks that my mind even had to go there. It is one of the worst displays of mental gymnastics I've ever had to do. But I unfortunately live in reality, and reality is often gross. I didn't plan this show with the *Dobbs* decision in mind. I was, as many male comics (and absolutely zero female comics) said, "lucky with my timing." But I could not control how the *Dobbs* decision was intertwined with my career, and I had to recognize the substantial privilege of being able to make comedy during a catastrophic loss of human rights. Just typing that makes me want to throw up all over this shared workspace I'm writing from, it's awful. It sucks. I would trade it all away—the interviews, the ticket sales, the show extensions, Anna Wintour coming to my opening night—to guarantee protection for reproductive rights across the whole country.

I couldn't control the overturning of *Roe,* just like I couldn't control the years of our lives lost or altered by Covid. No matter how much I tried to control my life and my career, I now know that I can't. You can't hard-work and hustle your way through events over which you have no agency. That's the thing about creative work: It's still work that has to exist within systems that have nothing to do with passion. So rather than tie my own personal value to my career circumstances, I found it liberating to focus on one thing that ended up being a culmination of all of the sweat and tears and forcibly purchased Bud Light that flowed out of me on this journey. I immersed myself in writing and performing *Oh God* and it gave me what I had been chasing all those years. I was making something that was funny and important and uniquely mine. I felt like what I was doing ascended beyond career into something else, something more about self than work.

At the time of writing this, none of the major streamers or networks has bought *Oh God, A Show About Abortion* to become a special. That was my goal for it. I worked really hard to make that happen and it didn't. I spent a long time being sad about it. I felt depressed and rejected and confused and angry. At moments I wondered if the last thirteen years had been worth it if I couldn't get a network to produce this. But since then, I have learned that those feelings are me thinking about the *career* me. That anger is from the "my life is my work and my work is my life" mentality. I'm learning to approach it differently, from a more (ugh) enlightened place. I didn't get to cash a check from HBO or tell everyone to watch me on Netflix. This small piece of my big career didn't happen the way I wanted. But this hour of comedy that was seen by thousands of people and deeply felt by countless women? My goal of talking about something that no one talks about being funny, thoughtful, and approachable for everyone? That's something the work me can't appreciate. But it's something that the person me does.

I'M POLITICAL

E very single time a major political crisis or tragedy occurs, I have the same thoughts. First, I think, *Oh my god this is terrible*. And then my brain immediately follows up with, *Thank GOD I don't work in late-night anymore*. Today, writing for a late-night television show is just taking horrific events and turning them into the cleverest little tongue-in-cheek joke that the network will allow on air because it won't alienate the masses of people who still allegedly watch late-night television and offend their allegedly moderate political views. It's spending an entire day looking for a punch line about immigration bans, grisly bombings, and the loss of our reproductive rights and ultimately ending up with the 350th-funniest thing that was already said on the internet six hours earlier. I absolutely do not miss it.

The first chunk of my television writing career was in late-night television. It didn't start out as political, but eventually all late-night became political late-night and I, along with the rest of the world, went with it. My first late-night job was actually a silly pop culture show that ran for all of four episodes on E! in 2015. *We Have Issues* was part game show, part talk show, hosted by two comedians chatting about the dumbest news we could find for the week: the end of Bennifer 1.5 (Affleck's divorce from Garner), gushing over Channing Tatum's abs, the meteoric rise of Left Shark.* These were the kinds of stories we spent our days in a windowless conference room in the E! offices on Wilshire finding a funny angle on. The stakes felt high from a professional standpoint because we all wanted E! to actually pick up the show for a whole season, but culturally, we knew our lane. Even though other shows certainly covered heavier political stories than we did, most of writing comedy for late-night up until Trump's election felt light and fun, based on human interest and pop culture and niche corridors of entertainment (lol, remember the existence of the channel G4?).†

E! did not pick up our show to series. They had just canceled *The Soup,* the long-running and genuinely laugh-out-loud-funny clip show about pop culture, covering everything from prestige A-list stars to the third-most-important cast members of *Duck Dynasty.* E! was moving on from that show, and from comedy in general, becoming a network that mostly featured women shaking to-go containers of salad without moving a single facial muscle. But while the network that red-carpet interviews built leaned further into reality television programming, the rest of the television landscape went the other direction and became incredibly political.

---

* If you don't remember or are extremely young, Left Shark was a dancer in a shark suit during the 2015 Super Bowl halftime show that starred future astronaut Katy Perry.

† G4 was a deep cable channel with some talking-head clip shows that gave hot women who were brunettes their first hosting jobs.

Politics and pop culture collided in figures like Arnold Schwarzenegger and Donald Trump, when they were still a governor and a long-shot presidential candidate, respectively. At this same moment, the internet and social media gave everyone their first taste of "online discourse," and news stories that usually don't register to the average person began to dominate screens big and small. The success of *The Daily Show* taught other shows the wrong lesson. Where Jon Stewart specifically zeroed in on politics, politicians, and the journalists* who spend twenty-four hours a day dissecting them, broader late-night shows saw his ratings and chased them, asking every silly sketch writer to somehow work in a reference to the Iraq War and forcing goofy, lovable hosts to address global geopolitics in a two-sentence monologue joke every night. It was, to sum it up, not fun.

Thankfully, I actually grew up consuming a lot of news and a lot of political comedy, so I felt prepared to pivot to what the networks wanted, even though I wasn't exactly aching to work in that corner of the industry. My parents had multiple newspapers delivered every morning and they both managed to read a big chunk of them before work, an incredibly impressive feat when you consider that my mother was a teacher, so she got up somewhere around four forty-five just to read *The Baltimore Sun* while she had her coffee and buttered English muffin. WJZ, the local Baltimore news station, would play on the kitchen television in the background in case something was breaking. Once my mom had left for work and the sun came up, my dad and I would change the channel

---

* Only some of these people are actual journalists with research and opinions and credibility; most of them are sycophants cashing checks for promoting propaganda at best, and spreading hate at worst. We could have made any genre of television twenty-four hours and for some reason we chose news. We're all idiots.

to *Good Morning America*. In the evening, *Time* magazine would provide a glossy(ish) full-color read before dinner, and afterward, we watched local evening news on WBAL before turning over to the seven o'clock *CBS Evening News* for national stories from the trusted Dan Rather. On Sundays, naturally, we also added *60 Minutes* and *CBS Sunday Morning* into the mix, two shows my parents still regularly ask if I've watched each week, as if I have ever been up before noon on a Sunday.

Every night, we also made sure to watch the rerun of the previous day's *The Daily Show with Jon Stewart*. In 2000, when I was sixteen years old and didn't have an adult grasp on politics, this was the first time I was being given a thoughtful look at a fraught political situation (the Bush/Gore presidential race), as well as a meta-analysis of the way the news media was covering it. Jon Stewart and *The Daily Show* may not have radicalized me into political action, but I do think I saw it at the exact point in my life when many people either get interested in politics or turn away from them entirely. I got interested.

Even before I started doing comedy my mom used to say, "You should work for *The Daily Show*." I always scoffed at her, especially in my early stand-up days, when I was writing long bits about Doritos and submitting humor pieces reimagining Kim Kardashian's Thanksgiving-dinner conversation. I was interested in silliness. I wanted to work on funny sitcoms, I didn't want to sit around and make jokes about the news. But once I started seriously pursuing a career in comedy, I realized that the first and easiest leap into television writing for a stand-up is through late-night. So I started submitting to shows, which basically meant completing a long homework assignment. *Submitting* is also the perfect word for what it feels like to apply for these jobs. You are literally being submissive: taking the comedic voice that you've honed for years in dark basements and empty bars and refitting it so these jokes sound just as good coming out of the mouth of a rich white man on network television as they do in your brain. I had to write a page of monologue jokes based on the news, and then, depending on the show, pitch a few pages of segments and sketches. The work itself was straightforward, and if you've watched a few episodes of *The Tonight Show* or *Conan,* you understand the assignment. For the run-of-the-mill, nonpolitical late-night shows, the monologue breakdowns in general were 30 percent politics/hard news and 70 percent focused on pop culture or strange human interest stories, like someone finding a leaf that looks like Stanley Tucci or a town having the world's largest birdbath.

Political late-night shows were a different beast. To submit to those, you had real homework. Coming up with fun games is one thing, but writing a long-form news essay with video clips and sources (oh, and some jokes) is a much taller order. I submitted to *The Daily Show* twice, and both times the assignment was more work than my current full-time job. You had to watch the news. You had to choose a story that you understood and that was also the right fit for an act 1 desk piece on the show. Then you had to find video clips to include, plus other headlines and ancillary support to flesh out the segment. You had to understand the rhythm of the jokes (you need a joke coming out of a video that refers to the video, otherwise why did you include that video?) and possess a broad background knowledge of American and global politics. I did not get hired either time I submitted. I was disappointed but not shocked. Even though I had seen hundreds of episodes of the show and am better at writing a joke than signing my own name, this job was insanely competitive. And part of me was a tiny bit relieved. If this was just the job application, how hard was this job?

I eventually got hired by Robert Smigel to work on a political special for then-burgeoning streamer Hulu, featuring his beloved Triumph the Insult Comic Dog, in what was a deliriously fun and strange job. Unlike the complex storytelling of *The Daily Show,* the Triumph special was a series of sketches and field pieces centered around the political conventions ahead of the 2016 election. I sent pages of roast jokes and a few sketch pitches and was, to my surprise, offered a job. I had tried to write in the voice of so many hosts and comedians while submitting for shows, and the one I was most suited for was a dog who makes fun of people. It was my first job after a series of disappointments, and I was working with a legend. I almost cried when my agent told me Smigel wanted to use one of the jokes from my submission for the roast of James Carville at the Kennedy Center: "Donald Trump looks like the one animal we've been testing all of the cosmetics on."*

That joke, and the literal hundreds I wrote during my time with that show, was emblematic of the landscape of political comedy before November 2016. They were surface-level, rooted in physical appearance and fluffy mistakes that politicians had publicly made. Sure, that's kind of Triumph's whole thing, but it's also what other late-night shows were doing, too: making fun of people we thought were, to borrow a word I love that has been ruined by Trump, losers. No one thought a makeup-loving reality-show host/bankrupt fake billionaire would be the president, and the comedy reflected that. Making these jokes felt like it was helping, not hurting. We didn't need to be part of the #resistance because there was nothing

---

* God I miss when we could just mock his appearance and didn't know the depths of his evil yet.

to resist at this point. Some dumbass was running for president and a few dumbasses would probably vote for him, but nothing would really come from it.

For me, and for so many other people, Election Day 2016 started out so bright and devolved into a hell my brain could barely comprehend. It was like a bachelorette party: At first, it was fun and upbeat and positive, and by the end I was drunk and crying about my future and wondering why everyone hates women. I was living in Los Angeles and walked through my hilly neighborhood to cast my vote for Hillary Clinton, then treated myself to an obscenely expensive and mediocre breakfast at my local coffee shop, Lamill.* So I got an iced coffee and some eggs and toast for a super-reasonable $26 and did several takes of an I VOTED sticker getting stuck in my hair so I could post something on Instagram that telegraphed both that I voted and that I'm funny. I ran into my new friend Ilana Glazer, and we were like "YAY! VOTING! WOMEN!" Then I strolled up the hill to my house to sit and watch the counts slowly roll in. For all my hate for L.A., I guess it was a nice benefit that being on West Coast time meant I didn't have to stay up *all* night just to see Trump win.

I could go into the horrors of the next few days and weeks, but we all remember how it felt, and I have no interest in reliving it (certainly not here, for a third time). People cried in the streets. The world changed in ways that we're still discovering and recovering from. Surprisingly, a huge impact Trump had was on the world of comedy. A Hillary presidency certainly would have

---

* If you have lived or worked in L.A., you know Lamill. Whenever I wanted to tell people where I lived in L.A. I would say, "I live in one of the streets right up above Lamill," and they would respond saying, "Oh my god yes, I hate that place. I go all the time."

meant many things (slightly better reproductive rights policy, way more embarrassing girlboss merch), though I doubt it would have pushed comedy television to where it is today. Trump's run undeniably influenced everyone to talk about politics more than they did before. And then his win made it the dominant conversation in every room, every day, seemingly for the rest of our existence. You could feel that this unending focus on politics, and specifically on Trump, was atonement for the sin of not taking his run seriously. Every media outlet, television station, pollster, and Democrat thought there was no chance, yet here we were, writing words less likely to be together than "grounded influencer": "President Trump."

The next several months I spent aggressively submitting for every late-night job I was able to, which was many. Part of me just longed for an opportunity to write silly jokes, but I also felt some kind of obligation to participate in the mocking of our new world. I don't have other skills. I'm not a lawyer or doctor or activist. I don't know how to file petitions or organize rallies, so I did what I could: write political comedy. I submitted countless writing packets, getting close on some, but never getting hired. I watched as the network late-night packets I wrote went from fun stories about new Mountain Dew flavors and dog mayors to Trump's border policy and his cabinet's rare mix of evil and ineptitude. I used to love coming up with silly sketch pitches, like a game show called Are You Smarter Than a Crow?, but now I found myself deep in CNN's archives looking for coverage of Afghanistan so I could craft a perfectly accurate but not very funny joke. Jokes, at least in the world of late-night, became less about eliciting a laugh and more about eliciting an "mm, very true" and a nod of agreement.

This life took a toll on me. I spent all day ingesting the news, but instead of being able to take healthy breaks away from MSNBC or the *New York Times* home page, I was forced to regurgitate what happened in playful morsels and sharp punch lines until late at night. And then I woke up and did it all again the next day without so much as a moment of the fun that comedy and writing used to provide. Comedy began for me as an outlet for internal pain, a way to process it. But once I learned how to do comedy as a writer and performer, it became an escape from the negatives of the world, like horrific news or my literally negative bank account. Now here it was, back to functioning as a processing tool rather than a break from reality.

As I kept not getting jobs, the news kept getting worse. I was wallowing in self-pity and depression. Whenever I felt overwhelmed by the state of the world and wanted to bury my head in the sand of comedy, I instead had to dive back into the news itself to "focus on work." And when I was so discouraged by my job prospects and overworked with my submissions that I turned to the internet or television to unwind, it was infused with the horrors of our new political landscape that I had just been trudging through for hours. There was no relief.

Finally, in the spring of 2017, I did get hired to a job I absolutely loved, to write for a new Comedy Central show called *The President Show*. It was a job that existed only because of the hellscape of America: a classic late-night show in formula, but hosted by Donald Trump from the Oval Office late at night, with his VP, Mike Pence, as the Ed McMahon of the program. Trump was brilliantly played by comedian Anthony Atamanuik, who had been honing his impression over the previous year leading up to the election. I've worked on many shows now with many writers, and this one is still my all-time favorite. Our writers' room was filled with my comedy friends and people whose humor I'd always admired. I'm still proud of the jokes I wrote there and the pieces I worked on, which were super funny. There were lots of women in management roles, so it remains one of the healthiest workplaces I've been in to this day.

When I joined the show, the vibe was positive, considering we were making a late-night show about a president we all hated in a political climate that felt oppressive. We felt like we were pointing to the psychological elements of Trump that other late-night and political comedy shows couldn't reach. Our show felt both sillier and more subversive than anything else on television. We didn't get bogged down in the minutiae of exactly what Robert Mueller said, but focused instead on the bigger picture of power and oppression and how we got here, something that Atamanuik and our other executive producers Jason Ross, Christine Nangle, and Pete Grosz really understood. We felt like the comedy we made was both prescient and timeless, hilarious and devastating. Not only did we point our lens at the power players in the perverse game of politics we had to witness all day and night, the show often took on the media itself. We knew that the twenty-four-hour news networks and the print and digital periodicals were making more money than they had in years thanks to Trump. We knew the robust coverage of his presidency wasn't motivated by the desire to avoid this situation again; it was making some people a lot of fucking money.

The show helped me immensely. Instead of firing jokes into the ether in submission packets for jobs I'd never get or tossing political tweets into the universe that ultimately did nothing but inspire strangers and bots to yell at me, I was actually doing something. I'm not oblivious enough to think that our little half-hour political comedy on a cable channel many forgot existed was changing the world. But I felt an internal satisfaction, like I was more part of the solution than the problem.

I was reluctant for so much of my early comedy life to go the route of political comedy, but here I was relishing my identity as that kind of writer. When *The President Show* was nominated for a Writers Guild of America award, I imagined my future as someone who was literally shaping the culture, someone on a path to take the horrors of the world and filter them through sharp jokes that challenged the way people thought about politics, pushing them toward a more progressive, peaceful, and equitable world. That was the power of political comedy. I don't necessarily believe that every single political joke has the ability to move people to action or to reconsidering their views. Hundreds of jokes about Trump's hair have amounted to at best nothing and at worst getting him elected. But I did believe that thoughtful comedy about politics had real power.

But as Trump's first year wore on, the realities of the news and the tone of the comedy about it shifted to a much darker place, a seeming impossibility given the darkness of the world we were already in. There were more and more times when we had to stop and ask, "How do we make this funny?" and I was grateful that our show had the pathos to ask the question "Should we even make this funny?," too. The choice plaguing comedy rooms was: "Do we tell jokes and risk making light of something serious, tragic, and deeply real for many people?" versus "Do we eschew comedy, our actual job here, and talk sincerely about this, but if we do that how do we ramp back up to comedy and what the fuck are we supposed to say?" It was a precarious line to toe, and we did it every day until *The President Show* was ultimately canceled.

I spent a nervous month or two wondering what the hell to do, but thankfully landed at another show, solidifying my role in the entertainment industry as a political late-night comedy writer. I moved from one Comedy Central show to another and started writing for *The Opposition with Jordan Klepper,* where Klepper played a kind of Alex Jones–meets–Fox News far-right conspiracy theorist. I understood the game. I had spent the last eight months writing for "Trump," after all.

But at *Oppo* I lacked the hopefulness that I had at *TPS*. The problem with the show was foundational. To make *The President Show,* we all had to consume news about what Trump and his cronies and idiot kids did and said over the week, watching press conferences, scanning coverage on CNN and MSNBC, reading mainstream media reports about goings-on in the White House, and occasionally turning on Fox News just to see whether what they were jabbering about might help our episode. We just needed an account of what Trump said—arguably some of the worst things not just a politician, but any person, could say—and then we'd play around with his words. It was rough to have to live and breathe Trump like that, but it felt like we could really have agency over the comedy we made. That was not *The Opposition.* Jordan wasn't playing a figure who got covered, he was playing a figure who did the coverage, and to write that kind of comedy, we had to really consume and understand that coverage. Now, instead of reading a *New York Times* article about Trump's latest policy or watching CNN interview Kellyanne Conway, we had to watch hours of *Infowars* (a show so horrible and stupid I don't even feel I should have to italicize it here) and Fox News.

This job forced me into the belly of the beast. We had Fox News playing on the TVs in our offices at nearly all times. Our daily morning meetings were basically a rundown of everything the network aired after we had finished taping the night before and gone home to try and live lives. We scanned hours-long episodes of Alex Jones's show trying to find the worst, dumbest thing he screamed at the camera between supplement ads. We sifted through the social media of ultraconservative maniacs and incels and edgelords as we watched their fringe ideas slowly fold into the mainstream hate spewed by blond men with faces like melting candles on Fox News.

I was no longer hopeful or part of the solution. I no longer imagined a future of thoughtful discourse and Emmy nominations. It was a soulless grind with no end in sight. And it was worse, because even though I was getting a healthy paycheck every week, the news was taking a darker and darker turn every day. Even the other late-night shows had to begin reckoning with reality. It was no longer enough to make fun of Trump's silly hair or Mike Pence calling his wife Mother. The audience had seen and heard that day in and day out for over a year. It didn't help, and it had long since stopped being funny. The unignorable truths of racist, homophobic, misogynistic policies were now front and center. And the entertainment industry's obsession with making politics the main course of every meal was coming to bite us all in our asses. There was no relief. There were no light human interest stories about a restaurant that just sells toast or a frog that makes a noise that sounds like Adele. That was gone, we had killed it.

While I was working on *Oppo,* my parents came up for a visit. We were having lunch at a hamburger joint in Crown Heights near the apartment I was subletting at the time. Sitting at a booth in the back of the restaurant, my mom point-blank said to me, "Are you okay? You seem depressed."

I didn't even think I was giving off that impression. I hadn't seen my parents in a few months and I was happy to have lunch with them. Nothing about my life was depressing on paper. I had a job that paid me well in the industry I always dreamed of working in. I still ran my popular stand-up show and was busy doing spots most nights of the week. I had returned to New York after dipping my toes into the warm but wrong waters of Los Angeles. I had lots of friends and a vibrant social life. The me from a few years ago would have screamed in joy at the idea of this life. But my mom was right. I was depressed.

In order to do my job, I had to ingest hours and hours every day of the most disgusting and hateful programming in existence. No matter how much you hate the other side and know that the policies, opinions, and views you're consuming are wrong, that eventually erodes your hope for humanity and, honestly, your will to live. I didn't go from thinking that my television work was solving a national crisis to moping around a studio every day overnight. It happened slowly, like the sadness and apathy that has crept up on so many of us ever since Trump's first election.

There were certainly pieces and segments I worked on at *The Opposition* that felt invigorating both comedically and politically. We did a very silly bit about how Laura Ingraham criticized teen gun-control advocate and Parkland shooting survivor David Hogg. Because our host, Jordan, was playing a character with the same demonic views as Ingraham and her band of assholes at Fox, the segment looks like it is criticizing Hogg but is in fact criticizing the many Republican lawmakers who pretend to be pro-life and pro-safety and pro-children but routinely vote against stricter gun laws. Hogg retweeted it thinking it was funny (because it was). But each week there were fewer and fewer moments on the show that even approached that.

A problem with being informed is that the more you know, the more helpless you feel. The deeper some of our stories got into the way our society works, the more it felt like there was no way out. Sure, I was probably doomed to a life of trying to find a way to make welfare cuts funny (surprise, there objectively is not), but understanding how deeply ingrained hateful beliefs are in America, as well as across the globe, made me feel like we were on a roller coaster we couldn't ever get off. Watching and reading and writing about right-wing beliefs all day, every day, made me feel like we were the only ones on the left who really knew how bad things were.

When *The Opposition* was canceled, part of me was honestly relieved. I was terrified from a professional and financial standpoint since I needed paychecks to pay for things like rent and food and slight variations on the same style of jeans. But existentially, I felt free. After the initial blow of cancellation, the final two weeks were actually the most fun I had in my entire time at the show. We aired the stupidest jokes, the silliest ideas, and the wildest segments, all while drinking (at minimum) dozens of what became our signature cocktail during taping—tequila, Campari, grapefruit juice, seltzer, and lime. I stand by that drink recipe as one of the greatest accomplishments of my time in late-night.

After the show ended, I went on a cleanse of sorts. No stranger to a juice cleanse that toes the line of disordered eating, I applied that deprivation and scorched-earth mentality to my media consumption. I didn't watch even a second of CNN or MSNBC or Fox News. I immediately unfollowed every political outlet, thinker, and newspaper. The immense privilege of being able to remove myself from politics is not lost on me. There is no greater luxury than having the ills and evils of the world barely reach your comfortable life, and, even then, I was incredibly lucky that most of those evils had reached me only through a filter of reporters instead of firsthand experience. Of course I'd much rather have to sit through months of forced engagement with the worst pundits in history (I'm looking at you, Hannity) than have my family taken away from me, my housing denied, my healthcare made so expensive I have to choose between food and medicine, or any of the other countless horrors inflicted on people by even our "best" administrations.

So I used my immense privilege and unplugged from news and politics as much as I humanly could. After a few small, annoying jobs, I took the next step in my career and shifted into narrative television comedy by joining the staff of *The Marvelous Mrs. Maisel*. It was a job devoid of the tedium of hearings and bills and media literacy. My daily writing was focused on jokes about brisket and hats. I left my office drained every day, but not despondent about the planet. After years of blending my existential crises with my professional responsibilities, I finally had whatever the work-life balance of nihilism is. I spent two beautiful years able to separate the horrors of the world from the annoyances of my job.

And while my quality of life was vastly improved in my move from late-night to *Maisel* (the daily coffee runs, fresh berries and Rice Krispies Treats in the kitchen, and luxurious stays in some of the nicer hotels in Santa Monica and Miami make them almost impossible to compare), I did feel a piece of me was missing. I was doing stand-up every night, still honing my own voice and sometimes talking about current events, sometimes just about the experiences of my life. I was still friends with people who worked closely with politics and I tried to be involved in causes I supported. But though I didn't constantly have to hear the din of racist idiots praising a racist immigration policy or men weighing in on what constitutes sexual harassment, I missed aspects of being a political late-night writer. I didn't think of myself as informed anymore. I was satisfied with my work, but it never gave me the feeling that what I was doing was moving the culture politically. And while I finally got agency over my relationship with news and politics, I didn't feel powerful, I felt removed. Maybe streaming hours of Trump and Fox wasn't healthy, but in a world quickly spinning out of control, it did feel like some sense of control, even if that control was just finding the best, least depressing joke I could before we started taping a show.

Sometimes I look back on those years of writing for Triumph and submitting packets and working on *The President Show* and powering through *The Opposition* and spending all my time intensely consuming political news media and I wonder if it helped me or hurt me. Did it break my brain? Did it teach me anything? It certainly taught me some things. I learned a lot about my joke writing. I learned how to churn out work under intense pressure at rapid rates. I learned how much I hate the teleprompter writing software Scripto. I learned a lot about American politics and how our government works (and doesn't). And I learned what kind of political comedy writing makes me feel good: the kind I do on my own terms. Being force-fed ultraconservatism to mock is not my preferred corner of political comedy; I liked writing that felt more personal. I knew I couldn't tackle every single tragedy, misstep, horror, or event with so much swirling around us every second. I had to focus on what I could do best, which is tell my own political stories, and in a way that felt silly and fun. That's how I eventually came to understand telling the story of my abortion onstage.

As we all neared the 2024 election, everyone had their own predictions. My friends and I would share texts like "god, he's gonna win lol" and then immediately plan where we were getting martinis that night (the answer: literally anywhere). I knew in my bones that it was true. And that's not because of what I saw on the news. It's because of what I saw in comedy.

I don't even mean the late-night comedy I knew and worked in, I mean the entire world of comedians doing everything from basement bar shows to podcasts to sold-out arenas. The last few years I saw more and more mostly straight white men (but *certainly* some women who should not be let off the hook) get rich and famous peddling the exact same bullshit ideas, theories, and strategies that the dipshit incels and hate-mongering pundits did while I was forced to watch them every day searching for ways to make their hatred funny. It's not that I had some kind of ESP or deep political knowledge that my more hopeful friends did not, it's that I was seeing the ideas and views of once-fringe maniacs become the most popular comedy that has ever existed.

Right-leaning comics and fans will read this and call me jealous. Lol who am I kidding, they are *not* reading this. For starters, they're not reading. But that's the sentiment: If you're jealous of the theater-touring successful comedians who just happen to espouse and spew the same ideas as the alt-right, then you are just a failed liberal comedian who can't hack it in this industry giving people what they *really* want. I disagree with that and don't really give a shit, but I have to live in the world they have made. As much as making fun of Trump's big hair and small hands didn't stop him from getting elected in 2016, echoing Trump's vitriolic hate in arena acts and podcasts *did* get him elected. Their grift worked. And we're all suffering.

I hope that by the time this book comes out, in the not-so-distant future from my writing it (though from where I am as I write, every day seems like forty-seven years, so), somehow we're climbing our way out of this nightmare rather than wading deeper into it. I hope that somehow an alien spaceship has come to earth to beam down safe drinking water and money to citizens and beam up Donald Trump and Elon Musk. (I have to say that this is my dream instead of what my actual dream is, because putting that in print seems pretty risky from a legal standpoint.) If things are still as terrible as they are now, I hope I'm still finding a balance and that others are, too. I don't blame anyone for seeking relief in the form of political comedy. We all have our ways of coping in crisis. Some people's may be watching late-night and following political comedians online. Mine, personally, is staring into my cat's eyes and saying, "YOU ARE THE ONLY GOOD THING IN THIS WORLD!" We all have our tools. There certainly *is* good political comedy out there. The best of it is personal and coming from the people who have experienced oppression and are fighting back against the oppressors.

When I look at all of the essays in this book, this one to me seems like the least funny, like it has the fewest jokes. It was somehow easier to write funny things about my surgical complications, my abortion, my family, than it was to write jokes about my time working in political comedy. I think that's because the person I am today just doesn't want to make it funny anymore. Those years were, at times, validating and exciting, but mostly they wore me down. I've seen the writing on the wall—well, internet—before, and I feel a responsibility to constantly see it, process it, and know what is coming. And I know that in my work, I can continue to turn to my personal stories, make them funny and real and stand in the face of the horrific world we live in. And in my private time, I must remind myself what an immense privilege it is to be able to turn the news off.

I'M IN PAIN

I know this is a wild way to start an essay, but (cue calming-yet-terrifying female-robot-meets-yoga-teacher voice): What is health?

No, I'm not trying to sell you a nootropic juice for $54 an ounce. I'm just trying to figure out how to express my prickly relationship with the concept of health. As a lifelong athlete, I've been obsessed with being seen as "healthy" for as long as I can remember. I pushed my body to its absolute limits, which in my mind meant I was making it as healthy as possible.

Whatever your definition of health, I think most people share a similar idea of what a "healthy" person looks like: young and fit, with clear skin and thick hair. Hmmm . . . all the markers of "health" are eerily similar to those of "hotness." I know it's evolutionary biology, but that doesn't make it not annoying! It also doesn't necessarily make it true.

For years, I looked healthy when I was in extreme chronic pain. On the outside, I was a fit young woman in her twenties, but for most of that decade I was internally falling apart and gritting my teeth through everyday activities. It's bizarre to be treated one way when inside things are the complete opposite. The kind of chronic pain I lived in is often referred to as "invisible pain" mostly because it doesn't express visually, like a burn or a cut or even a broken leg in a cast that people can sign. That is one of the weirdest rituals in medicine. *I broke my leg skiing; can you write something on this plaster that a doctor will saw off of me in eight weeks?* Truly bizarre. But invisible pain, free from ogling and classmates' signatures, is like keeping a secret—and not in a fun way. It's like sitting through a dinner party knowing the host is having an affair and you just have to smile and keep eating your paella but it's impossible to focus on literally anything else because you have to do the hard work of not blurting out something that will absolutely ruin this party. And when you look like you aren't in pain, like you're an actual "healthy" person, that secret is even harder to keep. Everyone sees the shiny hair and vaguely athletic frame of someone who will crush their next checkup. But inside you're screaming, you know that things are falling apart, and you can barely complete a normal task without wanting to cry.

When I got back to Cornell as a sophomore after almost dying from the blood clot following my first back surgery, I felt like a healthy person who suffered a tragedy and was on the road to recovery. My back was a problem, and my surgery fixed it. My problems had solutions, and I did what the doctors told me to do to solve them. It was painful, but it was over. I thought a lifetime of sports was still ahead of me, that with time and physical therapy I would be back on an NCAA Division I crew. I thought my medical problems were finite and finished. And for some time, that was true.

A lifetime of competitive sports has always made my relationship to exercise complicated. I've never been able to do it in a casual (read: "healthy") way. And my body could handle the intensity because, as I would remind myself, I was healthy. In the years after college, I tried to find a way to be physical that felt right. I had no specific goals, just to try and exercise enough to punish myself. I had a gym-rat phase after graduating because I had nothing else to do but go to the gym and run for more than an hour before my shift at Nordstrom. When I moved to New York and was searching for both identity and a fitness routine, I fell back into Bikram yoga.

Bikram made sense to me. The more I practiced, the easier it was and the better I felt. I went to a studio on the Upper West Side about ten blocks from my apartment. It had just enough of a cult-y vibe to feel spiritual, but also enough of a chic Manhattan gym vibe for me to feel like I wasn't going to be recruited into a group suicide, just an expensive membership and some overpriced accessories. Also, this was all before the Netflix documentary (arguably before the existence of Netflix) exposing the abuse by the guy who founded Bikram.

What I loved most about doing Bikram four or five days a week was that it was the most "healthy" I had felt in years, probably since my freshman year rowing. My body was in the best shape it's ever been in, I was much more flexible (still not able to touch my toes, but definitely closer!), and my skin was incredible from constantly sweating out anything that had ever been inside my body. Sure, here and there I felt a twinge of pain in my back or leg, but I was sure that was something I would be dealing with for the rest of my life after the surgery. Plus, I reassured myself that this occasional pain wasn't disruptive to my life at all. Until it was.

The morning of September 15, 2008, I was getting ready to head to my job at Random House. I had emailed my bosses that I was running late because I had to pick up a prescription at Duane Reade that wasn't ready yet. It was a lie—I was just avoiding leaving the apartment—though I thought it was a pretty reasonable excuse for being a half-hour late for my job of stapling papers together for other people to hand out in a meeting. I was putzing around my tiny, dark bedroom, which had a window, technically, but it just looked into the air shaft. I had my little black brick of a Verizon flip phone on the edge of my desk. I pulled on my gray cotton pencil skirt from the Gap and was putting on my bra (securing the hook and eye in the front, spinning it around, and then putting my arms through the straps because despite the yoga I'm still not flexible enough to do it the other way). Suddenly, searing pain shot through my back and left leg. This was a new pain. This wasn't the little twinge I felt when I bent forward sometimes. It had all the hallmarks of the same back and leg pain I'd had before my first surgery, but much worse. I fell to the floor on my hands and knees.

Fortunately, I had grabbed my phone on my way to the floor. I gave it a minute, figured clearly I needed to wait out a cramp or relax my muscles and then I'd be fine. But instead, it got worse. The pain was brutal enough that I did what I do in any crisis: I called my dad. I don't know what I thought he could do from four hours away in Maryland, but I had to tell someone. Predictably, his response was, "I don't know what to do for you, buddy." (My dad calls me buddy a lot, probably because he wanted a son.) But then he smartly suggested calling one of my friends who was actually in New York to see if they could come by. Genius!

I called Divya. She was in law school not too far from my apartment, so the odds that she could get to me seemed pretty good, or at least better than those of my dad somehow teleporting to me.

Thankfully, she could come right over. Problem solved! Until we realized that she would need to get into the building, which would involve her buzzing an intercom that I couldn't reach because I couldn't move. I was stuck on the floor, looking like I was on the receiving end of doggy style. My super let her in, seemingly unconcerned that 1, he had to do this, and 2, when he opened the apartment door he found one of his tenants, a healthy-looking young woman, on the floor on all fours, sweating and crying. He just shut the door in a "not my problem" way. Only in New York!

Despite regularly practicing Bikram and being in the best shape of my life, my body was losing the ability to stay in my all-fours position. When you first get on your hands and knees you think, *It's not so bad, I'm stable as a table!* When you're stuck on your hands and knees for more than an hour in excruciating pain, you start to struggle. I was shaking and sweating and panicking about what would happen when my arms and legs finally gave out from the exhaustion. What were Divya and I going to do? Our first thought was to call *her* dad, who at least is a doctor. This man was in Arizona, so despite being a medical professional, he was even less helpful than my nondoctor dad in Maryland. He suggested ice, so we placed a bag of frozen edamame on my back like I was a Costco shopping cart. Then we called my dad back and he was (surprise) still not much more helpful. Finally, we took the advice both the dads involved had given us and called 911.

The paramedics showed up quickly, and thank god Divya was there to let them in. I was expecting two giant EMTs who could each toss me over their shoulder like I was a gym bag, but in walked two women who were roughly my size. They didn't look like they could haul my groceries back from Fairway, let alone get me off the ground and out of that apartment. But they each grabbed under one of my arms and ripped me off the floor. I screamed louder than I have ever screamed in my life and didn't stop until they had me in a stretcher and loaded into an ambulance on West Eighty-first Street in broad daylight with half of my block trying to see what all the yelling was about. It must have looked confusing: I wasn't bleeding. I wasn't throwing up. I wasn't bruised or convulsing. I didn't have a swollen ankle or a bent joint or a weak-looking limb. There wasn't a knife stuck through my hand or any other dangerous kitchen implement lodged in any other part of my body. I looked healthy. And here I was being carted away in an ambulance crying.

When we got to the emergency room, they rolled me into a curtained-off area to wait in agony. I was Lamaze-breathing when I wasn't screaming, but the most they could do was give me two extra-strength Tylenol and discharge me with the advice to call my doctor and probably get an MRI. So I was sent home with two pills I could have found in my medicine cabinet and no path toward being able to stand up on my own. We somehow got in a cab, and when it dropped me off back at my building, it took me more than twenty minutes of agony to climb the three stairs of the stoop that led up to my first-floor apartment. I cried the whole time. I'd never been more relieved to live in that sunless ground-floor apartment than I was when I finally got inside.

Not only was I stressed out and still in pain when I got home, but I was also exhausted. When you're in this kind of pain, you have to reconfigure your body to try and lessen it, to lean on the parts that aren't hurting. I took only about seventy steps the entire day, but my body was tired. My muscles were weak from being on my hands and knees for almost an hour and from walking with super-tiny steps, taken with my knees bent and my feet angled outward to feel more stable, as my core had basically collapsed. My legs and abs quivered from being tense for the entire day. It felt like doing nine hours of Pilates but without the benefit of having actually worked out. And when my mind could finally take a break from focusing on the pain, I could only focus on the fear. Did I need another surgery? If I had surgery, would I end up near dead, or worse, actually dead this time? Or would I be like this forever? Would I ever be able to stand and walk without screaming? Would I ever put on a bra safely again?

My mom took the train up to help me out, and I was able to start seeing a doctor who prescribed me some real pain pills. Every few days Duane Reade called me up to tell me they had another ninety-pill bottle of Percocet for me. After a week or so I was at least able to get off the couch/bed enough to kind of go back to work. I was a twenty-five-year-old walking through the office with a cane, drugged out of her mind. I was a pair of pasties and a fedora away from the worst burlesque show anyone's ever seen. I was popping pills left and right and hadn't stood fully upright in weeks, but the doctors I saw seemed in no rush to help me. I don't think they didn't believe my pain, but they seemed to think I would be fine without any intervention because I was a healthy young woman. Never mind that a few years before, I'd had back surgery, or that now I was screaming and crying every time I had to put on a shirt. I was healthy! A week ago I was doing intense hot yoga. My body would fix itself, they told me.

But it didn't. When I finally got an MRI, it showed a herniation in the same disc I'd had operated on when I was nineteen. I didn't think we needed imaging to tell us that, but hey, I was just the person feeling the pain they were diagnosing, what did I know? My doctor recommended I get steroid injections in my spine to stop the inflammation from the herniation and hopefully relieve me from the pain I was in so I could go back to normal. I remember sitting in the waiting room at my first appointment for the injections, looking around and surveying my medical peers. I was about fifty years younger than any other person there. Everyone had white hair and orthopedic shoes and walkers and here I was with my just-developed frontal lobe, leaning on my cane and still quivering in pain through a hazy, drug-addled consciousness.

They called my name and I slowly made my way to the exam room. I had to lie face down on a table under an X-ray machine that was positioned above my lower back so the doctors could watch the needle going in while performing the injection. I was nervous in a way that even the pain meds couldn't numb. The doctor preparing me for the procedure wanted to be clear that it was not a pleasant experience, because they were injecting a nerve with drugs, so it was very sensitive and would be painful. He explained how it would feel: "Like getting struck by lightning."

Was I supposed to . . . know what that feels like? Being struck by lightning is an image we use to describe things that never fucking happen. The doctor then revised it to "like being electrocuted." Oh, phew. That's so much better. I was also warned not to move, especially when the needle was going in. So just stay perfectly still while I feel like electricity is coming out of the sky and violently striking my spine? Got it, no prob.

I lay there alone and freaked out while the men—well, the neurosurgeons—stood over on the edge of the room looking at the X-ray that would tell them where to inject me. Then I heard one of them say, "What is that?"—the worst sentence you can hear in a medical setting. Well, besides "Hi, I'm Dr. Joe Rogan, let's get started." I was freaking the absolute fuck out while lying completely still like they told me to even though we hadn't started yet. Then they brought in a third guy, who was also perplexed by the image they saw on the screen. Part of me was relieved that perhaps I didn't have to do my insurance-covered electrocution today. Finally, a nurse walked into the room. She looked at the screen for one second and said, "That's a tampon. She's wearing a tampon." She looked at me and asked, "Do you have your period, dear?"

"Yes," I replied. Mystery solved. A *tampon*. Three NEUROSURGEONS couldn't identify a tampon. A tampon that was in the part of my body it was supposed to be in. It wasn't in my head or something; in that case, sure, let's call in a committee to figure it out.

What's worse than three doctors not knowing a tampon when they see one is that then we still had to carry on with the shots. I've never been struck by lightning. I've never been seriously electrocuted. If either of them is anything like this, then they're extremely painful. I cried throughout the whole procedure. There's something uniquely hellish about signing up for intense pain to help relieve your chronic pain. And it didn't even help. I was in slightly less pain (but not taking any fewer drugs) for a couple of days, and I was a little more mobile. I think I made less noise when I bent down to put on socks than I did before the injury. So getting these serious nerve shots from a few men who didn't know a tampon from a Good & Plenty didn't fix anything.

Pain makes you feel trapped in your own body. My specific memories of this time are rather blurry thanks to popping Percocet all day like they were Tic Tacs, but I still remember the feelings. I remember always breathing heavier than normal to power through the pain and also to have something to focus on aside from the constant buzzing, burning feeling in my hip and leg. I remember being so frustrated that I couldn't just hop out of bed. In my entire time on this planet, I've never been someone who bounds out of bed at the crack of dawn ready to start the day, but at least before this I could get up without pausing every few movements to tell myself, "You can do this," just to get my feet on the floor. I remember being absolutely exhausted just from leaving my first-floor apartment, going down the three front steps, climbing into a cab, and then taking the elevator up to my desk at work. Those simple activities felt like a marathon to me. The noise from my body was drowned out only when I would go to a friend's apartment and top off the pile of pills in my stomach with the cheapest white wine we could find.

The hardest part is that just weeks before this my life was entirely different. I was running around the city in my (Loehmann's-purchased) Michael Kors Collection three-inch heels, standing around at bars, climbing the stairs to rooftops filled with finance bros and the women desperately trying to change them. I was sprinting down the subway stairs to get on the 1 train and make it to brunch in Chelsea on time. I was walking the length of the Upper West Side to and from work every day because the long walks gave me time to think about what the hell I actually wanted to do with my life. At least four nights a week I was pouring sweat trying to make my toes touch the back of my head in a Bikram class. And then suddenly all of that was gone. My agency. My freedom. My identity as a "healthy" person came crashing down. I was now a person in pain.

And the pain was relentless. The doctor I was seeing* was hesitant to suggest surgery, but the injections had almost no effect. Was I destined to live like this forever? Was I just a drug addict with a cane who used to be an athlete but now had to take a cab

---

* Lol "the doctor I was seeing" is a phrase my mom has been desperate to hear me say my whole life, and every time I do, it's the opposite of what she is hoping for.

five blocks? Could I never do my favorite thing again? And I don't mean Bikram or rowing; I was thinking about grocery shopping.

But when I considered another surgery, my mind jumped to the worst-case scenario: another blood clot, perhaps not one I could survive this time. And even if I did survive, I didn't feel like I could relive that experience. How could I have done everything right—the surgery, the blood-clot procedure—just to be back here again: trapped in my home, in my body, and gritting my teeth through excruciating pain with no end in sight.

After a month or so, I finally found a new doctor at the Hospital for Special Surgery. He could see that I needed real intervention, not just the mask of pain management drugs. He told me a simple discectomy/laminectomy should relieve my pain. I don't remember that surgery being so simple when I was nineteen, but maybe this time was different. Maybe the scientific community had spent the last five-ish years intensely focused on perfecting this procedure so that not only did it work, it was quick and easy. Whatever happened, I could not go on like this.

And it turned out this surgery was different. For starters, I entered it with a bizarre mix of relief and trepidation. I was desperate to be free of my debilitating pain, but I was also terrified that I would die from complications. I would also be recovering not in my parents' comfortable suburban home, but in my cramped Manhattan two-bedroom apartment that my roommate had very kindly vacated so my parents could come up and take care of me. And my motivations were different this time around. With my first surgery, I was more optimistic; the goal was to fix the problem and start recovering so I could go back to Cornell and row. This time I was just trying to end the monotonous hell I was in and hope I didn't make it worse or die in the process.

I pushed past all those fears and anxieties because living in extreme chronic pain, at this point for several months, was unsustainable. Pain changes who you are. It's not just that you're trapped at home or taking drugs, it makes you angry. It makes you want to give up on everything in your life. The energy normally spent on humor or critical thinking or passion is spent mentally managing pain, compartmentalizing it, and pushing down the thought that you can't keep going like this. You lose your personality; you lose who you are. You become this shell of someone who was once a person, capable only of surviving rather than having a chance to thrive.

A day before the main event, my doctor gave me a bonus little procedure to protect me from blood-clot complications. They inserted a little metal umbrella structure into a blood vessel in my abdomen that, were there to be a clot in my bloodstream, would catch it before it got to my heart and lungs, preventing a catastrophe. They obviously inserted this device through . . . my neck. Makes total sense. The way to a man's heart is through his stomach, and apparently the way to a woman's stomach is through a vein in her neck. I did this procedure in the morning and then I went back to work with a giant gauze bandage on my neck, still walking with a cane and loopy as hell from the drugs. No one in my office seemed concerned. They all knew I was going out on surgery leave the next day, but it still felt like people in my department—particularly the older men—viewed my condition as an exaggeration, the histrionics of a twentysomething girl who's being dramatic about her body when, actually, it's fine. I caught them rolling their eyes at how slow I was moving. They were very focused on when I could get back to work, and never asked if I was okay. Understandably, these were men who needed a job done and I was not doing that job, but the dismissal of my physical deterioration felt less about late administrative work and more about how this all seemed a bit much to them.

This surgery went incredibly smoothly. The nurses and doctors even walked me through the best ways to get in and out of bed in under an hour. Also, in the years since my first surgery, the medical community had moved on from barbaric staples, and this time I had stitches, which felt much more humane. What a difference it makes to maneuver through a day when you aren't feeling the ten pieces of metal crammed into your back at every second. My mom spent the first week with me, the most intensive period that involves help in the bathroom and help getting dressed. By the time I was nearly self-sufficient, save for cleaning and taking out the garbage, she and my dad switched places. He stayed with me for a few days partly to help me around the house or take me to doctors' appointments, and partly so that we could walk a block or two to an Italian restaurant and crush a bottle of red wine with dinner.

After those first two weeks, I felt like I was actually getting better, like I was on the path to having my life back. The months of herniation likely caused some permanent nerve damage, but the acute pain was mostly gone. I had a few weeks of recovery from surgical pain, but I was, as Taylor Swift would say, out of the woods. Once I finished physical therapy, I was able to do the things I did before. I was hauling bags of groceries from Fairway to my apartment. I was bounding up and down subway stairs to catch trains and see friends. After a few months I even returned to Bikram yoga, starting slowly and skipping some positions, but eventually regaining control over my practice and feeling in touch with my body. My personality returned because, instead of using my brainpower to manage my instinct to scream all day, I could talk, read, have opinions, and regain the little charm I used to have. Sure, some of who I was had eroded and would never return, but at least in the day-to-day, I felt like a person again rather than just a husk trying to survive.

A year to the day after my disc had re-herniated, I was sitting at my desk at my museum job. My phone rang and as I reached across the vast expanse (two feet) of desk to reach the landline, I felt a very familiar twinge accompanied by burning pain down my left side. I froze in my office chair, unable to move. It wasn't quite as severe as the last time, but I knew the feeling all the same. I knew it had happened again. Though I don't know why or how it happened *exactly* one year later. If you are an astrologer reading this book, please advise me on what I should be doing on September 15 every year so this never happens again. I'm a Capricorn, if that helps.

My first thought was that at least I was sitting down and wouldn't have to be on my hands and knees in my office, something the staid museum would not have entertained no matter how serious the medical reason. My boss called me into her office shortly after to go over something, and I walked in crouched down and leading with one foot like I was doing some bizarre Tracy Anderson exercise that focuses just on your inner thighs and upper calves. She wasn't so much concerned as confused. What had happened? Why was a healthy-looking young woman suddenly acting like this? I wasn't crying (because I was busy grinding my teeth through the pain of every breath), so she seemed to not take whatever was going on with me seriously, like when a dog hobbles around and the vet tells you that it's faking an injury for attention and treats. Eventually, my boss excused me for the day and I spent a half hour getting downstairs and into a cab home, knowing the road ahead was a bumpy one, both literally and figuratively.

People who don't understand pain expect that it always comes with an outsize reaction and emotion. They think that you'll be able to tell them how terrible you feel and they'll be able to easily understand it. I've discovered that's not how pain works. In that moment, I wanted to scream and cry and throw office supplies against the wall in a rage that I had to suffer *again*. But I know pain. I know my pain. I know that no one knows how to handle any outpouring of negative feelings in any context, certainly not physical ones. And I know that there is nothing anyone around me can do for me. I also know how to push all of it down, steel my face, and move through my life in an agony that would destroy most "healthy" people's souls.

My body had betrayed me. I did everything right. I was physically active, I didn't rush into surgery until a doctor knew it was the only solution, and I took the proper time to recover afterward. I ate lots of vegetables, I did yoga, I had been without opioids for seven months. Now I was right back to my old dosage of "a handful a day keeps the pain away" and closing down my brain function so I could get through the day. I was confined to my couch or bed, and moving from one to the other was a miserable journey. Why would my body do this again?

An MRI confirmed what I, of course, already knew: The same disc had another herniation that was pushing on my spinal column and causing pain and immobility. Great. It was like a toxic old hookup that keeps popping up to ruin your life for a few months. At least this time my doctor was faster to suggest surgery. Instead of months of drugs and pain it would be only weeks. Even with a solution in sight, I was scared. What was stopping this from happening to me every year? Was I trapped in this cycle of excruciating pain, then surgery, then brief relief, then back to excruciating pain forever?

We once again scheduled surgery, and once again it went relatively smoothly as far as these procedures go. My mom helped me recover, then my dad, and then I was on my own again. I was on my own to wean myself off the piles of pills I was taking. I was on my own to figure out how to move forward with my life, how to live without the constant fear that any minor movement could cause the kind of pain that, according to professionals, makes people consider killing themselves.

In the course of about fifteen months, the label of "healthy" that I had claimed for myself was gone. I wasn't healthy, because health isn't having defined triceps and clear skin. Health is how you feel, not how you're perceived. No amount of muscle definition or bouncy hair or old college athletics sweatshirts could change that, inside, I was on fire and felt like I was dying much quicker than everyone around me. I know that fearing your own body, losing your agency, watching the life you built slipping away, is the tough stuff that fortifies who we are, that makes us strong. But I also know that the months of agony and drugs also took something from me. Pieces of me are gone forever. Being someone in pain means being only a part of yourself while the other part of you deals with the pain. And you deal with that pain yourself so others don't have to. You don't want to be a burden, you don't want to be a chore, you don't want to be doted on or consoled or pitied. What you want is to just be yourself. And when you lose that, you begin to wonder who you'll end up being.

I'M TOO ONLINE

I refuse to look at my screen-time report. It's like getting on the scale during a week when I had a lot of dinners out: I know it's bad, I don't need a number to prove that to me.

I love the internet. I loved the internet when I could access it only through our home computer, I loved it on my own smooth white iMac late at night in college, and I love looking at it all day, every day on my phone. I have always been good at being online, at finding ways to use the internet for fun, at mining the best parts of it for my and my friends' enjoyment. I read once that my particular subgeneration of millennials (everyone born between 1980 and 1985) is called the *Oregon Trail* generation,* which feels right to me because computers are a defining characteristic of we who are now in our early forties. We grew up without smartphones,

---

* If you are not familiar with *Oregon Trail,* it was a computer game that the lab of every elementary school in America had in the early nineties. The "game" was to get your family and farm animals to Oregon without everyone dying of drowning or dysentery. No one has ever met a single person who "won."

wifi, social media, or even digital cameras. But we did grow up with the ever-evolving internet, and we became adept at navigating its many iterations while also knowing how to function without a phone in our hands that connects to the entire universe (well, mostly—unless I'm lost or trying to do work or waiting on a line, then I am sent into a spiral of terror that only Instagram can cure).

Some part of culture always gets blamed for being the downfall of a generation. When I was younger, video games and television bore the brunt of that criticism. These days the internet and social media get all the hand-wringing. But I'm glad I was the right age at the right time to experience many forms of the internet before people worried about it corrupting the youth.

In high school, I stayed up late chatting on AIM on my graphite-blue bauble of an iMac. I mostly messaged with my friend Andy, whom I loved talking to but hated actually IM'ing with because his preferred aesthetic was a dark blue background and neon-green Comic Sans text. And while that was murder on the eyes, I respected him doing him. It used to be free to show who you were online. You didn't have to buy hauls from Nordstrom or display hundreds of dollars of Sephora makeup to show people your personality, you had an array of fonts and text colors to play with depending on your whims. You could put up cryptic away messages that were mostly song lyrics if you were sad or in love (or both), or movie quotes if you were trying to be funny, or inscrutable inside jokes for literally one other person if you wanted to exclude everyone. You didn't have to worry about using a sexy photo for your profile or trying to display wealth or status. Your online existence was for people who already knew you, not for people who didn't.

While I chatted on AIM, I would browse my favorite corners of the internet. I was constantly downloading songs from LimeWire, a Napster competitor that I understood slightly better, trying to find the music they played at Abercrombie & Fitch. I'd burn CDs that mixed pop music with songs by Donovan and Bob Dylan to listen to when I was driving to school or to rowing practice. And then I would make entirely different mixes filled with DMX and Lil' Kim songs for cruising around at night with my friends, heading to some guy's house to try Smirnoff Ice for the first time.

Being on the internet when I was in high school wasn't exactly "cool." Someone who was logged on to AIM every day from the minute you got home from school until after midnight wasn't a person everyone wanted to be. Knowing your way around the digital world too well wasn't something anyone envied. People who loved the internet were mostly geeks and nerds. At best, they were portrayed as cool hackers with short spiky haircuts and platform combat boots who said things like "I'm in" while typing at Mach 1 speed. But mostly they were considered losers who had to turn to the digital world because they couldn't make friends in real life. On the spectrum of being online, I was up there. Despite having a robust life off my computer, I really enjoyed sitting down at my desk and fucking around for hours.

At one point during our senior year, Andy and I stumbled across a page of ecards on Tom Green's website. (My friends and I were huge fans of Tom Green during high school, and of course he had a website.) But these weren't normal cards adorned with stuff like birthday balloons or a graduation cap. No, this was Tom Green. The cards were all just esoteric photographs of average office furniture. One was a desk lamp. One was a swivel chair. None of it made any sense, but it made Andy and me laugh for hours. Terrific site, but dangerous for two high schoolers who were easily bored and had a strange sense of humor. Unlike today, where when you do anything online your browser and device both know your email, name, and every identifier you have down to your blood type, you could send someone an ecard just by putting in whatever sender and recipient email addresses you wanted. Weeks earlier, our AP Calculus teacher had handed out a list of everyone in our class's email address and distinctly warned us not to use this list for anything other than calculus. That tells you how new the internet still felt in 2001—someone handed me a piece of paper with a list of email addresses on it. Obviously, Andy and I could not help ourselves. So late one night we divided up the calculus class list and started sending Tom Green ecards to and from different students. Because we disguised our email addresses, no one would have any idea that we were the ones at the digital helm of this psychotic ship.

The next day in class, Andy and I eagerly waited for the conversations to begin as we settled in after a quiz. My heart raced as we looked around the room. Finally, Andy couldn't help himself and said, "Al, did you send me an ecard last night that was a picture of a file cabinet?"

In what is probably the best acting I've ever done to this day, I said, "Wait, I definitely didn't, but I got an ecard from Steve and it was just a watercooler?"

The floodgates opened. Suddenly everyone was saying they got a weird card from someone else, but of course none of the "senders" actually sent them. It wasn't a *mean* prank. We didn't send nasty messages or only pick students who were "unpopular." (This was AP Calc, none of us were popular.) We saw that the internet let us create very funny chaos, and we did it, and then we laughed so hard that I think I lost consciousness for several minutes. I think that's what appealed to me so much about my early experience on-line: It was the first place I could really "do comedy." I was funny with my friends in person, everyone was, but here was a new venue to try and make people laugh. I was hooked.

If AIM defined my high school internet experience, Facebook ruled my college years. I started at Cornell in 2002. By my sopho-more year, it reached us, high above Cayuga's waters. It seemed like everyone was joining, so, of course, all my friends and I did, too. At that time, Facebook was another way for elite universities to feel like elite universities because it hadn't yet gone far outside the Ivy League.

I had a blast on Facebook in the early days because it was still evolving, and every time they added a new feature, it was a new way to goof off and be funny. Sometimes, I would fully change my profile from my actual information to a parody of some col-lege archetype just for lols. At one point I made my entire profile a sorority-girl caricature. I had many friends who were members of sororities, and I regularly went to fraternity parties. I also love 98 percent of the things typical girls in sororities love, like shop-ping and the beach and doing shots with my friends and hooking up with men who unfortunately wear flip-flops. I wasn't parodying sorority girls to make fun of them, but rather to satirize the way that my peers used this new medium to communicate their identi-ties to the rest of the world. My friends and I laughed about it for a week and then I switched it all back. I did it again a few weeks later to parody a group of rowers we knew on the heavyweight men's team who defined themselves by loving long rows, classic rock, and being huge. I made my profile picture a photo of a grill filled with steaks.

At this point, my digital persona (which was just me, but online) was still only for the people I knew in real life. I didn't have an online "brand" the way everyone does today. This was before anyone became an internet celebrity or influencer. We were just people using the internet as a space to work and play and just kind of exist, as a new method to gossip, complain, and joke. I was on Facebook to connect with people whom I met on campus or knew at other schools. When I made my account into a parody, it was just to make my group of eight friends laugh.

My internet existence significantly shifted during my adulthood. I went from using the internet to reach people I already knew to using it to reach total strangers, and as many of them as possible. I heavily blogged in my pre-comedy existence, mostly in the fashion sphere because I like clothes and, well, fashion blogs were a thing. I had one called Black and Bleu, where I posted trends I liked or roundups of designer collections from Style.com. I had no authority, but I wanted to practice writing, and I thought I might as well do it about something I loved (clothes, shopping, and spending money I didn't have). That later expressed itself through another blog I created with my friend Divya devoted entirely to the weirdest finds (jeans with built-in boots, black leather ruffled bloomers) in the furthest corners of the online shopping universe (mostly Yoox.com clearance pages). It was called Heavy Browsing and we had some serious heat before realizing neither of us was really set up to run a successful fashion blog.

The biggest part of my professional digital life has been Twitter. What can I say, I loved it before it became a Nazi playground! I am aware that technically its name is X, but I'm sorry, I cannot call it that. "Twitter" is a social media platform I was on for more than a decade that has functioned as a digital town square, a marketplace of ideas, and a place for comedy, information, and connection.

"X" is a letter overused in energy drinks marketed to men who are always "playing devil's advocate." I also like that calling it Twitter pisses off Elon Musk, something I will make any amount of effort to do as often as I can because, and I truly mean this, fuck that guy.

I still remember when I first joined Twitter in 2010 and had a new place to try to be funny every day. I had been blogging and doing stand-up onstage, as well as freelance writing for websites (remember those?!). And while Facebook was still a place to connect with people you knew or wanted to meet in real life, Twitter felt like the Wild West. If Facebook was the Rolodex of everyone you've ever met, Twitter was the yellow pages getting dropped on your front stoop,* full of strangers and bizarre companies. Sure, I followed a bunch of people whom I either knew or wanted to know as comics, but my goal was to be a personality, for hordes of strangers to follow me as a source of entertainment. I didn't want to know *them,* I just wanted them to know *me.*

My first tweet was: "It's 4:30 p.m., was the sandwich I just ate lunch or dinner?" It's certainly not a joke, but it is a thought. That about sums up my early tweets. Back before Trump and Elon and #resistance, most of my feed was comedians and writers joking about whatever was right in front of them. My Twitter personality was clear from the beginning, which I probably owe to those old parody Facebook profiles. I learned early how to telegraph a lot in only a few words. My tweets covered what my life included: snacks and sandwiches; weird comments I overheard; air, train, and subway travel; dating; and, of course, wine.

---

* For those who didn't know what *Oregon Trail* was a few pages ago, I'm sure I should explain that in the past, the phone company delivered a printed-out book of every phone number in your area and that was how you called people. I know, it feels made up.

Weirdly, I made a lot of friends on Twitter. Not strangers who lured me to meet up in a dark alley or anything. In fact, I think millennials are perhaps the safest group online because of how the internet evolved as we grew up. When messaging and chat rooms emerged, our generation was told that basically every single person you talked to online was a pervert, pedophile, or murderer who would find you and kill you. Were there perverts, pedophiles, and murderers in chat rooms? I mean, are there peanuts in trail mix? Duh, of course, and they suck. But we entered digital spaces with a certain trepidation that younger generations lack. Ironic, too, that those in my parents' generation were the ones warning us that everyone online is dangerous and now you can't look at Facebook without seeing boomers sharing AI-generated content and falling for scams.

My Twitter friends were people in the comedy/entertainment/writing community whom I knew only through social media before we hung out in real life. They were mostly women, but we always met up with groups in public places, because, you know, murder! Twitter also helped me better know the people who were in the comedy community around me. Standing in the back of a show was certainly a place to get to know comics, but they were mostly men, so it could be intimidating as a woman to hop into a conversation and joke around casually. When those relationships could be forged online, it made the room a little less scary.

My friend Alyssa and I were already on our way to a closeness that some would consider clinical codependence, and I'd be lying if I said Twitter wasn't a catalyst for our relationship. We built our personas there, both individually as comics and together as friends, replying to each other's idiotic jokes with an even more idiotic tag. People knew us as a pair, which helped us get jobs writing together. But we didn't just exist as BFFs online; we would combine the physical and the digital. We'd sit on her studio-apartment couch drinking wine, or go to Tolani, the bar in our neighborhood where we'd get kale Caesars and meatballs and, you guessed it, wine. We would be talking and joking IRL, but we'd also be on our phones live-tweeting our hangs. We'd come up with new tweets and ask each other, "Could this be a real bit onstage?" Pouring pinot grigio and debating ordering the hummus plate was punctuated by gleeful exclamations about which big comic or writer had just followed us or that a silly joke about Hershey's Kisses was suddenly getting lots of retweets. Twitter wasn't just a place online to mess around, it was a genuine part of the comedy ecosystem. It was a place to test material, to find your voice, and to network with people in the industry. And a place to read a lot of really funny, really short jokes.

Then Twitter (and the internet, and the world around us) began to change. My feed, once dominated by dumb thoughts and wordplay and people promoting their latest *McSweeney's* list, slowly became more politicized. Twitter became a place where you absolutely had to make your politics known. Most of my peers, at least in 2015, were still doing that with jokes, and I was no different. One day I tweeted: "As a woman, I just hope that one day I have as many rights as a gun does." It's not a particularly original joke and I am absolutely not the first person to write something to that effect and blast it off into the internet, but I wanted to make my opinion known: I'm a woman, I don't feel like an equal in our country, and I feel like guns are strangely overprotected. Seemed harmless enough.

A few days later, I was at my friend Laura's apartment helping her move to a unit upstairs. There is a unique hell in moving within your own apartment building. No matter how much crap you have, it feels like you should be able to just carry it all in a few trips. It honestly takes as long to move within your building as it does across town. Laura had garment racks and boxes all piled up and ready. We drank red wine and gossiped about old co-workers and shitty situationships while we loaded coats and dresses on hangers. We took a brief break so Laura could make us her signature grilled cheese, and I checked my phone. When I opened Twitter, my mentions were flooded in a way they had never been before. At this point I hadn't had a single tweet blow up, and now it was happening. It was thrilling, in a way. I'd seen others have tweets go viral, catapulting them to minor digital celebrity. Enough of those and you could get hired to write for a late-night show. But as I scrolled through Twitter, my excitement faded into disappointment and then terror. This was finally happening for me, but it was happening with the wrong tweet for the wrong reasons and thanks to the very wrongest of people.

A conservative user with a massive following somehow came across my simple joke about guns and women's rights. He retweeted it with a reply that completely misinterpreted the joke, saying that if I wanted to be treated like a gun, I would be locked in a box or something. One misogynist intentionally misreading my joke in bad faith to prove he is "funnier" and "smarter" than I am? Sure. Truly, who could care. But that misogynist blasting out my tweet— and my name—to two million gun-loving, woman-hating assholes was much worse than I was prepared for it to be.

My mentions were flooded with some of the worst things I have ever read, even to this day. Skip this paragraph if you want to spare yourself some truly disgusting misogyny. Lots of men said that I should be banned from polling places and schools. Many more said

I should be bought and sold. Some truly outstanding individuals claimed I deserved "to have all of my holes cleaned with a rough brush" (which I GUESS is how you clean a gun????). Those who couldn't keep the joke going replied that I was a dumb bitch or that someone should rape me or that someone should kill me. Every word in the dictionary that can be hurled at a woman negatively was used to reply to my tweet. My phone alerts were going off nonstop, but I kept checking them hoping that maybe this time it was something positive. Every time it was just a variation of "fuck you, bitch," but I couldn't stop looking, which led to me doing a terrible job helping Laura get all her throw blankets upstairs.

The flurry of hate was difficult, but not the most terrifying thing that has ever happened to me. It's devastating to see in action the intense misogyny that I know is out there but am lucky to rarely have to interact with. I already knew that these people existed. Their profiles were all the same, too: an extreme close-up of a white guy in wraparound sunglasses not smiling, and some combination of the words *father, husband, patriot, Christian*. It was even more chilling when the hate came from one of these guys' wives, often a profile picture of a woman with terrible highlights and a spray tan or a wide shot of a family of six. Also a *wife, mother, Christian,* and the appropriate Bible slogans—wait, that's not the right word, what is it, *passages*?—Bible *passages* to indicate they are good and pure and love everyone. That is, unless a stranger tweets something they don't agree with, and then all that wholesomeness fades away into murder threats.

The hate stopped existing just in the mentions tab of my Twitter account and started making its way into my messages, then into my Facebook inbox and onto my wall, and eventually to my personal email—none of which were linked on my Twitter account. Which means people went out of their way to find me on other platforms just to tell me I was wrong or stupid or fat or going to die soon. This felt scary. And it made me miss when my experience with the internet was just the digital representations of people I knew and trusted in my life. Until this point, I had never felt the internet was actually a scary place, but this was the internet our parents had warned us about. Because while I knew that it was 99.9 percent unlikely that any of these gun maniacs was going to find my address, come to my home, and kill me, it wasn't 100 percent impossible. These were people who read a joke that wasn't directed at them and immediately threatened to kill me. I didn't know what they were capable of.

Obviously, I was not murdered by a stranger from Twitter. If I had been, you wouldn't be reading this book. (You'd be reading a very interesting true crime book probably titled *140 Deadly Characters: The 2A Twitter Murder* that would be adapted into a Netflix limited series where I would hopefully be played by Lizzy Caplan.) But the experience of going viral like this did shake me. I made my DMs accessible only to people I actually followed, and then didn't open the app for a few days to avoid seeing the fresh hate that was still pouring in. I always knew the internet was unkind to women, but this was the first time I had personally experienced its violence, and at this volume. And the irony of my tweet was that I'm a wildly privileged woman. In my offline life, this kind of misogyny existed more in theory than in practice. I'm a straight white woman with money in a liberal city. I have so many rights that other people don't that my joke barely even made sense. I was even privileged that this happened digitally, that this hate wasn't screamed in my face the way so many other marginalized people experience it on a regular basis.

After a few days I wrote a little blog about my experience and posted it on Medium, and had the inverse experience I had after my initial tweetstorm. So many people shared it, from friends of mine to big comedians I respected. I had my dose of positive reinforcement from the internet and moved on, back to my normal online life of joking about wine and bad dates and sending what were clearly inside jokes with Alyssa out into the universe for no one else but us to understand.

Nothing too notable happened to me on Twitter for a long time after that. I moved into the new phase of the internet just like everyone else, eventually joining Instagram and learning about angles and filters. I kept writing for online outlets like *McSweeney's, The Huffington Post,* and The Cut and promoting that work on social media. I climbed my way through the comedy-writer Twitterverse and had some stupid jokes go viral here and there. One such joke demanding that chicken fingers not be only on kids' menus got so many retweets that Bella Hadid posted it to her Instagram stories, which I think means I'm a model now? Also, writing all these descriptions of retweets, posting, and virality feels absolutely insane, as I imagine you are (hopefully) reading this book on paper years after any of this terminology is remotely relevant. Kudos to me! This is the "email addresses on a piece of paper" portion of the essay.

Fast-forward to November 2020, because literally nothing happened between 2015 and then, right? The vibes were all over the place, because while we successfully elected Joe Biden over Donald Trump, we were still in the throes of an airborne illness killing thousands while we waited less and less patiently for the vaccine to be available. The country, and especially those citizens like me who lived on the internet, had been a disaster for years. We were more divided than ever, and it seemed like there was not one thing anyone could come together and bond over anymore. Even people with brief positive fame were quickly found out to be idiots, menaces, and not-so-secret racists if you had three seconds to google them.

I was packing up my little apartment for an impending move to a slightly less cramped one-bedroom thanks to a Covid deal. After piling all my books and pottery and rarely worn accessories into reusable bins, I made a Negroni and lit a tiny joint while alternately watching *Seinfeld,* fucking around on my phone, and tossing back Cape Cod chips and Goldfish. This is, to this day, my absolute favorite way to spend my time and I'm positive that nothing else will ever come close. The next most fun thing I can imagine is being asleep after a hot shower. So I was LIVING IN MY OWN PRIVATE HEAVEN and jumped over to Twitter to fire off a not-yet-too-drunk-but-drunk-enough-to-not-think-much-about-it   tweet: "People who live outside of NYC and don't have bodegas: where do you go to buy two Diet Cokes, a roll of paper towels, and oh also lemme get some peanut butter m&ms since I'm here, why not." And then I went into my broom-closet-sized kitchen and cooked dinner.

When I brought my pesto pasta (with tomato, kale, red onion, and basil, for those who are curious) and some wine back over to my couch through the maze of boxes in my living room, I noticed that tweet strangely had a ton of engagement. I didn't think it was particularly interesting; it was a joke about how I am literally always buying candy. Suddenly, it went from a few hundred retweets and replies to a few thousand. My feed was updating so fast that every time I refreshed it, I couldn't even see the most recent activity because every two seconds someone new was weighing in. It looked like a slot machine after you pull the arm, spinning fast and impossible to read or predict. Everyone was latching on to the elements of the tweet I didn't think twice about: New York elitism, a white woman saying the word *bodega,* the usual. I simultaneously got Diet Coke, paper towels, New York, and bodegas to trend on Twitter. Everyone started replying with where they buy basic necessities as if it weren't a rhetorical question. So many people did that that Walgreens was actually trending, too. I should have demanded sponsorships or at least a thank-you note for making them so relevant for forty-eight hours. People replied to me in outrage. "Um, the gas station!!!!!!," "I can get all of those things at a grocery store that I can drive to!!!!!," and my all-time favorite answer: "Amazon."

Huge celebrities like Chance the Rapper, Padma Lakshmi, Chrissy Teigen, Desus Nice, and even Mr. Kellyanne himself, George Conway, all had takes—most of them defending me from something I didn't know I needed defending from. MSNBC hosts, internet thinkers, fellow comedians, anyone with an opinion on anything jumped into the conversation. And I loved every second of it. Sure, some people were calling me stuck-up or stupid, but I'd been there before and in a much scarier way. I laughed and laughed as I watched my follower count keep climbing because people either hated me or thought I needed defending from the people who hated me. And all because I can't stop eating M&M's. I have a rule that 99 percent of the time I don't respond to rude/useless/bad-faith replies to my tweets, so instead of jumping into the fray, I kept tweeting and replying to myself, saying, "If this isn't on NY1 tomorrow then it was all for nothing." And then it WAS on NY1. My favorite gals Jamie, Annika, and Ruschell (who has since tragically passed and was a delight to watch every day) all sat around the round table and discussed the tweet, the many celebrity replies, and weighed in with their own love of NYC bodegas and what they buy there. It's the happiest I have ever been in my life. I reveled in my forty-eight hours of Twitter "main character" fame. Friends who aren't even on Twitter or familiar with the viral moments that happen there were texting me. My friend Divya texted one of the group threads we are on together, "Alison what did you do?" And we all just laughed.

I laughed because I knew that my mid-dinner-prep, slightly stoned and drunk, apartment-packing-up-panic tweet gave people something to focus on beyond the horrors that lived both on- and offline. Part of why I still love the internet, and Twitter in particular, is the potential for there to be one person, one idea, one thing we could all collectively participate in discussing, no matter how different or divided we may be. Monoculture is almost nonexistent, but it had some dying breaths thanks to Twitter. It's not always the most thoughtful discourse. Okay, it's rarely, if ever, thoughtful discourse. But I was on Twitter for Cat Person, Bad Art Friend, Cinnamon Toast Crunch Shrimp, How Do Dogs Wear Jeans, and countless other day-or-two-long digital events that everyone in my corner of the internet was weighing in on. That shared conversation is something that's missing from our culture in general, and by late 2020 was something noticeably missing from my life outside the internet. There was no gathering to talk about anything. At best I would be out with three friends and all we would discuss was how strange it was that some people ate inside at restaurants or the latest vaccine update or what the hell to do with all this sourdough bread we were making. Deep in Covid, just barely past a difficult election cycle, the world was not a fun place to be and an even less fun place to talk about. My stupid tweet was a respite from the swirling hell of the world.

The internet is permanent, but it's also, in a way, ephemeral. While tweets will exist online forever (unless Twitter implodes, which is extremely likely given its leadership), the domination of my 140-character thought over the world lasted barely a weekend. It sometimes still pops up with brief relevance, usually when someone tweets, "What's the worst tweet you've ever seen" and then people tag my old bodega tweet. When that happened, I used to break my own response rule and usually reply, "Thank you!!!!" After all, I stand behind my words. And I want everyone to always remember that it was me, I wrote the bodega tweet.

I have permanently left Twitter now. As the throngs of Nazis and bots grew, I realized the party was over. In late 2024, I no longer got any of the things I had once loved from Twitter. Even when I could curate my feed to just the users I liked, it turned out they had given up weird jokes in favor of sharing news stories about the worst things happening on the planet and donation links to try and raise money to help. I wasn't meeting friends, I wasn't refining jokes, I wasn't promoting things well, so it was time to go. I also left Facebook back in 2020, though I recently tried to return when a friend sent me a link to a Facebook Marketplace listing for lamps I was desperately hunting for, minutes before a panel show I was doing in Mobile, Alabama. A woman on the Lower East Side was selling two H. T. Huang toucan desk lamps in excellent condition for a great price. I panic-joined Facebook again, feverishly trying to plug in enough information to have a functional account. My profile photo imported sideways and I didn't even try and fix it, I just rushed to message the seller: "Hi are these still available, I live in NYC and would like both I know this is a new account I am not a bot." Within seconds I was suspended for being a bot. All of this to say, I no longer have Twitter, I no longer have Facebook, and I didn't get those lamps.

Articles and studies point to the countless problems the internet has created for people who spend too much time on it: the body dysmorphia, the overspending that turns into inescapable debt, the radicalization of young white men to the far right, the purchasing of illegal weapons and images, the overall dumbing down of the global population. Those things are real, and I've seen or experienced them. But I still love what the internet has given me, what being too online has provided. For every influencer with a twenty-four-inch waist who made me hate myself, I've connected with someone in the comedy world who helped me or made my life offline even better. For every filter that smooths your skin into what looks like velvet, I've had the chance to develop my own comedic voice in writing. For every incel who told me to kill myself or misogynist who used something I wrote to "prove" that women aren't funny or anonymous message that told me I was unfuckable or . . . where was I going with this? Right. For all the horrific online hate I've dealt with, the internet has still proved to be a source of creative fulfillment, personal improvement, and human connection that I'm better for having experienced. Oh, and there are SO many cat videos there. It's worth being too online for that alone.

I'M SINGLE

. . .

Women are expected to be romantics. Flowers, sonnets, Valentine's Day, over-the-top marriage proposals with doves and fireworks (hopefully not both at once)—these are all things women supposedly want. We are raised on the idea that we must be wooed with pretty things and gentle surprises. We are encouraged to believe that romantic love is something magical.

But I am not a romantic. I never took love all that seriously. In high school, I would get together with my friends Meg and Erin at our favorite coffee shop, City Dock Café, which was tucked away in a busy corner of downtown Annapolis. In the evenings, after we were all done with sports and extracurriculars and having dinner with our respective families (in my case, watching *Jeopardy!* while eating roast chicken), we would park ourselves at a high-top table with three stools. We'd each get our favorite drink, a Milky Way latte, which I'm not unconvinced was just old coffee with a candy bar dropped in it (I mean this as a compliment). I would also get a toasted sesame bagel with butter—at eight o'clock after a full dinner—because my metabolism was that of a hummingbird spin instructor. After we settled in with our snacks and drinks, we'd get down to the real reason we'd all convened: to read sections out loud from romance novels we got at the library.

I remember bringing these worn paperbacks up to the checkout desk at the public library, giggling and refusing to make eye contact with the librarian as she yelled a return date at me, then sprinting out the door. This, I imagine, is the girls' version of trying to buy *Playboy* for the first time.

Once we'd pulled out our supposedly contraband reading material, it was time to begin the, well, performance. Erin and Meg were much better at reading these out loud than I was; they were both involved in theater and could bring a hilarious tone to their dramatization. I was an avid reader, but I was also an athlete with little to no theatricality in me. (And yet somehow, of the three of us, I became the stand-up comic.) The book titles alone made us laugh so hard we'd have tears streaming down our faces and into our candy-flavored night coffees: *To Tame a Highland Warrior. Once a Pirate. Loving a Dowager.* The covers all featured wasp-waisted women clawing at ripped, shirtless men who had the kind of hair I would show a stylist as inspiration to this day.* Meg would clear her throat and begin, "He smelled of honey left out in the sun . . ." and we could barely get to the end of the sentence before bursting out in giggles. We weren't so much making fun of this style of romance as we were laughing at this foreign language that we felt we didn't, and wouldn't ever, understand.

Today, in my forties, I'd probably read those novels with the same amusement and eye-rolling that I did in high school. At this

---

* No, truly. If you want perfect beachy waves, forget influencers hawking Airwraps and just bring a few sexy novels from the nineties to a salon.

point I have a physical understanding of what it means to run your dainty fingers over rippling abs, but the actual drama of romantic love still feels confounding to me. And romance novels aren't the only thing that tells women we need drama in our love lives. Almost every aspect of "female" culture sends that message: glossy magazines with windblown actresses on the cover, romantic comedies packed to the brim with meet-cutes, will-they-or-won't-they television arcs, every advertisement that subtly threatens that if you don't buy this product no one will ever love you and you will die alone and miserable and with visible pores. I still consume all of the above, but with a distance from this narrative because I just don't connect with the core concept of romantic love being the governing force in every woman's life.

There is a lot of talk these days about "decentering men," and I absolutely love it. I've done it. More women and nonbinary folks should do it! If you're unfamiliar, decentering men isn't about hating men or ignoring them or living without them (though sometimes that sounds nice, sorry!). It's about trying to structure your time and energy in a way that isn't instructed by patriarchy and the systems created by and benefiting almost exclusively men.* I believe I have decentered men significantly in my life. I've stopped going places just because I could meet a guy there. I've deleted dating apps because I don't like how they make me feel. Because of those things, in recent years, I've also found myself decentering romantic love. It's not that I don't like or understand the idea of romantic love (I would like it!). For me, it's about reorienting my priorities. I don't consider a life without romantic love a failure,

---

* To be clear, the patriarchy also deeply hurts and damages men by creating a system where they become reliant on others and don't develop skills. But in terms of benefits, yeah, only men get those in this system.

because it's at the bottom of my list—behind friendships, career, and family.

I was single in high school, if that wasn't wildly apparent already. While I flirted and made out with boys, I wasn't one of those girls with a long and storied romance playing out in the locker-filled halls, like Juliet in Abercrombie jeans. Nor was I the kind of girl who was the subject of passed notes and bathroom whispers. It's not that I didn't want to be "dating" in high school—which meant sitting together at lacrosse games, sneaking out of your parents' houses, and having a default for prom if your relationship could make it to the spring—but romance was never something that felt all that realistic or even desirable for me. I never watched high school soap operas like *Dawson's Creek* or *Gilmore Girls,* which aired while I was busy at swimming or rowing practice or holed up in my room cranking out AP English homework. I saved my precious hours of television time to turn on Comedy Central at ten P.M. and watch *Strangers with Candy.* I didn't have an idealized will-they-or-won't-they best-friends-turned-lovers-at-the-homecoming-dance fantasy. I had a stomach cramp from laughing at Stephen Colbert and Amy Sedaris sparring in front of a chalkboard.

My home life didn't leave me rhapsodizing about passionate love affairs and whirlwind connections either. Growing up, I considered my parents to have what I'd classify as a really nice relationship: They've always seemed to actually like each other, and they don't fight. It's not that they never disagreed in front of me or got short with each other—they were raising an annoyingly precocious child in the high-stakes world of suburban Maryland as two professional adults, so there was plenty to be annoyed about every single day. But unlike a lot of my friends' parents, they didn't put up the weird "everything is fine" façade that clearly hid lots of tension behind the surface, nor did they have knock-down, drag-out screaming matches that required me to hide in my room. They just kind of . . . loved each other and mostly got along?

Where a lot of my friends had wedding photos on display in their homes, their mom in a white princess gown and fluttery long veil, arm in arm with their tuxedoed (and often mustached) dad, my parents had a tiny wedding picture that for a long time I thought was from a work lunch they were forced to go to. My dad didn't even wear a jacket. Their civil ceremony at the courthouse was so short that when they got back to their car, they still had time left on the meter, and they had only put thirty minutes on it.

The funny thing is, my parents actually have an outrageously passion-filled origin story as a couple, but they didn't spell it out for me until I was much older. I understand why: Very young me would have been confused, and tween me would have been running my mouth about it to everyone I met as if it somehow made *me* more interesting. When my parents met, they were both in marriages that weren't working. They taught at the same school: my mom English, my dad shop class. They struck up a friendship, which turned into a romantic connection. When they realized how strong their feelings for each other were, they decided they'd be better off together than in their respective marriages, so they each got a divorce, and then they married each other. Now they've been together for fifty years. THAT is passion! THAT is romance!! THAT is the kind of love you spend your life hoping you find!!! That's the stuff of rom-coms that we can only dream of!!!!

I wonder what my perspective on romantic love might have been if I had known from a younger age that my parents were so in love that they blew up their lives to be together. Maybe I would have been more interested in dating, knowing that I wasn't neces-sarily trying to find The One and that I might have to be with someone who wasn't right before finding someone who was. Or maybe it would have turned me off more on the idea of romantic love, because it seems like a lot of work to be married twice. Who knows. Instead, I grew up thinking that weddings aren't fairy-tale beginnings and the idea of magical romance is for maniacs and stu-pid people. So dating lots of people in hopes of falling in love with my soulmate was never high on my priority list as a teenager, when I could focus on things like sports or getting into an Ivy League school or having the most enviable tan of anyone I knew. You know, the important stuff.

I don't know if I've had bad luck or bad timing or if I've genu-inely not cared enough to try, but I've always been the single one of my friends. (Often, I was not alone in that role as everyone jos-tled between wrong fits and complete losers.) The only time in my entire life that this wasn't true was the spring semester of my fresh-man year in college. My friend group was made up of the other rowing girls, most of whom were either single or had a slowly wan-ing long-distance boyfriend they would inevitably break up with because, duh, college. I ended up dating a guy on the lightweight men's team because sports like rowing are basically speed dating with weight training. There is an equal number of men and women just milling around the boathouse in spandex, so eventually you just start pairing up, intentionally or not.

On paper, Matthew* was exactly the kind of guy I thought I was

---

* Names of all these gentlemen have been changed because it's too easy to be an internet detective and I want to protect everyone's privacy. I mostly wanted to change one name, and if you change one, you have to change them all, like decid-ing to wear flats, and then realizing you need to change your jeans, and because of that, your top.

supposed to be dating: He was tall and athletic with a mop of curly blond hair, and he somewhat cared about wearing clean clothes every day and took the steps to ensure that happened. But in reality, the only thing we had in common was that we both had to show up at the same boathouse six days a week to shred our quads and rip the skin clean off our hands. He was a science major who thought playing techno while his roommates were working was a really funny bit, and I'm not entirely sure he ever finished reading one book that didn't have equations in it. Our relationship of talking about training before awkwardly hooking up in my twin bed was not long for this world.

Eventually, things ended because he met a younger, blonder, smaller girl back home over the summer. She had a hot-pink Xanga journal* that I found and stalked for a few months. It wasn't unrequited love, but I did NOT like the feeling of being dumped for someone else when I'm clearly perfect in literally every way.

The next fall, I ran into Matthew at a Halloween party. My friends and I were dressed as a fake boy band made up of hunters that we called *N Season (hunting gear was all we could find at the Ithaca Kmart last minute). I had my hair in a low ponytail and was wearing camo sweatpants, a neon-orange nylon safety vest, and aviator sunglasses, giving the impression of a middle-aged man who could dance as well as he could hunt. When I saw my ex in the corner of a house party, he was dressed as a woman and was easily ten times hotter than I have ever looked in my life thanks to his tall, lean build and thick curly hair. It was the perfect reminder that we were NOT a match. (Though, in a way, weren't we?) My

---

* For the non-millennials out there, Xanga was like a written version of Instagram, a diary of slightly customized colors that now gives a humiliating view into who you were in 2003.

friends and I laughed about it all night before going back to our house, pouring crushed Doritos into our mouths, and falling asleep with our aviators on. It says a lot about this relationship that I didn't mourn it particularly long when it ended. I thought that had more to do with us being objectively mismatched as a couple, but in retrospect, it was because I didn't really care about being in a relationship with anyone at that point.

I spent the rest of college just doing what most college students do and hooking up with guys here and there, kind of having a crush every once in a while. I had a weird, brief long-distance thing with Jack, a guy I knew from my hometown who was in a questionable place with his maybe-ex-girlfriend. (She was blond, and went to the same college as he did, so I was zero for two out the gate.) Jack and I hooked up when I was home on break, and he put up cryptic away messages that made me think there was real romance between us, at least when it came to AIM. Despite the murkiness of our situation, I liked the excitement, the slightly less awkward sex, and plenty of time to do whatever the hell I wanted while I was off at school living my life. He eventually stopped talking to me because he met an even younger, even blonder woman than his maybe-ex.

At this point, it may seem like every man I've ever been with left me for a hot young blonde. But really, I think these guys all just found women who actually wanted to be with them on their terms, and they were like, "Oh, this makes way more sense to do than tolerating this other woman who both seems too busy for me and has expectations I don't feel like meeting." Hot blondes, I don't hate you! You can have these guys!!!!!!! I'm good!!!!!

My twenties in New York were exactly what you're expecting a dynamic young woman's urban dating life might look like:

constantly hanging out in chic cocktail lounges across from a hot guy with a full head of hair who doesn't even look at his glass of whiskey when taking a sip because his eyes are so locked on to mine, then he suggests we go to Paris for a weekend where we have sex on a hotel bed that faces a glittering Eiffel Tower. LOLOLOLOLOLOLOL. Imagine. Just like, truly imagine that life. I'm fairly confident people do experience that outside of sleek, quickly canceled television dramas about being single in the city, but I have yet to meet anyone who has actually lived it. No, most of my interactions with men were post-bar hookups that never went anywhere, and one blind date organized by a friend of my aunt's co-worker (terrific!) where I had infinitely more chemistry with the bartender than with the guy I was actually meeting. Scream-talking in loud bars to guys in Diesel jeans, bumming cigarettes under an awning from cute dudes with stupid tattoos, ripping shots with a bro in a backward hat. These are all the highly romantic sparks that can fly when you're twenty-six, single in New York, and spent your last $8 on a mostly soda vodka soda.

I didn't have a particularly jaded or cynical approach to meeting guys and dating, but I also wasn't overly hung up on the cinematic romance of what that might look like. I was mostly interested in the *idea* of being interested in someone rather than the person himself. I saw other friends bouncing from crush to crush, so I subconsciously forced a romantic curiosity about guys I thought made sense. I had such low expectations that when things were even *slightly* nice, I was floored.

During my Upper West Side era, when I would regularly hang out at neighborhood bars drinking Brooklyn Lager and whiskey shots, there was a cute guy my age in the group of regulars I befriended. We'd always flirt, but I didn't think he'd be seriously interested in me because I have a weird inferiority complex about guys I find "hot." I think I'm the smartest, funniest, coolest person on the planet, with a decent set and thick hair, but for some reason, I'm convinced that any man with a slightly visible jawline would think I'm a swamp creature. Then one night we actually hooked up, and he ended up coming home with me and sleeping over. The next morning, I set off down Columbus Avenue to work, and since he lived a few blocks away, he walked with me, both of us awkwardly trying to act like this was totally normal. When it was time for him to peel off toward his apartment, he very sweetly kissed me. On the lips! On the street!! In broad daylight!!! I couldn't believe that level of romance, of chivalry. I basically floated my way to my office and immediately texted all my friends about the outrageously passionate gesture.

My excitement was mostly met with responses like "He kissed you, and . . . is that it?" To which I replied, "But, like, during the DAY!!!!"

In my deeply unromantic world, this was akin to proposing at the top of the Empire State Building with an eight-carat diamond, a bouquet of roses, and a custom Birkin. In retelling this story to friends, I realized that kissing you goodbye after fucking you the night before is probably baseline human behavior and not exactly something to send a newsletter about.

That guy and I never hooked up again, let alone live happily ever after in a classic six on Riverside Drive. So many of the guys I went out with or hooked up with throughout my twenties were (I assume) perfectly fine people with whom I ultimately just didn't have a ton in common. Even with my college boyfriend and my long-distance whatever, I didn't actually share much beyond being in the same place at the same time, and with Jack I didn't even have that. Though I had these two "relationships" under my belt, I still didn't feel like I had experienced the romance that many of my friends had as young adults. I hadn't been in a relationship that lasted more than a few months or even gone on a real "date" that didn't start in a university dining hall or end at his mom's house. At this point I wasn't feeling behind or "undatable," but I was starting to sense that something about romantic relationships just wasn't for me. At the time, I told myself I was avoiding the heartbreak of learning no one would ever love me. You know the drill: You dump him first so he doesn't dump you. I thought I was doing that but with the entire concept of romantic love.

In my teens and early twenties, I had forced myself to care about relationships because every piece of media and culture I consumed told me that the most important thing I'd do with my life was find the right man, have a fairy-tale wedding, and be in love with him every day for the rest of my life. Even the failures in that pursuit were valuable. (Thank you, Carrie Bradshaw, and also every other woman on television.) And yes, I think relationships are valuable! I think failed relationships are valuable! I think that vulnerability and sexual chemistry and longing and comfort and all the ups and downs that come with pursuing a romantic love are hugely important to the human experience. I also think it's okay if those things aren't necessarily on the front burner for you for most of your life.

The first guy whom I actually *did* have a ton in common with was Jason. We're actually great friends now. When we met, it was an instant spark: We cared about the same things and had the same sense of humor; we both loved *King of Queens* and we both hated the same guy named Kevin (not James). The length of time between the first texts we sent each other and making out in a bar after a birthday-cake vodka shot was impressively short.

This relationship is not one of my great loves in the sense that we actually belonged together and perhaps I've missed my chance at happiness. It is one of my great loves in that I still have a ton of platonic love for Jason. While the messy sorting out of romantic love didn't end in a committed relationship, it taught me (and I hope him) a lot about parsing the feeling of closeness. There's a strange phenomenon that I think a lot of us experience when we're young and single: You meet someone whom you have chemistry with, and there's an instant rapport; you crackle with excitement talking to each other. And because you're both single, you assume that you want to date each other. It seems like the start of all love stories, the stuff of romantic comedies, teen dramas, and gossip you share over dinner with your friends.

Jason and I exchanged numbers, we hooked up, we went out and got late-night drinks. We met a few of each other's friends. But we weren't dating. Whatever our relationship was never quite elevated to a recognizable romance. The whole time we were together, we never broke the friendship part. Even when weeks or months went by without going out or sleeping together, we still talked every single day, texted nonstop, or sent each other funny pictures of our drunk exploits.

But things began to change, and Jason's interest in romance ended before mine did. We both saw other people the whole time we knew each other, but he certainly seemed more focused on them. Any exciting momentum had slowed. It was painful to have to process "a breakup" without having actually been in "a relationship." But I learned that sometimes you meet someone and you are destined to be . . . friends! I love friends. I love having them, I'm super close to them, I make time for them. Sometimes those friends are men. A lot of my male friends are guys I met when I was much younger, or when only one or neither of us was single, or we didn't have that extra spark of attraction. In your twenties it can be so easy to confuse romantic and platonic love, to confuse the desire to be with someone and the desire to be around someone. Through a little heartbreak, some honesty, and a sabbatical from texting him daily, I learned that this kind of friendship can be deep and satisfying and still a little electric, but ultimately entirely platonic. There's no special test you can take to define your feelings for someone, and in a world where all of us—particularly women—are conditioned to think the goal of adulthood is marriage, most of us just assume our interest is romantic when we have a meaningful relationship with someone we find attractive.

The longest thing I have had that even approaches a relationship is actually about as far away from what most people consider "a real romance" as can be. If a real relationship is Midtown Manhattan, this thing was the edge of Yonkers—in the same general space but truly worlds apart. But before I go any further, Mom, do not read this next chunk of the essay. Dad, DEFINITELY do not read it.

Charlie popped into my life at just the right time. He was, for lack of a better term, a sex partner. He was good at it. Really, really good at it. (In fact, I'm sure he still is, I'm just not privy to his current talents, but kudos to the people who are—you won the orgasm lottery.) He was so good at it that I know at least half a dozen other friends who have all hooked up with him, and no one has ever had even a pubic hair's worth of jealousy over that fact. We basically just high-five about it. At points I *wished* that I could sign up a friend for sex with him because it really was a cure-all for the mind and body. He's like a public utility. And I don't mean for this to be demeaning in any way. I'm not trying to reduce him to just a dick and a mouth, but rather to highlight how rare it is to feel true physical pleasure and excitement as a woman who sleeps with men. At that point in my life, I was deeply immersed in stand-up comedy, and I spent all night, every night listening to men who didn't have savings accounts talk about how annoying their girlfriends were. It often felt like every eligible man in my circle low-key hated the idea that I existed, but Charlie was the exception.

There are a lot of straight men who seem to not actually like women at all. They think our interests are stupid, they hate how we talk, but they tolerate spending time with us to get things like sex. Charlie was different. He seemed to actually enjoy talking to and spending time with women. He flirted with every woman I ever saw him interact with, and our friendship was no exception. This man would have sexual chemistry with an upside-down rake. We hooked up a few times and fell into a yearslong on-again, off-again casual sexual relationship. There were lulls, like when I moved to L.A. or when he was seeing someone. But whenever the time was right, the sexual relationship was just where I'd left it, like clothes on the floor before you go to bed drunk. You know, the way your jeans and bra lie there like you were raptured into space but really you're just sleeping off three martinis and drooling into your own hair. Our relationship was reliable, and Charlie seemed to take care of both my sexual and my quasi-romantic needs. We'd text, and he'd come over to whatever weird sublet I'd found myself living in. Maybe we'd grab a drink first, or maybe we'd just skip that part and chat on the couch for a few minutes. No pressure, no dressing up, no awkward breakfast or wondering if I'd ever hear from him again. For years we did this dance, and it was exactly what I wanted and needed.

Maybe this seems like an underwhelming way to fulfill your needs. Maybe you're questioning what my needs really are or if I'm totally detached from my humanity. But both then and now, I felt absolutely complete in this casual relationship. I didn't need to be in a "real" relationship, thinking about when we would move in together or whether he'd want to take the next step. That slice of my life was incredibly satisfying. And because it was just that—a slice, not the whole pie—I could focus on other parts of my life without being distracted by pressure to find The One. I was in the throes of a turbulent but exciting surge in my career, bouncing back and forth between the coasts and up and down town; I was navigating the changing friendships of my thirties; I was in constant conversation with my body and pain levels. Having occasional sex with Charlie wasn't just what I wanted, it was really all I had the energy to care about. And that is absolutely fine. Romantic love doesn't need to be at the top of your list of priorities. It's okay if it's hovering around number six, after "committing to Pilates."

A long time after things ended with Charlie, I worried that all those years in this kind of casual situation prevented me from focusing on real, serious relationships. Was I lazily relying on intermittent casual sex for fulfillment instead of searching for someone to spend my life with? Was I too comfortable gossiping for twenty minutes before getting my guaranteed orgasm from someone who most likely wouldn't murder me and steal my stuff instead of pushing myself to go on dates and be emotionally vulnerable over mediocre ricotta toast and rosé? I worried I had wasted valuable dating years, and wondered if my lifetime of eschewing romance in favor of professional advancement or friendships or marathoning *Veep* alone was the great tragedy of my life. But then I realized that I don't really care about being in a committed relationship. The great discovery of my heart and soul in my late thirties was that ultimately I'm kind of apathetic about having a romantic partner. And that's TOTALLY OKAY!

Maybe *apathy* isn't even the word I'm looking for. I'm *neutral* on being in a committed relationship? I'm fine either way about it? I'm whatever about it? I don't think there's a perfect word for the way I feel because no one ever talks about this perspective on relationships, at least not publicly. Would I enjoy a lifetime with someone who complements me and treats me well? Yeah, of course, that sounds great. Would I also enjoy a life that continues on a lot like the one I have now? Absolutely.

I have hard opinions on a lot of things. I think perfect jeans are worth the price. I think being a morning person isn't morally superior. I think that excellent lettuce is the key to a good sandwich. I think it's okay to get really tan in the summer and that Lorrie Moore is one of this era's most gifted writers and most cities would be better with car-free streets and health insurance should be free for every person and that it's okay to put ice in your wine! But the one thing I don't have a hard opinion on is whether or not I need to be in a relationship. I need to spend time with friends one-on-one. I need my job to take priority as long as I need money (aka forever). I need to always have access to cocktails and snacks in my home. I need to be able to cancel plans if my back and leg nerves are bothering me. I don't need to be in a relationship. I don't need to get married. I don't feel like this is a particularly radical or shocking outlook, but for some reason it's typically met with confusion at best, and at worst a mix of harsh judgment and pity.

Women never get to be apathetic when it comes to marriage and children. If a woman doesn't really care much about her career, no one says anything. But when she doesn't care much about being in a relationship, suddenly all her motives are questioned, doubted, and discussed. It's often as subtle as a friend asking, "But you do want to get married one day, right?!" or telling me, "So many great guys are divorced now," as if I'm obviously searching for someone and hadn't even thought about that entire group. But why is it so bad to not care about being in a committed romantic relationship? Where is *that* rom-com? The one where the chic, city-dwelling lead who carries designer bags and never has a hair out of place goes through a turbulent courtship and decides, *Yeah, I don't need to bend my life around this guy just because we bumped into each other at a coffee shop once, spilled hot liquids on each other, and had a cute but ultimately annoying trip to urgent care together. I'm good just living my life the way it is.*

The thing is, I *am* good with my life the way it is. Sure, the older I get, the more complicated it has been to make time for good (and safe!) sex, but otherwise I really like my setup. I like my apartment. I like the work I do and the flexibility with which I get to do it. I like my weird cat and all his toys. I like going out and seeing friends every single night of one week, and then spending every single night of the next week home on my couch rewatching season 2 of *Vanderpump Rules*. In fact, I'm a bit like my cat in that way: I need to be left to my own devices, I have a lot of boundaries and take a really long time to warm up to people. But I still can and one day might!

The worst part of feeling this way about relationships is no one ever believes you. I'm happy alone! I promise!!!!!!!!!!!!!!!! And I am the first one to admit that, like, three times a year I think to myself, *I wish a man was here.* But it's a rare occurrence. In fact, it's probably rare for any woman to be like, "You know what would make this whole thing better? A guy being around." Sorry, men, I love you, but you sometimes make things harder. (Do NOT read that the way I know you're all reading it.) Yes, there are times when I know I'd be happy to have a partner with me: weddings where the guests are mostly couples, some industry events with tuxedos and long gowns and professional photographers, Best Buy when I'm trying to get a new TV. Those times I genuinely feel a bit of a loss. But other times in my life I don't feel like anything is missing. Weddings that aren't as couple-y, fabulous work events where I want to talk shit with my comedy colleagues and not have to walk my partner through whom we hate and why, picking out bedding.

It's frustrating that being neutral on romantic relationships is so confusing to others. I wish more people understood it and more people who felt it would proclaim it loudly. It's true that it's hard to take a bold stance of ". . . sure, maybe, or maybe not, either way is fine!" Extremes are way more understandable to people (and make for compelling entertainment).

I know at my core that I am fine being single possibly forever because I am the perpetual third wheel, the single person amid married or coupled friends. And I don't know why third wheels get such a bad rap. That's how a tricycle stays up! (Though I'm also a unicycle in that sometimes the most annoying man on the planet is on top of me.) And while many people will doubt this, I do genuinely enjoy hanging out with my friends and their partners because most of them are just . . . my friends. They don't pity me. They aren't constantly trying to set me up with some guy just because we're both single so clearly we're both just dying for a partner. They aren't including me in weird mixers or excluding me from couples-only events. They also aren't studying my life to get an inside look at the bizarre, incomprehensible world of modern dating when they themselves were also part of that world, like, eighteen months ago. They don't ask to see my dating app profile (mostly because I'm not on any), nor do they downplay the things they do together so I don't go home sulking in singledom. They're all just my friends, and I like spending time with them.

The occasion on which I most struggle with my feelings on romantic relationships is when I confront how romantic love is presented to women. Our whole lives, from every direction, women are taught that the only exciting and magical experience we'll ever have is finding someone to love us and then suffering the dramatic ups and downs of making that love work. We're taught about *the spark, butterflies, the right place at the right time*—all these metaphors to describe the indescribable when it comes to love. And love *is* hard to describe and *can* be magical. I just don't know that I've ever felt that magic. The closest I ever got was being hit on by a magician and it was, in a word, chilling. I'm all for the serendipitous magic of romantic love, but in my life, I've experienced far more magic in the non-romantic parts. Being late for a meeting that's two subways away and both times, as I'm stepping onto the platform, the train is pulling up and I somehow make it on time? Magic. Meeting the right person at the right time who put me up for the right job that changed my professional trajectory? Magic! Buying a pair of Ferragamo sandals online and accidentally entering a credit card that has already expired but somehow the transaction goes through and your current card never sees a charge and you never have to pay for the shoes? MAGIC!!!

Sitting next to someone at a bar and simultaneously ordering the same strange drink and then talking to each other, realizing there's a spark, and then living happily ever after? That's magic, too. But never experiencing that doesn't make my life a failure.

Sometimes I wonder if my way of living comes from being an

only child. Not that I think all only children don't care about relationships—many of my friends who are only children are partnered or want to be. I just mean that it prepared me for this option. I got really good at being alone as a child, so now I actually enjoy solitary time. Because I didn't have siblings, I learned to build really important and affirming friendships that I truly value, and I'm grateful that I ended up with a robust group of friends as an adult. Being a true third wheel to my parents' happy and healthy relationship made me enjoy hanging out with my couple friends and have really fulfilling relationships with both men and women. Being an only child is why I'm so happy being an only adult.

But if you're a guy who loves alone time, doesn't care how much I spend on jeans, and likes ice in your wine . . . DM me. I'll at least consider it. Sorry, cat allergies are a deal-breaker.

I DON'T HAVE A BEST FRIEND

■ ■ ■

I was convinced I ruined the first wedding I was ever a bridesmaid in.

When we were in our early twenties, my close friend Siobhan
asked me to be a bridesmaid in her wedding along with her sister
and her best friend. *This is it,* I remember thinking, *the major
leagues. I'm not just a silly college student anymore, I'm a bridesmaid. This is adulthood.* Granted, it didn't quite feel like adulthood, since my parents were invited as well; it kind of felt like
being chaperoned.

The wedding was very traditional, but Siobhan is a pretty low-key
person, and thus was a pretty low-key bride. When we were sorting
out the bridesmaid looks, I pitched a pair of gold d'Orsay heels from
Ann Taylor that matched the spring-green dresses we were wearing.
Everyone agreed they were perfect. I didn't order mine right away
because I'm a procrastinator, and at the time I was on an assistant
salary in New York City and had been living off canned soup for
meals and asking my friend, an associate at a fancy nonprofit, to

steal tampons from her work bathroom every twenty-eight days. I figured I could get the shoes closer to the wedding, with the hope and dream that at some point between planning and execution, my parents would offer to pay the $68 to complete my look.

When I finally remembered I needed to get these shoes, they were sold out. My heart started to race. My first big task as a bridesmaid, my first responsibility in this pastel-hued version of adulthood, and I had already blown it. I called a few stores near me and no one had a pair left in my size. (My size is "cinder block," because that's a rough estimate of both the size and shape of my feet.) My mom took me shopping, and after traipsing to a dozen stores, it became apparent that these shoes physically did not exist. I found a pair that was close enough and figured I wouldn't say anything, but the day of the wedding, when we were all getting ready in the hotel room, Siobhan looked down and said, "You're wearing different shoes."

I panicked. My laziness coupled with the fact that 58 percent of my paycheck went to rent each month might have ruined my friend's wedding. For eternity the photos of her special day would be marred by my poor planning, my mismatching shoes a sparkly memory of my failure as a friend. "Sorry . . ." I said.

I was ready to give a speech about how apologetic I was and how much being in this wedding meant to me, but before I could, she cut me off: "Whatever, it's no big deal."

Relief washed over me. I hadn't ruined the wedding. I wasn't a bad friend.

Siobhan's wedding was what I imagined all of my friends' weddings would be like: fancy but not stressful, fun but not dramatic. The bridesmaid job seemed like a glamorous one. A reward for more than a decade of being a good friend. A thank-you for supportive phone calls and inside jokes in the form of a free hair and makeup session and some pretty photos to use for Facebook profile pictures.

Female friendship is very hierarchical, and bridesmaid is a very special category. It's almost more about how other people perceive your friendship with the bride than the actual quality of your relationship. You stand in a special place. You dress in a certain way. You are in professional photos. It's like getting drafted into the NBA: "Come put on a jersey that matches this group of people, you're on the team now." And maybe you don't know your teammates because some of them went to college together and some went to high school together and one is a co-worker from two jobs ago, but you're a team. You're the bridesmaids.*

And if you're important enough to be the maid of honor, well, you're basically the vice president of that wedding. The chain of command goes: bride, maid of honor, groom, brides' parents, everyone else. You are the BEST FRIEND, which is the biggest role in any woman's life, arguably even bigger than the wife role that the bride is about to step into. Taking care of a partner involves a lot of compromise and care. Taking care of a best friend means standing outside a bar *screaming* at her ex even though she doesn't care anymore and neither do you, but you haven't seen him since the breakup and it's time to defend your best friend's honor.

The cornerstone of female friendship is the best friend. For as long as any woman can remember, we all wanted to have a best friend, and we wanted to be a best friend. I can still list all the pairs

---

* The Bridesmaids would honestly be a great name for a WNBA team, because what on earth is more threatening than a group of women assembled for a wedding? The Lynx? The Storm? Tell me how those are scarier or more competitive than drunk girls in strapless dresses.

of best friends at my elementary school. Lindsay and Megan. Lauren and Jen. Rebecca and Elizabeth. (Okay, those last two were twins, but still, they were also best friends.) I think that this obsession with claiming a best friend is partly biological. Not that I have any of the scientific evidence to support this, but the general theory about women preferring intimate, one-on-one connection rings true. And this push toward best friendship comes outside in, too. The "best friends" necklace is iconic. It's the warm-up for the engagement ring: a piece of jewelry that tells the world you're taken, that you have found your someone special.

My relationship to best friends and friendship in general has always been complicated. I feel very lucky to have had a lot of friends, who usually come from different places and groups. In elementary school, I had friends in different grades and at different schools because I played sports outside of school. But even in those days, I had lots of friends rather than one group, and thus didn't have one best friend. During that time, I had a neighbor, Shannon, who was the same age as me. Our parents became instant friends, and though we spent a ton of time together, she and I just didn't quite get each other. But the proximity of our front doors and having to walk to school together every day forced the relationship. One day while we were walking home from school, Shannon was being extra annoying. She kept saying, "Everyone has a best friend, Alison, who is *your* best friend?"

I insisted truthfully that I didn't have a best friend, but Shannon wouldn't let it go. She knew how to push my buttons.

She carried on: "You have to have a best friend."

I kept trying to make it stop, but she was relentless.

"Everyone has a best friend. You have to have a best friend. Who is your best friend??" Shannon begged.

Finally, I said, "Jessica Barth."

It shut her right up. Until she got home and cried to her mom that I had told her Jessica was my best friend, not her. I don't think Shannon even really liked me, but I think that I was the closest thing she had to a best friend, and she just wanted to be someone's. I think she thought I wanted a best friend, too, because we were girls and girls have best friends. Though I spent the rest of my school days secure in my constellation of friends, Shannon did hit on a truth about many women: We just want that special person.

My college experience was a rare one, because I had been recruited from high school to be on the women's rowing team, so I showed up on campus with built-in friends, girls who all had something in common. While other students were meeting people in their majors and debating a spring-semester sorority rush, I was part of a group before I even set foot on the quad at Cornell.

A small group of us became the kind of close-knit circle of friends I'd never had before. Two of them—Natasha and Laura—were the kind of friends who just made sense from day one. Natasha and I initially bonded over realizing we were the two shortest recruits on the team, standing a whopping five feet six in thick socks. We walked from our first team meeting to pick up our gear at Teagle Hall and realized we knew people in common from back home and had the same taste in seemingly everything from hairstyles (super long) to chicken tenders (crunchy breading, lots of black pepper). Laura, a six-foot-tall blonde from Alaska with an infectious laugh, had a maternal streak in her that I think is the only reason any of us made it out of college alive.

Our group also included another six-foot-tall girl, Sarah, who had curly hair and a very calming presence that I mostly attributed to her growing up in Vermont. There was Marnie, a modern-day hippie with messy hair who rode her bike everywhere. Tucker was a slim and quiet recruit from a private school in D.C. with a tortured vibe that made every man on campus want to "fix" her even though she was fine. And finally, rounding out our clique was Brynn. The first time I met Brynn, I hated her. While the rest of us showed up at our first practice in spandex unisuits from JL or RegattaSport, Brynn was wearing those cotton short shorts beloved by cheerleaders and sorority girls, rolled up a few times at the waist, as is legally required when you put them on.* She was not, in my mind, one of us. But after a few practices and hangs, I realized Brynn was actually funny and cool, and I was an asshole for using shorts as a reason to completely write someone off.

It wasn't enough for our group to just be friends; we had to make sure the rest of the world knew it, too. During our winter training trip to Cocoa Beach, Florida, Natasha and I bought cheap drugstore aviator sunglasses with dark lenses and shiny gold frames. We were very ahead of our time, as aviators came back into style a few years later, so now I associate them both with college but also with Tiger Woods's mistress/luxury-baby-store owner Rachel Uchitel. After that, the whole group wore aviators to practices and parties. We called ourselves Team Aviators, or TA for short. Once, a junior on the men's heavyweight team called us Club Aeroplane because he couldn't remember our group's name, just the vibe, so we also adopted that moniker.

At the core of this group was the quartet of Natasha, Laura,

---

* I believe these are Soffe shorts, which as a swimmer and then rower I never wore. I assumed they went out of style when I graduated high school, but I have heard that like all things Y2K they are back.

Brynn, and me. Over time, who was closest with whom shifted along with class schedules, study-abroad plans, and whom we were sleeping with. But over the last two years of college, Brynn and I became incredibly close. I traveled with her family over winter break to the Caribbean. We lived in the same big college house junior and senior years and shared a ritual of sitting in Brynn's room in our pajamas after everyone else was asleep, turning on the rainbow-colored paper lanterns she covered her ceiling with, and getting stoned. We'd stare into the bright colors, thumb through the dictionary and read aloud the definitions of words that felt fake, like *hangdog,* and we'd giggle between handfuls of popcorn until the wee hours of the morning. When so many students were making out at bars or pounding away on laptops in the library, Brynn and I were laughing our way to what I had always imagined a best friend was. I loved it. I felt like I unlocked a new level of girlhood. After years of always having so many great girlfriends that I was close to in different ways, for the first time in my life I started to feel like I had a real best friend worthy of the title. This was what television and movies and books told me was the pinnacle of young femininity. Here was someone whom I did everything with, who could practically read my mind, whose life I would be in forever. She'd for sure get the other half of a BFF heart necklace from me if either of us had been into that.

When college ended, we all parted ways. I moved home briefly before reuniting with Laura in Brooklyn to begin our adventure of working and living in New York City together. Natasha stayed in Ithaca to work for the local newspaper for a bit. And Brynn bounced between East Coast cities and Europe, where the boy she met during her study-abroad time lived. She spent the years after college flying back and forth across the Atlantic the way most people drive across town, funded by family wealth that I began to understand more and more as we got closer. It would be a lie to say her family money didn't make me jealous. It would make anyone jealous. When we went to the Caribbean, we stayed at her family's compound on a somewhat private island, where we drank at outdoor bars among celebrities and supermodels. As I stressed about my life of incredible privilege—I had grown up comfortable, playing fancy sports and going to Cornell debt-free—it was always hard to not want more. My parents helped me financially when I moved to New York and was working as an unpaid intern at *The Onion* and a part-time sales associate/dressing-room crier at the SoHo Bloomingdale's. But Brynn never had to work. Brynn got to have charity jobs where she could take a tiny salary and still afford to fly to Europe for the weekend to see her boyfriend.

Despite work, travel, distance, and money, Brynn and I were able to stay pretty close in those years after we graduated. She came to the city when she could, and we talked on the phone and emailed and Gchatted for hours a day. We also made sure everyone knew we were still best friends, leaving inside jokes on each other's Facebook walls* and uploading albums of forty-nine photos of just the two of us from a weekend we spent with her family in Philly.

But over time, like almost all relationships, ours wore a little thin. Brynn spent more and more time abroad. I began doing open mics and dove headfirst into my stand-up comedy career. It became harder and harder to see or talk to each other as often. Transitioning a college friendship to the real world is always challenging.

---

* The "wall" on Facebook used to be an exciting feature where you could publicly establish your connection to the person whose profile you were writing on. I think today "wall" on Facebook is usually associated with "build the."

College is a bizarre time where not only is everyone in the same place, but you all have roughly the same level of responsibility—school, maybe some clubs or a job—so for the most part everyone's life is flattened out to be similar. After graduation, it's like the cops are breaking up a high school party: Everyone scatters. They go on to different things in different places for different reasons with different responsibilities. The further we got from college, our lives naturally became fuller, and there was less time for our friendship.

Then Brynn got engaged, the first of my college friends to do so. And to be honest, she's still one of the only ones. Knowing Brynn, I had a feeling this would be an incredible wedding. Surely the same woman who came to New York for the day to buy Manolo Blahnik sandals and had hard opinions about buttercream frosting would throw a party for the ages. When she began planning, she asked me to be her maid of honor. I was floored: That is best-friend status. Even though I didn't really consider Brynn a best friend anymore because of the way our lives were expanding and changing, I was thrilled and flattered, if a bit surprised.

In the wedding-industrial complex, maid of honor is a high-intensity role, with lots of responsibilities and expenses that come along with it. It varies from bride to bride, but it usually requires you to be a project manager, a party planner, an emotional support dog, a fashion consultant, a managerial accountant, a transportation coordinator, and, on the day of the wedding, a bathroom attendant. Meanwhile, I had a brutal schedule of working multiple jobs while pursuing comedy, and so little money that I still needed to ask my parents for help if I had to do anything more expensive than taking a cab from Manhattan to Brooklyn.

But then Brynn told me about her expectations for the role and I nearly fainted from relief. There wasn't going to be a full bridal party, I didn't need to plan things, I could wear whatever I wanted. First Siobhan, now Brynn: My friends were chill brides! All she needed of me was someone to stand next to her while she married the love of her life and give a speech at the reception. This was the dream. I don't have to wrangle a group of seven other women who don't know or like one another on a trip out of the country? I don't have to sit through multiple events with your sister-in-law who cries about her life when she drinks too much? I don't have to sink hundreds of dollars into a pastel gown and painful heels that I never want to wear again? I won the maid-of-honor lottery.

So I began working on the two things required of me for this event: a great dress, and a heartfelt and personal but also funny speech. Speeches are no sweat for a comedian, but the dress was a little trickier. My evening preference is always simplicity, like Jennifer Aniston on a red carpet or Gwyneth in her Calvin Klein phase, so I got Brynn's approval to search for a long black or navy dress. She invited me to join her at the legendary wedding-dress shop Kleinfeld, where her mom and I watched Brynn try on different configurations of duchess satin and ivory lace. It was hours and hours of sitting on settees sipping champagne and watching a flurry of opalescent beads and rivers of organza flow in and out of the Flatiron showroom. Randy, the iconic associate on TLC's *Say Yes to the Dress,* was the one helping us, and I've never made a better impression on anyone. Put me in front of someone who deals mostly with maniacs and I WILL make them laugh.

Brynn's ancillary events around the wedding were also pretty relaxed. She decided on a fancy luncheon for her shower, followed by a night out with a small group of friends for dinner, drinking, dancing, and likely screaming (as most of our nights ended provided at least one Journey song came on). As the maid of honor, this seemed so doable, and so preferable to the gauntlet of travel, activities, and financial hell other brides expect. Even the best versions of a bridal shower are a nightmare. You have to dress up during the day for a fancy lunch and have some wine and it's like, well, what the hell is the rest of this day? Do I take a nap in my makeup? Do I hit happy hour in a dress? Do I eat a second meal at four-thirty P.M. because half a wedge salad and a piece of salmon didn't quite do it for me?

Of course, the date Brynn picked for the shower was the same weekend as the Bridgetown Comedy Festival in Portland, Oregon. I had submitted myself but didn't have high expectations of actually being accepted; it was a prestigious festival usually populated by the coolest stand-ups in what was then the alt-comedy scene. But I was aching for a big opportunity, and there were plenty of stories of comics performing at Bridgetown and then getting signed to an agent or manager or getting booked to perform on television.

In my memory, I thought maybe I mentioned it to Brynn, in passing at least. On one of our planning phone calls, I likely tossed it out there as a "this could happen, but honestly probably not," because I didn't want to force Brynn to plan a bridal shower around the slim chance I got into a festival at the cost of some of her family not making it, so I just crossed my fingers that this didn't backfire on me. I'm still not sure whether she knew or not. While friendship now is a permanent record, written in the indelible ink of texting and email and the internet's ability to vomit up evidence from the past at the worst time (Facebook, my memories are none of my business), so much of my relationships at the time lived in the ephemeral breath of phone calls, AIM, or in-person hangs that weren't documented for all your other friends to see. And even if I did tell her the dates of the festival, could I really expect a busy bride to keep my tentative work plans in her head? No. What I do know is I told her all the time about the dream I was chasing, the career I was mortgaging everything for. I told her about the high highs of getting booked on big shows, the low lows of bombing in front of someone you respect, and how exhausting it all was, the good and the bad. She may not have known what the Bridgetown Comedy Festival was, but she knew I cared deeply about my dream, just like I cared about hers, because that's what friends do.

My saving grace was remembering how chill Brynn had been about her expectations. She wasn't a bridezilla; she wasn't making me fly to Puerto Rico or pay for a spa day or plan a banquet for a gaggle of middle-aged European women. She would surely understand that if I ended up getting into this prestigious festival, that might change my life, right?

Well, I got into the festival. And even though I expected Brynn to ultimately understand my situation, I knew this wasn't going to be our most fun call. When we got on the phone, I decided to just rip the Band-Aid off: I explained that I didn't want her to plan this event around me and I hadn't expected to get into the festival, but I did, and I didn't have any choice but to attend. It would be my biggest career opportunity thus far and I'm so so *so* sorry and I'll make it up to you ten times over.

She was silent. Every second felt like an hour while I waited for her to say, "Ugh, it sucks, but I get it, we'll miss you." I held my breath until she finally replied: "I can't believe you would do this to me."

I was floored. But maybe her initial anger would recede into understanding? Brynn and I supported each other. I was her maid of honor. I was her best friend. But that wave of acceptance never came. Long pauses broke briefly for her to utter "I can't believe this" and "Wow." I tried to explain that with any other thing I would choose her, but this just was too big a deal for me. But she continued, "I can't believe you would skip one of the most important weekends of my life for your hobby." The phone call was over.

Within me was brewing a special cocktail of extreme guilt and unbridled rage. My HOBBY???? I was working more than I was doing anything else at this point in my life, including sleeping. I woke up at seven A.M., got to my office and did whatever it was I did all day while also sending booking emails and tweeting and writing jokes. When five o'clock hit, I hustled out of there to do open mics and shows all over town, some nights heading home "early" around nine so I could do my *Top Chef* recaps or other freelance work. I fell asleep somewhere between one and three A.M. every night and then woke up and did it again the next day. I was exhausted but loved it. I was living my dream.

How could the person whom I stayed up with every night not understand how much of my life I had already neglected to pursue this career? How could my best friend and I be on such wildly different pages about our lives? One day we were arm in arm chasing greatness together—winning the silver medal at Eastern Sprints, launching ourselves into careers—and the next day she was mad at me for doing exactly that.

I barely had a hold of which emotion I wanted to lean into before I received an email from Brynn's mother. It was two sentences. That was all she needed to tell me that I was a disappointment and a bad friend to Brynn. While I was still processing, Brynn had already told her mom and her mom had composed and sent a devastating email to me. It's one thing when your own mom calls you a disappointment, but when someone else's mom gets on Beyoncé's internet to call you a disappointment, well, that's a new low. What was I supposed to do at this point? Say no to a festival I had begged desperately to be a part of and possibly forgo taking the next step in my career? I told myself that because I probably didn't make Brynn aware of the possible conflict, it was my fault that this happened.

After taking a few days to cool down, I started texting and calling, hoping we could figure this out. No response. She was icing me out. I wanted to do something to make it better. Every single day I was waking up with a pit in my stomach formed from shame and guilt (and dollar pizza). I hadn't just fucked up a little. Regardless of my understanding of the events, I had fucked up a lot. And I wanted so badly to take it all back, return to being best friends. I ordered a set of champagne flutes off her registry to arrive at the shower without me, thinking maybe they would be better friends to Brynn than I was. While I was busy running around town refining new jokes before the festival, I was also assembling goody bags filled with mini vodka bottles and packets of Advil and special mix CDs featuring songs from our college partying days to send to the bachelorette party in lieu of my presence.

By the bridal shower weekend, Brynn still hadn't been responding to texts or calls, so I headed to Portland. The Bridgetown Comedy Festival was everything I hoped it would be. Festival staffers shuttled me around town, and I was handed free Bud Lights and vodka sodas instead of having to pay for them myself. I had great sets at packed shows. I performed in front of prestigious bookers I never got to see in New York. I made real-life friends with successful comics I knew only from a great distance. We stayed out until two A.M. smoking weed and talking about who bombed and who crushed and who surprisingly hooked up. It's hard to put into words how slippery comedy success is, but you can tell in the moment when things are changing for you, and this was absolutely one of those times. I took a red-eye home on Sunday night after getting way too drunk and cried the whole next day at my desk job as I counted the minutes until I could go home and crawl into my bed. And all of it, even the exhaustion tears in the office bathroom, provided a much-needed break from the constant torment I felt as Brynn cut me out of her life for what felt like a scheduling issue.

When I still wasn't able to reach Brynn two weeks before the wedding, I started to wonder if I even existed anymore. Were my texts getting through? Were my calls getting dropped? Did my goody bags get tossed out the window of a van on the way to the hotel?

Finally, she called me back. My heart stopped. I stared at my phone knowing that this was either the moment we proved the best friendship that was promised the day she asked me to be her maid of honor, or this would be the end of the road, and our friendship, best or otherwise, was over. I answered.

I don't remember if we exchanged pleasantries or caught each other up on our respective weekends from the previous month, I remember only the information she called to relay. "We all discussed," she started, which I immediately knew meant her and her mother. What they had discussed was rather than me being her maid of honor, standing next to her during this huge moment and making a heartfelt speech as we all raised a glass to her everlasting love, I could be nothing. Just a regular guest. I was not the maid of honor, and I definitely was not the best friend.

It hurt. It hurt because it always hurts to disappoint someone. It hurt because I am an overachiever and any opportunity falling apart feels like a failure. It hurt because aside from missing Brynn's shower and bachelorette, I thought I had been a good-enough friend to her over the years that we could get past this. It hurt because it showed me that along the way, my comedy career was going to cost me things, real things that I cared about. It hurt because it was the first time I saw how the expectations created by the label "best friend" can come between people.

There was no way I could go to the wedding. I would eat the money I had spent on the dress, the gifts, the bachelorette goody bags, the train ticket, the hotel room, the Tums I had been swallowing whole to settle my distraught stomach for the last month and a half, so I could spare myself the humiliation of showing up to watch my former best friend get married while knowing I was once supposed to be the maid of honor. Sitting in the crowd with all the other not-best friends felt like I'd be wearing a sign telling everyone I had failed. Guest of dishonor. *Fuck that and fuck her,* I told myself, *I'm staying home.*

But then I spoke to my own mother, who told me I should go.

I replied, "You're right, this is growing up and maturing. I should be the bigger person, swallow my pride, and support my friend on a very big day for her."

My mom clarified that she meant I should go because Brynn should have to feel the consequences of this decision and that I had the rest of our college friend group to rally around me if I felt bad. That settled it: I was going to the wedding out of spite.*

The weekend itself was actually fine. Team Aviators/Club Aeroplane all took the train to Philly together; we ate bagels and lox in the café car and laughed and reminisced about college. At the wel-

---

* This was the second wedding I'd gone to out of spite. The first was a kind of weird semi-family wedding at a country club that my mom dragged me to in order to support the father of the bride. Halfway through the reception, I went to the bathroom and found my dad reading a book on a couch in the lobby.

come drinks, Brynn's mother pulled me aside and I prepared my-self for a "how dare you show your face here" monologue but was pleasantly surprised by a light apology and an "I'm glad you made it" hug. The morning of the wedding I had plenty of time to myself to walk around Philly and make phone calls while browsing a Ba-nana Republic. I got a few great photos of me in lipstick and sun-glasses, and by the end of the reception, Brynn and I danced around to Erasure like we were back in the main room of Sigma Phi on West Campus, ignoring everyone else around us and celebrat-ing a friendship forged in early-morning rows and late-night par-ties, a friendship we were sure would never die.

I'm still sad about how this wedding went. I'm sad that I disap-pointed Brynn. I'm sad that Brynn's disappointment was so deep that she demoted me from being maid of honor. I'm sad that this one event created all these bizarre expectations for our friendship that never existed before and were absolutely the reason for its end. I don't know if Brynn and I were going to be friends forever or what would have happened without this fight. Our lives were al-ready starting to go in very different directions, and I suspect over time we would have gradually drifted apart. Instead, we reached a violent end from which we never recovered. Why did a wedding turn our friendship into a transaction? Brynn had missed dozens of important milestones in my life up until this point. She hadn't seen my first comedy shows or been to my new apartment. And I hadn't been there for anything non-wedding in her life, like her first job or getting accepted to grad school. I'm also pissed that I'm sitting here calculating who had been the better friend when that's not at all how friendship works.

Maybe being a best friend isn't the dream role the heart neck-laces and beaded bracelets tell us it is. Or maybe I'm not quite cut out for it. The standards are too high, the expectations are too final. I don't know if I have a best friend today. I know I have lots of friends whom I love deeply. I think a lot about one of my favorite quotes from *The Mindy Project:* "A best friend isn't a person . . . it's a tier." Nothing has ever been more true to me. I don't have one friend in my life responsible for all of the requirements for my happiness and picking up all of the pieces in my sadness. The best and most equal version of friendship is by far the least exciting. There are no transactions. There's no hierarchy. There's no running score or tab or counting. It's just love and support and as much fun as you can have. And sometimes, matching sunglasses.

I'M
A
BRAVOHOLIC

I still remember the hardest I laughed at my TV in the last decade.

It's a moment from season 11 of *The Real Housewives of New York City*. Allow me to set the scene for those unfamiliar: The women are on one of their contractually obligated group trips to Miami. Tensions are high between Luann de Lesseps (formerly known as the Countess) and the rest of the group—Bethenny Frankel, Tinsley Mortimer, Dorinda Medley, Sonja Morgan, Ramona Singer, and Barbara Kavovit—because they feel Luann has been selfish and detached. These are the women who ran her intervention only a few months ago, protected her from paparazzi, prevented her from running down the street in a nightgown during a relapse, and funded her rehab treatment following her arrest for assaulting a police officer after drinking through the sadness of divorcing her husband of a few months. This is the rehab that, of course, she left early so she could begin touring her cabaret show where she sings three original songs in different sparkly gowns.

Earlier in the episode, while the rest of the women had a lovely day at the beach club, Luann walked herself to a nearby theater to stare at the not-quite-life-size poster advertising her cabaret show. Her hand over her chest, a swell of emotion takes over Luann, and she asks a stranger nearby to take a picture of her in front of her own image. "Is that you?" the passerby says.

Now, as the gals gather for a big group dinner that night, the scene is brightly lit, as if indicating to the other diners at the restaurant that this will be dinner and a show. The show is this group of women, all dressed like they are attending different events, like an over-fifty Ice Capades or a salsa-dancing class in a Loehmann's basement, screaming at one another.

Luann is the last to arrive at dinner because the hairdressers who came to the house to provide glam were packing up by the time she returned from visiting her poster. She starts passive-aggressively detailing her day alone, as if it were something the women did to her and not something she did to herself. She emotionally retells what happened at the theater. "It's a big deal," she says, pissed that the other women didn't go with her, or at the very least praise her for the booking.

You can feel everyone wanting to say something, but being obviously careful as they tiptoe around Luann's newfound and delicate sobriety. The group is doing their best and has been all season. They have, as a company, coddled and taken care of this woman through an undeniably tough time in her life.

When their cocktails arrive, they have all the showmanship of Barnum & Bailey. Two drinks come with a dinner-plate-sized black-and-gold gong, liquid nitrogen creating a rolling white smoke to spill off the tray and onto the table. Sticks of cotton candy are dissolved in vodka, and neon-colored rock sugar adorns metal martini glasses. Once again, Luann feels left out. Her nonalcoholic mojito is just a boring glass of sparkling water with mint leaves and lime in it. No smoke, no candy-colored accessories, no appropriated Asian culture providing whimsy to her plain old soft drink. "A toast," she declares. The women hold up their beverages, raising them to "girls and fun" before Barbara puts hers down and says, "Lu, I have to say something that's bothering me." It's the perfect segue from a toast to a roast.

The women begin going around the table, chiming in on the ways in which Lu has been selfish and delusional all year. About how she doesn't engage at all with the group and then complains when she isn't catered to at every moment. Barbara is trying, as a real friend and not just a television friend of Luann's, to explain her hurt over the last few months after bending over backward to help her in a time of need. When Lu won't acknowledge their feelings, the others jump in.

Bethenny doesn't want to fucking hear it. Even though her boyfriend Dennis passed away from a drug overdose, she was still there to help Luann through sobriety. And now she's had enough of her shit. Bethenny lists all the ways she's been there for Luann despite Lu never once asking her how she was doing after Dennis's death. "You're insufferable!" she screams as other diners crane their necks to see exactly what is happening center stage. Luann fires back, "Oh, so we build women up just to tear them down?"

As she throws out this ridiculous defense, a waiter arrives and places in the middle of the table a GIANT NOVELTY MAGENTA-AND-CHROME TOASTER. Resting in the slots are lobster "pop tarts." It's easily three to four times the size of a regular toaster. It looks like a tabletop Smart car being driven by two beige and likely flavorless pastries. The toaster sits in the foreground as Bethenny interrogates Luann, her voice fast and breathless as she demands an answer she knows Luann can't give her. Lu blames her strict cabaret regimen for why she's been less available. And as more servers approach the table to serve the ladies a massive old-timey popcorn maker containing fried shrimp, Bethenny stands up and screams, with the kind of dynamic performance Luann wishes she could deliver onstage: "Cabaret! Cabaret! Life is not a cabaret!"

Camp wishes it could be this camp.

In some ways, what is happening in this scene is the opposite of funny. It is a fight among women about difficult times in their lives as they navigate addiction, divorce, starting over, and death. But the fight is in front of gongs and fog and novelty appliances. It's so funny. It's art. It's like nothing I've ever seen before. It's both serious and funny, flippant and earnest, real and not real.

Real Housewives and the other programming on the Bravo network are often considered "guilty pleasures." It's the candy of television. You know it's bad for you, it's okay to have a little, but too much might rot your brain. But I don't believe that. Bravo to me isn't candy, it's more like those brownies that secretly have puréed broccoli in them that you're supposed to feed to picky children. It isn't all fun and unhealthy, it just looks that way. It's secretly pumped with good-for-you, mentally nutritious things that make life better.

And yes, it *looks* like vapid, superficial, exploitative reality TV that's heavily produced for drama and devoid of anything real or good or valuable. I get it! I understand why people feel this way about Bravo. Everyone on the network is slowly injecting their face in a way that seems to push the limits of science. The fights are sloppy messes that usually get traced back to an offhand comment that the cast focuses on for years yet means nothing. The relationships seem produced, and the events are often staged. If you just drop in and watch an episode of *The Real Housewives of Beverly Hills* or *Southern Charm* or any other show on the network with no knowledge, that's probably what you'd take away from your viewing experience.

One thing that doesn't take long to recognize when watching any Bravo show is the humor. In my opinion, the editors of Bravo reality shows should get nominated for comedy-writing Emmy awards. There are the subtle moments, like how they'll follow up a cast member saying something ridiculous with a reaction shot from a pet—usually a small, fluffy dog. Bethenny Frankel will ask Sonja Morgan, "What about your toaster-oven cookbook?" and then the camera will pan to Cookie the dog with a confused look on her face as if she were a stand-in for us, the viewers, all equally confused by the fact that Sonja has been hyping a nonexistent book for years now. Then there are hours (and I mean HOURS) of Kyle Cooke, resident party animal on the Hamptons-set show *Summer House,* drunk-eating. The rest of the housemates are fast asleep in a hard-seltzer haze and he's pouring an entire bag of crushed tortilla chips into his mouth, managing to actually ingest some while the remnants form a corn-chip carpet around him. These moments feel like outtakes from *Animal House* or the party scene of a fun nineties rom-com, the kind of drunk high jinks that are less about drama and more like the stories you'd tell around the brunch table after a big night out.

But Bravo isn't just drunk pratfalls and silly goofs. Shows from this network tap into fundamentally meaningful parts of life so seamlessly that you barely realize it's happening until you're crying alongside a woman in $900 worth of fake eyelashes. Over a decade of Bravo's reality supremacy, no societal stone has been left unturned. We've witnessed devastating friendship endings, heart-breaking fertility journeys, affecting substance-abuse stories. Breakups and divorces are par for the course across the network. When Ariana Madix from *Vanderpump Rules* very famously discovered her boyfriend of ten years was cheating on her with a younger cast member and close friend in a drama that became known as Scandoval,* the world stopped and rallied behind her. You couldn't open social media without seeing pictures of a broken, flawless, and makeup-less Ariana or an angered and angular Tom. *The New York Times* wrote about it. About *Vanderpump Rules*. Let me repeat that: *The New York Times* wrote about *Vanderpump Rules*. That's how big it was. And it wasn't because the scandal itself was so shocking, it's because viewers saw the hurt and tapped into their own betrayals; they connected deeply with what they were seeing on their screens.

We've watched the casts of every show confront death in very real ways. The tragic loss of *Summer House*'s Carl Radke's brother to drugs, just as Carl himself was navigating his own sobriety. Love her or hate her, it was hard to watch *Real Housewives of Beverly Hills*'s Lisa Rinna struggle through her mom Lois's death, because even when she is ninety, it is absolutely gutting to lose your mom. The death of fellow *Beverly Hills* Housewife Taylor Armstrong's abusive ex-husband introduced some of the most complicated feelings most people have seen on television. Even *RHONY* cast member Tinsley Mortimer's raw emotions over the passing of her sweet dog Bambi resonated deeply, though I don't share her instinct to put a dead pet in the freezer. In the same way that a scripted drama like *Grey's Anatomy* pulls at our heartstrings by introducing death

---

* *Scandoval* is a portmanteau of *scandal,* which cheating on your partner of ten years with her co-worker/friend obviously qualifies as, and *Sandoval,* our aforementioned cheater Tom's last name.

and loss through beloved (or be-hated) characters, Bravo shows give us an outlet for processing our own grief.

But Bravo shows can make us feel even deeper, because these are real people. Patrick Dempsey didn't actually die, but Jill's husband Bobby Zarin did. And when these deaths happen on Bravo, you don't get expertly crafted dialogue about sadness and death and life and hope scored to the exact right indie folk song to make you cry into your couch. You don't get a perfect funeral scene choreographed to evoke emotion and show finality. Sure, Bravo cast members can sit down and give an after-the-fact, well-thought-out testimonial in a satin cocktail dress, but we mostly see the messy and real reflection of loss in a way that scripted television will never capture.

Bravo shows don't just connect viewers to cast members, they connect viewers to other viewers. The Bravo community is just that—a community! I know that people who watch *The Bachelor* have Bachelor Nation, which as far as I can tell is just being fans of dental hygienists who want to be fitness influencers. No shade to the fine citizens of Bachelor Nation, but gathering to see which makeup enthusiast a physical therapist chooses to be his short-term wife cannot compare to Housewives reunion watch parties. The group texts alone are a thing of beauty. I'm in four different group texts about Bravo programming that are all various combinations of the same eleven people. When the Scandoval episodes of *Vanderpump Rules* aired, my friend Julia hosted a viewing for superfans. We made fried goat-cheese balls (a SUR* staple) and drank Pumptinis (the shockingly delicious namesake cocktail of the neighboring Lisa Vanderpump bar, Pump), we submitted our

* SUR is the name of the restaurant where most of the cast of *VPR* worked during the show. SUR stands for Sexy Unique Restaurant. That is real.

guesses for what the big reveal would be, and we played a pin-the-tail-on-the-donkey-style game of "hang a TV on a wall in seven minutes" (a refrain from cast member Scheana Shay about her ex Rob, who, well, hung her flat-screen TV on the wall in seven minutes). And to know that around the country, thousands of friend groups were doing the same thing—that's something that transcends a silly reality show. That's something actually driving the culture.

I think there are several reasons Bravo doesn't get credit for its importance and pathos, but one of the biggest is that it's media meant for women. That isn't to say that lots of different people don't enjoy and connect to Bravo. Of course, there is a huge audience of gay men. Hell, there are even straight men who like it. (This is how to be an ally, gentlemen.) But the overall inception of the programming and the way it is produced has, for a long time, been aimed at women. And so much of content created for women is siloed off as "women's" whatever: women's television, women's fiction, women's sports. These aren't the counterparts to men's television, men's fiction, men's sports. Those things are just television, fiction, and sports. Stuff for women is niche. It's specific. And it's usually less than. There's an incredibly high bar for something made for women to not be considered dumb and valueless, let alone important and worthwhile.

Everything targeted toward women—reality TV, fashion, pop music, magazines, celebrity culture—is often categorized this way, as if these things are qualitatively less important than sports, cars, watches, and comic books. There are women who distance themselves publicly from what they enjoy privately because telling the world you love makeup gives people the opportunity to disregard your opinions on other things. I've even found myself qualifying my love of "women's" interests: "Actually, fashion is so referential you could technically call it art history with how far back its reflection of our culture it goes." "I love buying makeup, but like, I *know* it's just another tool of the patriarchy and capitalism to occupy my time and money." "Reality television is important for culture" (see: this entire chapter).

I take my role as a Bravo viewer seriously because it gives me so much. I'm so easily transported into these cast members' experiences that it almost feels like a substitute for therapy. (Note from my therapist: IT IS NOT.) Bravo encourages this kind of self-reflection. I watched Danielle Olivera from *Summer House* have a meltdown over losing her friend to a relationship and thought back to how I handled the same thing, and what I would have done differently. I watched Bethenny driving her Skinnygirl car around the Hamptons as the wealthier women mocked her, knowing that she was just hustling to make something on her own, and I saw myself in that logo-wrapped convertible, shuttling around to open mics trying to start a comedy career out of nothing. I think watching this version of reality television can feel so good and so cathartic because you can sense that the people onscreen really want to tell their stories. They chose to open up these parts of their lives so that we could follow along and end up interrogating parts of our own lives. I bask in the glow of my television for hours on end, indulging in an introspection that feels refreshing considering I'm doing it while rich women scream about hotel room assignments at a dinner. I value what reality TV gives me because I grew up with its evil sister, celebrity gossip blogs.

In the celebrity tabloid culture I grew up consuming, well, the stars splashed all over glossy pages and internet galleries didn't have that much agency. They didn't opt in to having people dissect what they wore to a nightclub or whom they were there with. And more important, reading these magazines and scrolling these websites didn't force me to imagine myself in their position, or to re-think conflict in my own life, or to process any complex emotions. Instead, I just looked at unflattering pictures and judged—harshly. Somehow a bunch of people sitting at home in front of a computer screen had more influence than globally famous actresses, models, and singers. And I'll spend the rest of my life trying to make up for my participation in that culture.

I was born in 1983. I was a freshman in high school when Britney Spears debuted ". . . Baby One More Time." I was about to turn eighteen when 9/11 happened. I was in my early twenties before the financial crash of 2008 changed the country. I lived through the worst of celebrity tabloid and gossip culture at the most vulnerable and impressionable times in my life. My frontal lobe wasn't fully formed when stills from Paris Hilton's sex tape were posted all over the internet or when Perez Hilton started drawing white cum drops on actresses' red-carpet photos. I was still navigating my own relationship with my body when *Us Weekly* began "bump watch" features on any celebrity who had eaten a sandwich within the week and *In Touch* ran a series of "Scary Skinny" photo spreads of clearly struggling starlets, not making it clear if these images were cautionary or aspirational.

I absolutely loved celebrity gossip media in my teens and early twenties. It defined my internet experience. Before Twitter and Instagram and TikTok, there were blogs. Between writing papers or looking for jobs, I had a bookmarked list of daily reading: I'd start with Dlisted, a blog run by Michael K., who had a knack for nicknaming famous people and knowing exactly how to space out posts so you would come back every other hour. Then I'd head over to The Superficial, a slightly slicker celebrity gossip blog that focused on starlets and A-listers with wry writing and through-the-bushes-style paparazzi photos. Next, I'd pop over to Go Fug Yourself, which was gossipy and fashion-focused but felt slightly less harmful than the others* (body talk kept to an absolute minimum, though dunking on formal shorts on the red carpet was at an all-time high, thankfully). Then it was time for "news," so I'd scroll through Gawker and Jezebel for my gossip that slanted more toward media moguls and writer darlings of New York but also conveniently included maps of where celebrities were eating and roundups of sartorial hits and misses at awards shows. Finally, I'd swing by Shopbop and browse the Citizens of Humanity jeans on clearance and lust after a pair of Marc by Marc Jacobs floral flats that I'd seen on any starlet under twenty-five in the blogs I was just browsing but which would absolutely shred my feet like a meat grinder. And by now it was time to go back to the top and start the whole process over again until the day was done and it was TV time.

When I close my eyes, I can still remember where I was when Britney Spears shaved her head, and see the magazine cover featuring emaciated Lindsay Lohan and Nicole Richie leaving a nightclub wearing flimsy dresses and carrying handbags large enough that they could climb inside. I have nightmares about men running blogs that called women "fat bitches" and "dumb sluts" and "whores" and the fact that female readers flocked to them, eager for more. Every corner of our culture was dripping in misogyny and racism and homophobia and fatphobia and every other kind of mis- and -phobia you can think of. And I consumed all of it. I

---

* The tone of GFY was clearly softer and less disgustingly hateful because it was a site actually run by women, not men who hate women.

thought myself *slightly* above the world of Perez Hilton and TMZ, but it doesn't mean that content didn't make its way to me and seep into the pockets of my brain that should have been reserved for learning to invest my income or remembering any phone number besides the Domino's Pizza in my hometown.

I distinctly remember these pieces of culture, these voices and tones used to talk about women, because I was an enthusiastic participant. While I didn't lurk in the comments section or run an anonymous vanity blog, I read and shared and talked about all of it. My friends and I would AIM message one another links to the funniest Dlisted post of Amy Winehouse smoking barefoot while we should have been writing college papers. Every time I boarded a plane or sat at a pool, I brought a stack of prestige misogyny (*Vogue, Glamour*), as well as every tabloid I could get my hands on, dissecting whether Christina Aguilera was pregnant or just fat, or whether the paparazzi picture of Lauren Conrad leaving the West Hollywood nightclub Hyde showed cocaine residue on the edge of her nose. I was part of the machine that was destroying not only me, but the lives of the (mostly) women they wrote about and our culture as a whole. I didn't gain anything from this. I didn't reflect or learn. It was pure, cruel consumption.

I also have a theory that tabloid culture was an underdiscussed driving force that led to the 2008 financial crash. I'm no Alan Greenspan, but when you look at the landscape, it's hard to let *Us Weekly* also get away as unscathed as the lenders and banks. Before gossip blogs and glossy tabloids of starlets, we didn't see celebrities that often. We saw some red-carpet pictures or television interviews during press circuits. Occasionally you could spot someone in the wild in New York or Los Angeles, having lunch a few tables over. But blogging and magazines brought a new wave of paparazzi coverage showing what celebrities wore in their everyday lives. A Givenchy blazer or a Bob Mackie gown worn at a premiere or the Oscars is wildly financially out of reach for most Americans. But if Lindsay Lohan was photographed with a $495 Botkier leather handbag, well, that was something a lot of people could put on a credit card. Jennifer Aniston's beloved Seven jeans were once $113, something extravagant but doable for so many people. Being able to try on these inaccessible lifestyles via slightly accessible items made a lot of people feel empowered to use their Visa to start dressing like an off-duty model, even if that money wasn't there. Sure, 2008 was heavily about unstable mortgage bonds, but I firmly believe some of the fallout was also due to consumer credit.* Bet you didn't think the editor behind "Stars—They're Just Like Us!" is as implicated in the 2008 financial crisis as the president of Bear Stearns, but here we are.

The women scrutinized by celebrity blogs and tabloids had no control over how the world perceived them. At the time, there were no avenues like social media to try to control their own narratives. It was like the high school nightmare of having a rumor spread about you and your only defense is to say, "I *didn't* use the handle of my electric toothbrush as a vibrator!!" The toothpaste is already out of the tube. Once someone speculates on your relationship status, your drug use, or the contents of your uterus, it's hard to undo. That's what tabloids were in the early 2000s. They taught me how to judge and be mean and reductive and dismissive. They preached hate in the form of snark, cruelty in the disguise of news.

---

* And I think we can all look forward to my next book, where I write about whatever financial crisis is upon us now and can point to TikTok Shop polyester dresses and influencers showing off their Birkin bag buying-appointment looks as the reason why no one owns a home and retirement is mostly about being a cashier.

I think I was the meanest version of myself when I was consuming pages and pages of celebrity gossip, transferring my judgments of Paris and Nicole and Ashley and Mary-Kate to the nameless women around me with whom I fought for male attention. I never went as far as exposing a sex tape or publicly claiming someone had a drug habit, but I was making those judgments in my mind all the time. Everyone I saw was mental fodder for the nastiest scrutiny my twenty-four-year-old brain could manage.

But other women weren't the only target of that kind of thinking. I became my own target, too. When you train your brain to be a complete asshole because all you feed it is asshole content, it's going to turn its assholery right back at the person it sees in the mirror every day. In my early twenties, I had my most objectively "attractive" body. I'm not saying it's the hottest I ever was (that would be a Thursday in 2013 when a perfect hair day aligned with a good skin day and I was two-days-post-stomach-flu thin), but it was the most conventionally appealing I ever looked (read: thinnest). My metabolism was still rolling along like I was a college athlete, but I'd lost the bulk of my rowing days. I had a twenty-seven-inch waist and my boobs were still in their original position in the top quadrant of my body, rather than where they are now whenever they are un-bra-ed, which is more of a fanny pack vibe. And still I would look in the mirror and it wasn't enough. I could see "muffin top" in Perez Hilton's handwriting around my midsection. A body that was actually healthy and functioning was considered a flaw.

But the tides turned on tabloids eventually. Celebrities became able to tell their own stories on social media. Our culture recoiled at some of the cruelty and eventually called for the "death of snark." The Peter Thiel–funded Hulk Hogan sex-tape trial killed

Gawker, and with it dozens of parasitic sites mimicking or piling on the sometimes-journalism, sometimes-gossip blogging. Money funneled in a new direction as print media embarked on its not-so-slow death march. And also, I grew up.

There is a gentleness with yourself that comes with age. When you start to actually live in the world and not look at it hoping for it to accept you, you stop caring about a lot of the noise. This isn't to say that one day I woke up, threw away every magazine I owned, and started meditating and loving myself just because I was twenty-eight. No, far from it. But at the media moment when celebrity gossip began to die, I didn't move on from it; I felt guilt about it. I felt dirty and gross for contributing to that culture, for giving my dollars and clicks and views to media whose entire goal was to tear down women just because they were young and pretty and successful. In the last few years, we've all collectively agreed that the public treatment of Britney Spears led to her crushing conservatorship. I can't open TikTok without seeing a video of someone reminding Gen Z that on *America's Next Top Model* a size 6 was considered plus-size and if you couldn't see Mischa Barton's ribs Perez Hilton would have plenty to say about it.

I don't know how much better it is today, but I think it's at least marginally better. People will complain that shows like *Real Housewives* and *Vanderpump Rules* are just glorifying the same things the tabloids were: wealth, beauty, vapidness. I'd argue no, and not just because I live for things like Heather Gay screaming, "Receipts! Proof! Timeline! Screenshots! Fucking everything!" and exposing her castmate Monica Garcia as the internet troll who has been spreading rumors about the women. I think Bravo and the Housewives usher in a new era that, while not perfect, is still better. These women have more control over their own narratives.

They're sitting in front of a camera and telling you who they are. They aren't having a guy in cargo shorts shoving a camera in their face while they try to go about their private business and then a bunch of strangers with dial-up make fun of them. These are women in their forties, fifties, even sixties, who are on TV, having fun and living life. Their stories aren't defined by the men in their lives or the men sitting at home and judging them.

The stars at the center of the celebrity gossip wave of the mid-aughts weren't allowed to own their messiness. It's not that famous young people didn't get sloppy drunk at West Hollywood night-clubs and leave with the wrong person or do drugs or even get in their car and drive away under the influence before paparazzi planted themselves outside. That has always happened. But in the mid-2000s, those missteps, that messiness, were wrestled away from the people involved and owned by the mean (mostly) men of the internet for us all to gawk and gossip. People on Bravo shows often get the chance to tell their side of the story, to explain themselves on camera both to their castmates and also to us, the audience that tunes in every week to see inside their lives. When they get too drunk, get too mean, say the wrong thing, invest in the wrong company, they have some control of the narrative. And in the words of Lisa Rinna, they don't have to, but they *get* to "own it."

One of the most iconic scenes from *Real Housewives of New York* is an early-season introduction to new Housewife Kelly Bensimon, a model turned magazine editor turned socialite and the ex-wife of famous fashion photographer Gilles Bensimon. In a voiceover, she's talking about her favorite thing to do in New York: go running. We watch her just casually doing her regular ol' New York jog down the middle of Fifth Avenue in Midtown Manhattan. She's wearing short spandex running shorts (I mean, if I had those legs, those are the ONLY shorts I'd ever wear) and a long-sleeve T-shirt with an owl on it. Her hair is down and loose with beachy waves, a far cry from how my hair looks when I'm working out (in a messy bun that is at once frizzy and soaking wet, somehow). She's bounding down the country's most famous and busy street, striding by luxury stores and condos. A classic yellow cab is rolling along right behind her as her afternoon exercise somehow slows down traffic on a street where cars already barely move.

Watching it, you think, *This is insane, no one runs like this!* Maybe that's true, maybe it's not. But what is true is that this wasn't sneakily captured and thrown on television for us all to judge like a stealth photo of Hilary Duff at Café Gratitude just trying to have a quiet lunch with a friend. This scene was carefully created. There were permits, there were crew members, there was a call sheet. The cameramen didn't catch her on a jog and think, *Oh, this is a perfect intro to Kelly.* Kelly, I assume, alongside the show's producers, decided she wanted to present herself as carefree and healthy and a woman about town. So they devised this scene to show the Bravo watching world who the "real" Kelly Bensimon is. You can scoff at how unlikely it is that she exercises with her hair down and blowing into her mouth. You can roll your eyes at someone going for a jog in the middle of the street in front of a cab like they're a Prius. You can complain that this is completely artificial and stupid. But you can't say it isn't Kelly.

Sure, Kelly curated a perfect-looking scene of how she allegedly works out in a way that the average person can guess isn't wholly accurate. But is it that different from any of us sharing our lives on social media? Her running on camera is just me strategically taking a picture of my hand next to an icy martini glass at a cool restaurant, but with a higher budget. She goes running, though maybe not always in the middle lane by the Louis Vuitton store. I did go out for a martini, but my night wasn't as chic as my post would have you believe. I didn't include the fact that I was in jeans with a hole in the inner thigh or that I bought the bodega bacon egg and cheese after this martini because I was starving and drunk and not going to spend $50 more on a meal. Everything is produced, almost nothing is real, and there's almost a sense of freedom in thinking about that (but not too hard). It's one of the invisible barriers between celebrity and regular person that has shattered. Everyone acts like a Real Housewife now.

I know the Housewives aren't aspirational in a lot of ways. I'm not out here dying to rent a Mugler bodysuit or plan a girls' trip to Cartagena. But there are so many ways the Housewives are aspirational because of the agency they have over their own lives. The patriarchy sells us a lie that liking celebrity gossip tabloids and watching reality television are two sides of the same vapid coin, but I don't think that's true. I don't look at *Us Weekly* headlines questioning someone's pregnancy or paparazzi photos on TMZ from the end of a sloppy night and wish that I had what these celebrities do. Those outlets broke my brain for years. I spent my teens and twenties treating myself and my own life like they were splashed across the internet for Perez Hilton to write insults all over. I scrutinized every inch of my face and body. I can't blame that *entirely* on celebrity gossip blogs, it's also the fault of the fashion world, the skincare and makeup industry, Hollywood, Barbies, Express mannequins, the mirror at the salon while you're getting a haircut, fitness cults, most men . . . I could go on, but we gotta wrap it up here. I reflected the attitude of celebrity tabloids back onto myself and was miserable for it.

But then came the Housewives, and they presented this better way of existence. These women are relentlessly themselves, unapologetically unapologetic. They don't say sorry for anything. They don't even say sorry when they've done something objectively wrong. In a world where most women say "I'm sorry" an average of forty-nine times a day (my rough estimate) for everything from eating lunch too late to bumping into a shelf, it's a breath of fresh air to watch women who don't apologize for anything. Not for wearing five-inch heels to lunch, not for sleeping with their ex-husband again, not for having too many pinot grigios and making a scene in a restaurant. They're living their lives.

The second I started to embrace some of the powerful agency with which the Housewives live, the better off I was. I've stopped apologizing for things that don't require an apology (like asking a bartender for a gin and tonic). I've stopped dressing exclusively for men and trying to look as thin as possible, and now I feel more myself than I ever have. Part of this is simply getting older and no longer giving a fuck, but I think the Housewives have helped. I don't think we should all try and live exactly like Housewives, because for most of us it would end in jail or liver failure or at minimum a broken ankle from a stiletto heel incident.

When I read celebrity gossip, I hated other women and myself. When I watch Bravo, I don't feel that. Sure, sometimes I judge a ridiculous outfit choice (shorts and heels in November??). But my criticism isn't necessarily just thrown back at the subject. I don't think to myself, *She sucks, and she's rich and thin and beautiful and famous, so if she sucks, then I probably suck. Anyway, off to work!* Bravo has been a great reminder that things aren't always what they seem. That living in an Upper East Side townhouse doesn't mean you don't have problems. (In fact, you might have more because of it.) And it's so much more enriching and enjoyable to follow the life of a woman bravely navigating those problems and providing her own thoughts and insights and fears than to see an out-of-context picture of someone leaving Hyde nightclub and judge their outfit. Life is messy, things get hard. And when they do, I don't want a guy behind a computer making snarky jokes about it. I'd much rather deal with it by screaming in front of a novelty restaurant toaster.

I'M CHILD-FREE

. . .

I have babysat exactly two times in my life. Once, when I was thirteen, I had to watch my nine-year-old neighbor, and we spent the evening talking about the swim team and eating Thin Mints until her parents were back. The other time was when another neighbor asked me to watch their baby for an hour while they ran an errand, and about twelve minutes in the baby started crying, so I called my mom to come over. Neither was much of a success (I ate too many Thin Mints) and both taught me that I never wanted to babysit again.

I don't think that my limited experience with babysitting is *why* I've decided not to have kids, but it's relevant. The only positive association I have with babysitting is racing my friend Lauren to read as many Baby-Sitters Club books as we could in fourth grade—though only after we had read every single Sweet Valley High. And in fact, the Sweet Valley books were much more aspirational to me than the Baby-Sitters Club. I desperately wanted to be older and popular and, most important, blond. Every girl I went to school with was like Jessica and Elizabeth Wakefield: blond-haired, blue-eyed, thin; beloved by boys and fawned over by parents.

Not only did I have zero interest in babysitting while the rest of my tween friends were stacking cash around the neighborhood, I wasn't even excited to play with baby dolls. Like every little girl, I was implicitly told I should want to nurture, but taking care of a fake baby just didn't do it for me. I was much more of a Barbie girl. From an early age I was obsessed with fashion, and who had more clothes than Barbie? (For this next paragraph or two, please refrain from thinking of *Barbie* as the Margot Robbie movie and try to think more about Barbie as the doll who ruined girls' body image from behind a motionless plastic face.)

I had tons of Barbies and all their accessories. The one with super-long hair who came with a variety of brushes and combs and wore a skintight minidress with a print that looked like if Pucci designed nineties movie-theater carpeting. The red Corvette, the baby-blue Chevy with a bubble-gum-pink dash, the magenta-and-teal camper with its now problematic Aztec-inspired wrap. The fucking BUBBLE BATH that you could actually fill with soapy water. I had all the Barbies and I loved them. But when I played with them, I wasn't pretending Barbie and Ken were making a beautiful home and raising a family. Most of my stories were ripped from *Days of Our Lives* plotlines I either actively followed or passively absorbed when my mom got home from work and watched that day's episode, which she'd recorded on a VHS tape. My Barbies were cheating on each other. They were faking pregnancies and throwing their friends off roofs. They confronted one another in the bubble bath. They lived by a code of sexy revenge and violence.

When I was making Barbie slap Ken because he was sleeping

with her twin, I wasn't subconsciously thinking, *I'm never going to have kids.* I spent most of my life never even considering that choice. In fact, my assumption was *I guess I'll probably have kids someday.* Even though I have never had any actual instinct to have children, it was something I just assumed I would get around to because that's what everyone does, like dyeing my hair or watching *The Sopranos.* You grow up, you go to college, you get a job, you meet someone, you get married, you have kids, you buy a house, you retire. It's a simple path, you just follow it and don't think too much about it.*

When I was younger, my friends and I would talk about when we wanted to get married and have kids. Twenty-four always seemed like the magic number, but even at twelve years old, I felt suffocated when I heard my friends say, "I want to meet someone in college and then get married and have my first kid at twenty-four." I didn't even have my period yet and I would think, *Eeehhh, I need more time for me!* But very rarely would I actually think about not wanting to be a parent. For a girl, it was always in the ether, even if I couldn't really conceive of what it meant because I only knew what it meant to be parented, not to actually parent. Nor did any of the parents around me make a particularly thrilling case for having children. They were parents! They never let me do cool stuff and were always saying things like "Don't stay up too late," and "Come turn this light off," and "Why the hell did you make the entire tray of Bagel Bites at once?" Who would want to be them?

As I got older, I was still waiting for my motherhood desires to kick in, but I attributed their absence to the fact that I moved

---

* It's a simple upper-middle-class path, I know that. But that's how I grew up, so that's the path I expected to follow.

to New York in my twenties. Everyone does everything late here, both at night and in life. People spend their youth as it is meant to be spent: staying up until four A.M., having long, loud brunches, working way way way too hard, getting fingered in the backs of cabs. New York, baby! Well, New York *no* baby, because those things all get harder if you have children. You do those things for ten years and only then do you start thinking about a family. The friends I grew up with in Maryland started getting married in the years after college, and then buying houses and getting pregnant. When I went to their weddings, I had fun, but felt like I was on another planet. How could two people who were the same age as me do something so serious and adult? We were literal babies who still had to ask our parents for money when a surprise dental bill showed up (right???). And once you're married, now you have to have kids, and that seemed categorically insane at that point in our lives!

By our late twenties, even the New Yorkers didn't think it was so bizarre anymore to be in serious relationships with engagement on the horizon. But kids were still nowhere in sight; a way-down-the-road issue to deal with, not the next step on the path to self-actualization/moving to Westchester. And even then, I still didn't clearly understand that I didn't want kids. I think I kept waiting for someone else to make the decision for me. I told myself I was okay with the idea of having kids as long as it was really far away. I continued to think that it was something I would likely end up doing, but I told myself it wouldn't even be a discussion before at least my late thirties.

While my city friends were slowly picking away at the ideas of marriage and children, I was just starting on a new phase of my life. My career hadn't been as linear as I anticipated when I was a tween planning out my future with my friends. I bounced around from industry to industry before finding the job I really wanted to do. I had to start from the beginning with stand-up and writing in my mid-twenties (and I want to stress is NOT LATE TO FIGURE OUT WHAT YOU WANT TO DO), which didn't leave a whole lot of time for anything else. I wasn't going on dates with the hope of finding a real partner or making the kind of money to put a down payment on a home I could fill with my family. I was spending what I thought were my last fertile years (lol, joke's on me) in the backs of bars and comedy clubs trying to find the best tag for a grocery store joke. And I knew that. I knew I was getting older and the task of meeting someone and getting married and having children would get harder the older I got. I knew that and still made absolutely no space in my life for those pursuits. I was subconsciously choosing every morning to not care if I had kids or not. To focus on myself and the career I was building more than the theoretical family I could have. I don't think I even realized what a choice I was making then, partly because I was around a lot of people doing the same thing. We were just living life, not consciously opting out of parenthood.

I don't think intensely pursuing a career is a substitute for children, nor do I think that all women who work the same way I do don't want or won't have kids. Actually, it's strange that as I write this, I feel compelled to make sure that no one takes my own personal thoughts about motherhood and assumes I am trying to make blanket statements about women and children and motherhood and non-motherhood. I don't want to speak for women who are mothers. I also don't want to be the voice for all women who choose not to have children.

I realize that this issue is fraught with personal feelings, and it feels particularly thorny because mothers and not-mothers are pitted against each other all the time. The patriarchy tells us that we're two opposing sides of womanhood who can't possibly understand, empathize with each other, or even have anything in common. A woman with children befriending a woman without children? How could they ever do it?? The woman with children is busy making cereal from scratch and dressing her offspring in matching overalls. The woman without children is still at work long after the sun has set, then goes out to drink martinis while wearing a suit. They are nothing alike!!! At least that's what the media has taught us for decades. I see it on television, in movies, in women's magazines, on Instagram and TikTok and whatever social media platform comes next to ruin our lives. It's a division infused into society, intended to keep women busy fighting with one another so that men can do stuff like shooting cars into space on the end of a stupid rocket shaped like their pale white dicks. Fuck that.

By the time I entered my thirties, kicking motherhood down the road took a sharp turn into complete apathy about having children at all. The late-night wine-and-hummus dinners I had with various friends always tilted toward the future. The married ones would say, "I'm happy either way. I could totally live a great life without kids." That was the most that the "no kids" lifestyle argument ever got: "I *could* be happy." Though I have many friends who are decisively not having kids, it wasn't a conversation we would have very often, because what was there to talk about? The lives we were living didn't require the planning and negotiating that having children does.

But this lack of a decision had me often feeling . . . left out. When married (or even unmarried) friends would talk about their plans to have kids, or the long negotiation of even making that decision, it took up all the space in the conversation. There was so much to think about. Where do you live? What happens to your work life? What roles will you and your partner play? What is it about being a parent that gets you the most excited? When you aren't going to have kids, there's less decision, less action, less "drama" to talk out, and you become more of a sounding board for someone working through their own choices than someone who gets to actively claim their own. The choice to not do something is rarely discussed or celebrated. When you're at a restaurant, you don't say, "And I'm NOT having an appetizer." You just don't order one.

There wasn't a specific day I woke up and realized, *Oh, I actually do not want to have children.* It wasn't because I saw a toddler melt down outside a restaurant or because I heard my friend tell me that during labor her "asshole ripped in half." (If you haven't given birth and didn't know this was even a possibility, I'm sorry. I'll pause for a moment to let you stop dry heaving.) It wasn't a fraught discussion with a partner. It wasn't the day before, of, or after my abortion. It wasn't a definitive moment in my life. It was a slow recognition of the absence of something. I didn't realize, *I do not want children.* I realized, *I've NEVER actually wanted children.*

Those thoughts may seem identical, but they're actually very different. I didn't suddenly change my mind after having wanted children in the past. Nor did I have a conscious awareness of having made that choice. But looking back, it was a choice that I made. The way I'd been living my entire life was rooted in the absence of desire to have children. As a kid, I didn't babysit, I didn't play with dolls, I didn't play house and pretend to be a mother. As an adult, I didn't date to find a partner, I didn't make room in my life to lay the groundwork for parenting, I didn't feel a pang of longing or recognition when I saw motherhood depicted in media or in real life. I just slowly realized that I don't want that and I'm not going to do it.

I truly hate invoking *Sex and the City* quotes to illustrate real-life experiences and decisions, but I do often think of the episode when Carrie learns her older boyfriend, the Russian, aka artist Aleksandr Petrovsky, does not want to have any more children, so staying in the relationship would mean she wouldn't ever have children. She says to the other ladies, "If I really wanted to have a baby, wouldn't I have tried to have one by now? I wanted to be a writer, I made myself a writer. I want a ridiculously extravagant pair of shoes, I find a way to buy them." I felt the same way. On the writing, and the shoes (but we're talking Gucci loafers here, not stilettos), and certainly on the kids. My inaction said it all. I didn't want kids. I never wanted kids.

I watched my other childless friends deal with pressure from their families, having to manage their feelings when their siblings had children. An older brother or sister having kids: *Well, you're up next.* A younger sibling having kids: *Now you're falling behind and better get your shit together.* But I'm an only child, so I carried both zero expectations and all the expectations. There was no yardstick to measure my childbearing accomplishments, no one to make me feel bad or behind. It also meant that all of my parents' dreams of becoming grandparents hinged on me and me alone.

Luckily, my parents haven't put intense pressure on me to start a family. Occasionally my mom would start to say, "Well, when you meet someone and have kids . . ." The definitive way she talked about it, like it was something I would eventually do, likely contributed to the reason I kept up the assumption that I would have kids without interrogating my own desires. It was always floating out there as an end goal that I never got closer to.

After I realized I didn't want kids, I would remind her from time to time when it felt relevant, like in the middle of a long phone call or milling around the Nordstrom shoe department. You know, the prime times to drop on your parents that they'll never become grandparents. Initially, my mom would wave me off, assuming this was something I'd grow out of. But as the years went on, she realized I was serious. Her response was often "Aren't you going to be lonely?" Look, I love my mom, but was I keeping her from being lonely? If so, woof, I was terrible company. The first few years of my life I wouldn't give her a moment alone. I made her spend all her free time on my stupid activities. Then as a teen I was a total bitch from morning to night. And after that I just left and kept calling asking for money? Is that better than being alone??

My mom certainly didn't grasp how many friends I have who also aren't having kids. When she was my age, my mom was, well, a mom. She was living in a community where every house contained a family. There were no single people in the neighborhood I grew up in, there weren't even apartments. Most of her friends were either the parents of my friends or the parents of kids I eventually had to befriend, too. My mom didn't have a huge network of child-free friends and colleagues the way I do. I live in New York City, where it's objectively difficult to raise a family without serious generational wealth. I work in the entertainment industry, which given its unstable nature in schedule and income calls to people who don't have and don't want kids. I'm also a millennial, living through an era where boomers hoard the housing, childcare costs are like buying a car every single month, and the idea of paying for education feels as reasonable as purchasing a small island. Because of this I have built an incredible network of friends, particularly women, who aren't having children. We already have plans for a retirement commune that will be heavy on cats and THC and light on anyone under sixty.

My mom's next argument, after my inevitable loneliness without a child, was the classic "Well, who is going to take care of you when you get old?" I watched my mother take care of her mother at the end of her life, and I will do whatever I can to care for my mother at the end of her life. But there's no guarantee that simply having a child means I have dedicated eldercare. And if that's why I'm having a kid, then it's going to be a brutal fifty years waiting for that planned benefit to kick in. There are plenty of reasons to have children, but this is definitely not one of them. On the off chance I live long enough to need that kind of care, my commune of child-free friends (and cats) will surely have a cadre of robots to keep the screen in front of my face constantly programmed to seasons 8–10 of *Real Housewives of New York* while my bloodstream stays steadily full of Dilaudid and Xanax. More likely a climate disaster will wipe me out before I can even collect what's left of Social Security.

My mom has actually started to agree with this last point. One morning when I was home visiting my parents in Maryland, I was having an English muffin and coffee while my mom was scrolling through her AOL home page. She came across yet another damning climate-crisis story and said to me, unprompted, "I think you're right about not having kids. What are people going to do?" It's unfortunate that the devastation of the planet by the fossil fuel industry is what helped my mom come around to my decision to not have kids, but I'll take what I can get at this point. Thanks, Shell and ExxonMobil, for helping my mom understand me!

It feels bittersweet to have my parents recognize and respect my child-free life when so much of our culture still does not. Of course, I am by no means an oppressed class. I'm a white lady with money and I don't have kids. Hell, parents are actually way worse off in this country than I am when it comes to actual support and resources. But moving through the world as a woman without kids is not always glamorous or comfortable, the way it is sometimes shown. It looks like a dream when it's portrayed well, but it's most often painted as the most depressing thing that could happen to someone. The world doesn't know if it should pity us or envy us, and either way, we're doing something wrong.

Pity is the emotion most people, especially other women, feel toward child-free women. It's condescending. It reduces all women to being useless and miserable unless they have a family to raise. No one has expressed it quite so clearly as whiny dipshit JD Vance when he told sentient wet fart Tucker Carlson in 2021 that the country was being run by "a bunch of childless cat ladies who are miserable at their own lives and the choices that they've made and so they want to make the rest of the country miserable, too." I know the stereotype Vance is referring to; I've seen it in pop culture my whole life, like Eleanor Abernathy, aka the Crazy Cat Lady on *The Simpsons,* with her gray hair and rundown home both crawling with screaming cats. There's the much younger but only slightly more sympathetic Angela Martin on *The Office,* who spends most of the series doting on her cats in the absence of children. Living with a bunch of cats instead of kids is cultural shorthand for being a miserable bitch who will die alone.

First of all, women with cats instead of children *should* be running the country. We'd crush it. We have the time and emotional availability to take on such a task. We deeply understand boundaries (our cats set many). We'd give every state a fun nickname, like CUTE-ah or Mr. Silly Pants Pennsylvania. But Vance invokes "childless cat ladies" to hammer home that women without children are sad. We're not doing the *one* thing that *all* women are supposed to do in his eyes: raising children. The culture feels sad for women without children. We're less than. We're pitiable.

That is, unless our lives are remotely comfortable or glamorous; then we're the point of envy for every person who has ever had to change a diaper. Women without children have no responsibilities and we have never once been tired. We have nothing to keep alive, nothing to love, and therefore we're always jet-setting around and sipping martinis late into the night when everyone else is cursed with waking up early to heat up a bottle. This is your Samantha Jones, the hedonistic powerhouse publicist of *Sex and the City,** who puts herself first. Everyone wants to be her and envies the lifestyle that she loves, and for that reason . . . she's terrible and we should hate her.

The problem with how our culture treats child-free women is that it's both of these at once. It's pity and envy, disgust and jealousy, and virtually nothing in between. As a woman who's child-free by choice, you just cannot win. If you acknowledge the parts of society where you feel left out, excluded, or even punished, then you're the sad lady who has nothing of her own and nothing to offer, and at best you can hope for sympathy without action. If you love your life and embrace the freedoms of being child-free, you're a selfish asshole who can't help throwing it in parents' faces that you can afford a much more fun life than they can.† You're someone to be jealous of, and thus hate.

---

* Omg two *SATC* references in the same essay. If I make one more, Michael Patrick King shows up at my house with a pair of Manolos!

† The irony here is that it's outrageously expensive to be a single person, which many child-free women are. Yeah, I don't have kids to pay for, but I also don't have a partner (and another income) to split literally every quickly escalating cost of being alive. Another fun lose-lose!

I'd like to note that there are no stereotypes about men who don't have children. They're all potential fathers until they're in a coffin. There is no pity or resentment, no need to categorize them, they're just men. Must be nice!

And while I fully expect the culture to label me as someone to pity or envy or hate (or all at once!), it's not something I expected real people in my life to do. Yet it happens all the time. Yes, I have my friends who are also child-free by choice and our grand plans for our menopausal utopia, but I also have a lot of friends who have kids. It would be a lie to say my relationships with them haven't changed since they had kids. That'd be a lie so big it could get me a job in the government. But they have, and that's okay. Friendships change. The superficial change would be easy to note: *Oh, we used to be able to hang out whenever, stay out late, and go on a weekend trip to Miami with a day's notice and now you can't because you have responsibilities to your family.* That's not untrue, but that's not the foundational shift that's really taken place.

Women who do have children can easily be left behind in the professional or creative worlds, or even the social world. The first woman in her friend group to have a kid always learns this the hardest. The freedom I have is something someone with a child cannot have. Being a mother (especially in the United States) is a grueling role where even with all the support in the world, it's hard to keep up all the areas of your life that existed before your child. It is undoubtedly harder to say yes to trips for work or vacation on a moment's notice, it's harder to stay out later for one more drink, it's harder to take the more creative but much less lucrative job. There are so many things that get harder once you have a kid. I am so, so aware of that. In fact, I'm so aware of it, I chose not to have a kid partly because of those things.

A quick prescriptive note to the women out there who have children and are reading this and saying, "Well, I have a kid and I *can* travel!!!" "I have kids and my job is creative and I don't make much!!!!!!" "Personally, as a mother, I do my best drinking at last call!!!!!!!!" Stop. Stop doing this. I'm not talking to all my wonderful friends with kids whom I often see and call late at night and travel with. You're perfect, never change. I see this mostly from the more anonymous mothers online who love to jump into any conversation that child-free women want to have on the internet. When a woman who isn't a mother gets online to say how happy she is she can travel easily because she doesn't have kids, it's not an invitation to prove how you're an exception. I assume you still had to manage childcare and pay for extra support or at the very least take a break from reading on a beach to feed your child, so it is, objectively, not the same thing we are talking about. Stop telling people without kids that you can do everything they can do. For starters, you fucking can't. And it's also incredibly insulting.

The reason it's insulting isn't that child-free women own the concept of vacations or that we want you to not have fun at night. It's that these are the benefits that we get from the choice we've made about motherhood, just like there are benefits that women with children get from their own different decisions about motherhood. Where mothers can feel (rightfully!) left behind in some areas of their life after they have kids, women without children also feel incredibly left out in a world that is built around the importance of family. There are conversations we're not part of, plans we're not included in, entire new social circles we can't enter. It can feel lonely when friends with kids cancel last minute, or decline a trip or a dinner or a phone catch-up because of their children. It's sad when a longtime friend moves out of the city for their family.

What's so difficult about experiencing this loss when you're child-free is you can't ever say anything, because family is the trump card. Nothing else in our society is as valued as family, not even close. Anything beyond family isn't even important. So not only am I sad when a friend moves to the suburbs and has a whole new group of friends because she has kids, I don't even get to say it upsets me because I just sound like a selfish bitch who doesn't get it because I don't have my own family. Like Mr. Vance says, I just want everyone to be as miserable as I am.

Recently, at a girls' dinner, my friends with kids around the same age got into a long discussion about school zoning and admissions while I sat quietly with literally not one thing to contribute. And even if I had something to contribute, I knew it would be immediately dismissed on the grounds of "Well, you don't have kids, so what do you know about this?" It wasn't the fact that the family conversation bored me; it's that suddenly I was excluded. If I were at a dinner with three friends who worked at the same company and one who didn't, it would be rude to constantly talk about the minutiae of our shared workplace. But when the topic that excludes someone is parenthood, there is an expectation that you sit down, shut up, and drink your wine until it's time to talk about something else because *you* are the one who opted out of this life.

I've had conversations with close friends who have implied that they need a job more than I do. In a scarcity landscape in the television industry, the last few years have been a fight for everyone to get into writers' rooms or to sell shows to streamers. I've been lucky to have many great jobs behind me and hopefully many ahead of me. But in a group of women all talking about the crumbling industry and the very, very limited prospects for employment, more than once I have had friends say, "I mean, I have a family, so I *really* need this job," as if I don't need that job because I don't have a family.

It's hard not to clock these changes and feel slighted. It's hard to not hear the culture call you selfish or stunted and start to wonder if that's true. No one has questioned my other life decisions like they've questioned my not having children. Living with extreme physical discomfort and pain has shaped a lot of decisions about how I live my life, for example. I spend money on upgraded air travel so I can be more in control of how I'm sitting or lying down. I take large chunks of time to walk all the way to the YMCA and swim laps for exercise because it makes me feel better. I don't do activities like skiing because I have a greater risk of serious injury because of my back. No one questions any of those decisions. But my life of pain is absolutely a piece of why I've decided not to have children, and yet that's something people feel no shame in questioning. When I've said I wouldn't get pregnant or give birth because of my back, I've been met with the reply, "What about a surrogate or adoption?"—two notoriously easy and inexpensive paths. When I talk about how much of parenting is schlepping stuff around and I don't have the ability to do that, I'm told I should move to the suburbs so I can drive, as if my life isn't in the city or you can just drive a car around the inside of a grocery store. Everyone has an opinion as well as a solution to combat any obstacle I try to raise. I wish people could treat my decision not to have kids like my decision not to ski and kindly shut the fuck up.

It's not hard for me to paint a picture of child-free life being, above all else, "easy." To some it's selfish and to some it's radical, but to everyone it's easier than having children. And most of it really is. That's what I like about it so much. But I can't deny that when I made the choice not to have children, I knew there were good things I was giving up, too. I know the love between child and parent is unlike anything else. While I have so much love in my life, I know I won't experience that specific type of relationship, which I imagine is wonderful. I do feel bad that my parents won't get to experience having grandchildren, and I'm bummed I won't get to see the strange and unpredictable ways they would spoil my kid. I'm aware that this is another milestone in life that I will not be celebrated for, and I'd be lying if I said that didn't make me a little salty. Like marriage, parenthood—and specifically motherhood—gets its own parties and outfits and presents and heartfelt toasts. Never mind that after the fancy baby shower, people rarely do things to help you or make your life easier as an actual pregnant person or parent, but I do love attention, and sadly you can't throw yourself a no-baby shower.

At the end of the day, I love my challenging and nontraditional career that involves a lot of travel and staying out late. I love taking advantage of living in a city like New York, where I can hang out with my friends until two A.M. and grab an Uber home easily. I love being able to take long stretches of time off from my work to refocus my creativity and not be so worried about money because my expenses are just me. I like deciding to join a friend in the Hamptons on a moment's notice and the only hurdles are fitting into a bathing suit and getting someone to pop in and feed my cat a few times. I love that when my back is bothering me, I can take a nap in the middle of the day. I love that if I want to just eat scrambled eggs for dinner after a long and draining day, that is all I have to cook. I love loudly watching *30 Rock* episodes in my apartment late at night without worrying about waking anyone up. I love being totally independent in all my decisions. I love that I can do every single one of the things I listed at once and without assistance or extra logistics or more money. I love my life.

A lot of people refuse to acknowledge that the choice to have kids is different from the choice to be childless in both good *and* bad ways. One isn't morally better. One isn't objectively more enjoyable for everyone. They're just two different choices. But one of them still needs a lot of defending. You don't see a lot of people getting online and making content *defending* having children. Glamorizing or grounding it, sure, but no one has to argue it was a choice that makes them happy. But in our culture, being child-free is still a position to be defended. The fact that I even have a chapter of this book dedicated to it is proof! And by loudly being child-free and enjoying my life, I hope I'm helping other people slowly understand that it's simply a choice, not a good one or a bad one. The less we dwell on that choice as saying something about your inherent value as a human being, the better we can all be treated in society. Don't bother me about my choices, and I won't bother you about yours, and we'll all be happy. I'm happy for my friends who have families just like I hope they are happy for me that I don't. Just don't ask me to babysit.

I'M OKAY

Hot take: I hate picnics. I hate them deep in my core because I hate sitting on the ground. I hate lowering myself from standing up to sitting on the ground. I hate how you have to constantly change positions to stay comfortable on the ground, leaning on one arm, then the other, then shifting to half-lying-down, and then you knock over a plastic cup of tepid rosé and it ruins a plate of sweating cheese and stale baguette. I hate maneuvering myself from sitting on the ground to standing back up. But in the summer of 2020, when sitting down at a table indoors to drink and snack with friends was a distant memory, I had a lot of picnics. And I hated them.

A large part of why I hated picnics so much during this time was because I was once again dealing with chronic back pain. Going on so many park picnic hangs is how I even realized I was in serious pain at all. Every time, I expected a living version of Manet's *Le Déjeuner sur l'herbe* with a basket of delicious pastries tipped over before a sexy threesome broke out. Instead, I had sciatica and nowhere to pee. Initially, I attributed the aching and burning to my new "never leave home" lifestyle and the fact that when I did sit for several hours, I was on the non-ergonomic couch in my tiny apartment rather than the very expensive ergonomic work chair in my office. But as I schlepped a heavy bag of sandwich toppings and quickly warming Pellegrino through Prospect Park and then struggled to sit on the ground for more than four minutes at a time, it finally clicked: This was not just an adjustment to a new lifestyle; something was wrong.

I know my body. I know back pain. And I knew that these weren't just the run-of-the-mill aches and twinges that everyone experiences as they get older. This was familiar, and not in the fun way like hearing the opening bars of "Return of the Mack" and realizing you still know every word. This was familiar like when you go back to the same restaurant where you once got food poisoning. I spent a few days walking around my apartment, straining to bend over and tie my shoes, grimacing as I dug through the bottom of my fridge for a block of cheese, and kicking my legs all night in hopes that just the right motion would make the burning feeling stop long enough for my brain to finally shut down and get some sleep. But even as it became more and more obvious that something was wrong, I was in denial. How, after three back surgeries, could I be having this kind of pain again?

Being in chronic pain during lockdown was uniquely challenging. Before, when my back was hurting, there were distractions and obligations that forced me to manage the pain. I was too busy and stressed out by work and gigs to dwell on it, and I was moving around the city so much during my day-to-day life that the pain didn't linger in my body and mind like it did now. In this new world, this incredibly small world that was mostly confined to my apartment walls, empty neighborhood sidewalks, and long nights alone, the pain was all I could think about. I had no real work to focus on, no stand-up to power through, no social events or parties or fun aside from long solo walks and the occasional picnic with a few friends. I spent most of my days home alone with my pain as my roommate, keeping me up all night and stopping me from enjoying a second of my day, as if it were blasting Rammstein and microwaving tilapia.

I also opted out of medication because the months of taking high doses of opioids for chronic pain after my three previous surgeries had left me with some addiction problems. I was always incredibly lucky that I hadn't ever slid too far into dangerous territory, but I had absolutely used pain pills heavily, finding myself extremely dependent on taking literal handfuls of Vicodin, OxyContin, and Percocet a day for months at a time both to ease the pain and to continue functioning. I had also suffered long and painful phases of withdrawal each time I stopped. Cutting myself off the meds cold turkey left me feeling sick, as I suffered sleepless nights in a cold sweat and vomiting while living in terror that I would resort to incredibly dangerous alternatives while weaning off them. The only reason I didn't end up in rehab or seeking out other drugs is that I was lucky. I'm not better, I'm not stronger, I was just lucky enough that opioids didn't destroy my life beyond the ways they already had.

And because I knew it was just the luck of the draw that things hadn't escalated, I was terrified to be prescribed opioids for long-term pain because every go-around seemed like another risky tempting of fate. This time, I was managing my pain with half a bottle of Advil a day and all of the weed and wine I could find. I knew this wasn't a healthy option, but at least I wouldn't be back on the opioid track.

I knew I needed to do something, but I didn't know where to start. I was so far removed from the life I'd had during my last two surgeries in New York. I was way out of practice in the back-repair area of my life, and had the added complication of navigating the healthcare system in the late summer of 2020, when we had only just gotten to the point where hospitals were functional again in New York. I made an appointment with my primary care provider, waited more than two months to see her, and when the appointment came around, she took one look at me and told me I needed to see a specialist. I already knew I needed an MRI, and I knew I needed a neurosurgeon or an orthopedic surgeon to look at the results, so this really could have been a phone call. But of course I had to do this step first because our healthcare system is so unnecessarily complicated that I assume it was structured by the same person who decides where you find your Uber when you're leaving the airport.

When I finally got an MRI, I jammed out to the faint tunes of Rihanna's *Anti* underneath the deafening BOP BOOP BEEP BOP D-D-D-D-D-DUUUUUUHN BOP BOOP EEEHHHHHNNNN of the machine and anticipated that the results would show I had a herniated disc. I was right, and my doctor had recommended a neurosurgeon whom she loved because he was very conservative about performing major surgery when other interventions might be possible. In theory, this is a wonderful way to practice medicine. To avoid immediately slicing people open for invasive and expensive surgeries when drugs and physical therapy might work is how all medicine should be done. But I was nervous because other therapies had rarely helped my back problems, so I didn't want to spend months on a futile treatment and then end up needing surgery anyway. I imagine this is how people who have children feel about being in labor for twenty-three hours just to have a C-section: Just give me the scar and the bill and let's get this over with.

I went to my appointment with my new surgeon on a fall day in 2020, nervous but also excited. There is a unique kind of hope that comes from seeing a medical professional when you're deep in pain. You latch on to the idea that maybe, just maybe, this person has the key to fixing it—even though you know in your heart that rarely does this happen.

My surgeon was kind and friendly without being too casual. No one wants a jokey spine surgeon, but you also don't want someone who sees you as a line item rather than an actual person lying on the table. He treated me like, what do they call it? A human being? He pulled up my MRI and told me exactly what I had expected: My L4/L5 disc, which had been through three operations at this point, had herniated once again, and little shards of disc were pushing on my spinal column. The best solution would be a discectomy, but because the disc itself was so destroyed from the previous herniations, they would need to do a fusion, which meant connecting the two vertebrae and inserting a prosthetic disc where the decayed one once was.

Maybe some people would find the news that you're getting a metal spine devastating. Not me. I remember I genuinely smiled under my face mask. I practically giggled out of relief. A real answer! No vague "maybe it's all in your head" or "let's see if whatever this is just takes care of itself" or "have you tried taking Tylenol?" I wasn't getting dragged through a gauntlet of useless physical therapy and being overprescribed opioids. Here was a solution not only to my immediate pain, but also to the possibility of future pain, because the fusion meant this disc would not shatter my life again. Sign me up!

I went home to "think about it" as my doctor instructed me. But there wasn't much to think about, so a few days later, I called his office to schedule the surgery. However, when my call was put through, the person on the other end of the phone told me in a rather accusatory tone that they couldn't schedule my surgery because I hadn't done all the other interventions yet, and I didn't seem like I was in the kind of pain to need surgery at this moment.

First of all, I never even saw this person during my appointment. Second, how do you know if I'm in pain or not? Can you tell just by looking? Like, oh yes, the hallmark of pain, the area that is bothering the person is glowing red like they're in an Aleve commercial. Never mind that someone who has lived with chronic pain might be incredibly good at masking pain, might be so accustomed to compartmentalizing pain, might be so hopeful in a doctor's office at the prospect of ending this pain, that they present as if there is nothing wrong at all, while just below the skin they are dying to scream out in agony. Here I was being dismissed again, being told that my pain wasn't real, that it was all in my head.

The person on the phone went on. I needed to do physical therapy and steroid injections for pain management before I could schedule the surgery. I had done both those things in the past, and of course, they hadn't worked. But now I had to find another doctor's office in Manhattan and commute there—during lockdown—all for something that felt entirely futile while prolonging the excruciating pain I was in.

I enlisted my car-owning friend Sam to chauffeur me to Midtown every two weeks. He would pick me up at my apartment in his tiny Honda Fit and I would sit shotgun with his dog, Scout, on my lap, and then we'd get spicy falafel on the way home. The office was lovely, the staff was kind, and the shots were painful and never worked. Yes, they still felt like getting struck by lightning. And no, I still don't actually know what that feels like, but they hurt like hell.

Five weeks later, after the third round of shots, the pain management team told me that if the steroids hadn't worked by now, they wouldn't, so I should let my surgeon know. When I called my surgeon's office to tell them I wasn't feeling any relief, they were shocked: "You did THREE rounds?"

What the hell? Before I wasn't doing enough injections, now I'm telling you I did it and you're saying I did too much? I felt like the Goldilocks of steroid injections; first I was a bad patient by not doing enough, now I had done too many. How many shots were just right?*

When my surgeon's office finally said they could start scheduling my surgery, I felt a wave of relief nearly knock me over. I wasn't thinking about the horrible recovery or having an operation during Covid or the newness of a titanium-enhanced spine. I was just thinking that I was going to be out of the pain that had been gradually worsening, and that this could be the end of a two-decade-long saga. I was ready to meet the final boss of back-pain relief, and I didn't care how tough the fight would be.

Having surgery in January 2021 was nothing like the previous three times. For starters, my parents couldn't come up and help me recover. They had both gotten Covid a few weeks earlier, and I re-

---

* I find myself asking this question a lot in nonmedical scenarios as well. If anyone knows the answer, please tell me. I can't keep sleeping with pizza in my bed, I'm in my forties.

fused to risk one of them being remotely still contagious, mostly because coughing post–spine surgery feels like someone hitting you in the back with a sledgehammer. I also couldn't bring anyone with me to the hospital, so I had to take an Uber alone at five o'clock on the morning of my surgery. The only times I'm ever in an Uber at five A.M. are coming home from a night gone off the rails or on my way to an early flight I deeply regret booking, and this was no better.

At the hospital, I waited alone to get checked in. I sat alone in my room between each doctor's coming in to brief me on the different things they'd be doing. I had no one to roll my eyes at when I met my anesthesiologist and clocked that he was about twenty-eight. I had no one to wave goodbye to as a nurse escorted me down the hall to the operating room.

Then, I got all my monitors on and IVs placed and lay down on the bed in that freezing room as they covered me in heated blankets and started the drugs and oxygen to lull me into surgical slumber. The last thing I remember as I counted backward was my surgeon grabbing my hand and squeezing it, indicating it was going to be okay; that even though I was alone, I was in good hands.

I woke up to the normal cocktail of loopiness from anesthesia and the shocking pain of having part of your body cut open. I was mentally prepared for it to be much more painful than my previous surgeries because of the added element of medical-grade Home Depot equipment permanently placed inside of me, but it felt the same as before. My surgeon told me that the surgery took several hours longer than expected because they had to clear out so much scar tissue from my previous procedures. It was so bad, he said, "we couldn't believe you'd been walking upright."

If my body and brain had been functional enough at that point,

I would have cried. I think I just gave him a thumbs-up with my eyes closed. The relief. Finally, someone had been able to see how bad things had been for me. I didn't have to prove my pain anymore: A roomful of people had opened me up and looked directly at its source. I knew it had been there. I knew it all along. This was the first time that pain was recognized, understood, and validated.

When I had first scheduled the surgery, I was told I might feel ready to leave the same night. Looking back, that idea was laughable. At seven A.M. they were doing professional welding on my spine, and what, by eight P.M. I could call an Uber for a late dinner at Hillstone? Not a chance. I actually stayed in the hospital for three days this time around, mostly to learn how to get in and out of bed with my new bionic spine, but also because I was having trouble peeing post-catheterization and you can't leave until you pee. A good rule to live by in general, just like your parents tell you before a car trip: We're not going anywhere until you pee first.

I spent my time in the hospital texting Divya, the helpful friend who was going to be taking care of me after I got home and had already settled comfortably into what we like to call "house hotel." I had all of the cable channels and all of the streamers, a fridge full of both healthy stuff and treats for recovery, and a stocked bar for whenever I was allowed to drink again. Every night, Divya would text me a photo of her order of Chinese food from Kings Co Imperial and a signature Campari-grapefruit-gin cocktail while she plowed through Netflix movies on my couch. I would text her back a photo of a can of ginger ale and empty saltines packets and a TV so far from my bed that I couldn't see which Housewives I was watching.

Finally, on the third day, I was pretty mobile and peed on my own for the first time, with the fervor of someone who had been holding it during a three-hour screening after finishing a large movie-theater bucket of Diet Coke. I just had to get discharged and Divya could come scoop me up and take me back to the comforts of home. I was sitting in a chair when a nurse and one of the surgical-team members came by. He echoed what my main surgeon had said about how bad my back was when they opened me up, but assured me that things went smoothly and I should finally be pain-free when I was fully healed. I was relieved. He also told me that my incision was closed with glue, so there were no stitches or staples to worry about.

"Have you seen it yet?" he asked.

I was like, "What?" Of course I hadn't seen it. I had barely gotten into this chair. I wasn't twisting around or grabbing a hand mirror like a girl finally discovering the power of her pussy. Whatever happened on my back was really none of my business at this point.

"Give me your phone," he said.

I complied, and he reached behind me, took a picture, and showed it to me. "Cool," I said, trying not to look at the bloody, glued-together wound for too long.

My first week of recovery was difficult, but doable. Divya's help was arguably better than my mom and dad's because we had none of the lifelong parent-child power dynamics to navigate, and had the same taste in television and snacks and conversation topics. We discovered Canada Dry BOLD Ginger Ale, made snack plates of sharp cheese and seed-studded crackers, and got hooked on *Patriot* (an incredible Amazon show from years ago that no one watched and everyone should—don't let the title fool you, it's not about whatever you think it is). I took little walks down the hallway. People sent gift baskets of famous pastries, bouquets I barely had room for, Boy Smells candles to set the mood for being on (prescribed) drugs. I went from being unable to get out of bed alone to taking a lap around the block. I had agreed to pain medication post-surgery because there was a clear tapering off of the drugs, and instead of my normal "could kill a moose" dosage, I was taking the recommended amount and able to function.

I started wearing jeans. I started meeting up with friends for walks or outdoor drinks under heat lamps. As winter turned to spring, the sun was shining and the world was getting vaccinated; I was back to doing a little bit of in-person work in television and stand-up, and I wasn't in pain. I was happy. I was relieved. I was free. And then I was really, really angry.

When I was fully recovered and living my life again, I realized what the true absence of pain felt like. And that realization crystallized into the knowledge that my pain had not started a few months earlier, during lockdown, among the picnics. I had actually been living in pain for years. I had been like the frog in the slowly boiling pot of water, not registering that things were getting worse and worse. I had become so good at masking my pain, so good at compartmentalizing it, so good at pushing through it. I was so accustomed to living in chronic pain that I no longer even recognized I was in it.

Chronic pain is difficult to describe if you've never lived with it. And realizing you're not in it anymore is even more challenging. The best I can do is compare it to hearing an annoying noise. Imagine you are trying to get some work done and outside your office window there's construction going on, maybe a jackhammer. At first, it's disruptive and you wait for it to stop. But then you realize it won't, so you try and continue with your work, even though it's impossible to focus. You spend a ton of time trying to solve it:

headphones, moving to the other side of the room, shutting a window, but it still persists. And eventually you give up and try and just force yourself through your work. You're able to somewhat get things done, and while it's probably not as good as a normal day, it's good enough. And then magically the jackhammering stops, and you hear silence. That silence is at first a relief, but then it itself becomes almost as deafening as the jackhammering. Like you had been so used to working with the noise that now it's almost difficult to work without it.

As you get older, time passes in ways you cannot fathom when you're young. Days and years bleed together, and you can decipher what happened when only by looking at the rise of your jeans and the thickness of your eyebrows in photos. It's harder to remember what you did, whom you were with, and how you felt. So I sat on my couch wondering just how long I had been living in pain. How much of the last several years had I spent pushing down my pain, and in that process losing pieces of who I was? How much of my personality, of my joy, of my passion, had been forced out of my life so that I could carry on with my daily tasks without buckling?

I was even angrier that I had just accepted the reality of living in pain, that I had let it control my life for years. I was so good at hiding this huge part of myself that even medical professionals didn't believe my pain existed. I was the Meryl Streep of spine pain. I put on such a good show that the doctors couldn't believe that inside of me was a spinal column full of so much scar tissue and decay I shouldn't even have been able to walk. My condition was worse than even *I* realized, and people in my life had had the audacity to question my pain, to devalue my pain, to discredit the pain that I had been living in for years.

I got angry with myself, too. I got angry with my body. It wasn't fair that I had to live with this condition for so much of my life. That I, someone who absolutely loved being an athlete, had been sentenced to several painful spine surgeries and years of being relegated to the couch because most activities were too painful or exhausting. But the "it's not fair!" argument was one I'd had in my head for years, every time I had surgery, so I was able to kick it out of my brain by telling myself how many people have it much worse and how lucky I was to be on a path to recovery.

This was replaced with anger about my future: that this condition would likely plague me for the rest of my life and that if anything my pain would be worse and my recoveries harder as my body continued to grind itself into dust from age. This, too, I could reason my way out of. I couldn't do anything about it, so why devote so much time to worrying about it? But then I started to reckon with how much of the last few years I had actually missed. As everyone around me was grappling with lost time from lockdown, I was looking back at how much time I lost before we had even heard about Covid. How many times did I bail on plans because I was exhausted from being in pain? How many shows had I performed on autopilot so that I could handle my pain while simultaneously joking about makeup and magazines? How many subway rides became Uber rides? How many nights out turned into days in? How many arguments with people were actually because I was managing pain and not mad at them at all? How many strangers thought I was a total bitch because they met me on a day when my nerves were on fire and my mind was busy pretending they weren't?

Finally, a new type of anger took hold. In all of the years, in all of the surgeries, in all of the spasms and scars, I had never felt this feeling before. For the first time ever, I missed my pain.

I couldn't believe it. I was floored. All this rage was flooding me and the most offensive feeling of all was that I somehow wanted my pain back??? I missed it like you miss a shitty ex-boyfriend. The kind of ex where everyone assumes you feel a thousand pounds lighter and happier after the breakup, but instead you're crying in your apartment being like, "Omg remember when he would make popcorn for himself when I had friends over for movie night? I miss him sooooo much!" My pain had been my toxic partner for twenty years. It had done nothing good for me. So how could I possibly miss the dark passenger that was responsible for so many of the times I had felt terrible?

But I did miss it. I missed it because my pain is part of who I am. It's who I was for two decades. I've known my pain since before I could legally drink. Me and my pain go back like me and Mike's Hard Lemonade in that both of them made me throw up at my parents' house. I recognized that being in pain for years without realizing it meant my pain really was a part of me: It was so close I often lost track of it.

The cycle of chronic pain and the surgeries to fix it ruined so much of my life and took so many things from me, particularly time. But it has also given me some undeniably good things, like teaching me compassion. It's hard to compare eighteen-year-old me and forty-year-old me in terms of human emotions, especially since most teens are assholes who don't care about other people because they barely understand themselves. But from age nineteen on, because I had to learn the language of pain—the nuances of every number on the scale from 1 to 10, how the feeling of aching is different from the feeling of burning—I am fluent in a way many people are not. I can spot pain in others, can tell when someone is hurting. Whenever I'd encounter the signs of chronic pain in another person, there would be a silent connection between us; we'd nod at each other the way people who have boats wave as they pass by, because we have this thing in common that other people don't get. A lot of my friends are shocked at how easygoing I can be about things like canceling plans. My outlook is just, you do you. I'm not interested in forcing anyone to do anything because pain taught me how hard it was to be forced to do things that I didn't want to or couldn't do.

Now that my pain was gone (for now, though hopefully forever), I didn't know what to do with myself. I missed it because I knew who I was with it. I knew what my days looked like, what my life was. I knew my limits, I knew what my brain and body could handle. Now, without it, I had all this space, all this ability, all this freedom, and I was at a loss. So much of my life had been spent managing this pain, and here I was again, facing the absence of the one thing my entire world had been built around, trying to figure out what happens when it goes away. When I had to quit swimming and then rowing, I struggled with the loss of my identity as an athlete. When Covid canceled my performances, I panicked at a world where I couldn't be a comedian. But here I was, finally free of something bad, something that had taken over my whole life against my will, and I was lost all the same. What would I do now that I didn't have to manage my pain? I never wanted to be someone who was in pain, and now I didn't know how to be someone who wasn't.

My back pain was a defining facet of my identity. I'm a comedian and writer. I'm addicted to Diet Coke. I went to Cornell and bring it up way too often given that it's the safety school of the Ivy League. I swim for exercise because I still remember the feeling of winning all those ribbons. I'm a Bravo junkie. And I'm someone with chronic pain. I'm someone who will cancel plans often because I have to, not because I'm flaky. I'm someone who overdoes it on wine and martinis from time to time, probably in an attempt to manage pain I don't even recognize consciously. But now what? Who am I when the pain is in my rearview rather than in my bones?

I'm learning that I'm . . . the same. Oddly enough, life without pain isn't really that different, except for having fewer excuses for canceling plans. Day-to-day, sure, it makes me freer and less exhausted and arguably nicer, but it doesn't change who I am. My pain is a part of me, even when it's gone. I may no longer spend hours awake while I try to find a sleeping position that doesn't cause a burning sensation down my legs, but that was my reality for a long time, and it made me who I am.

I think a lot about how bad I felt after I almost died at age nineteen. I think about my guilt for not becoming a perfect survivor, for not changing my worldview because I was lucky to be alive. For years I carried that around, and on some of my darker days I let it be the match to ignite the flames of depression. I felt bad about who I was just for being alive. But that's who I am. I'm glad that surviving the horrors of my spine surgery and blood clot didn't turn me into someone I didn't recognize. Who would that person be? How would that person have handled a life of chronic pain, of multiple surgeries, of so much loss? My pettiness and laziness and selfishness all weirdly felt like they prepared me to manage a life of pain. And now that my pain is possibly gone, I'm still grateful I am all of these things.

Our identity isn't just who we are *right now*. It's cumulative. It's everything we've been that brought us to this moment. I'm not one thing at a time, but rather this snowball of millions of moments and experiences and thoughts that rolled downhill into one person and is still gathering more every day.

It's the good and the bad, the nice and the nasty, the skinny jeans and the confusing wide-legs that seemingly work with no comfortable shoes. I've spent so much of my life obsessed with who I am at the moment that sometimes it's easy to forget I became her over time. We're lucky to pick and choose which parts of ourselves to lean on in different moments, because it means we (groan) contain multitudes! The "bad" things should be just as important as the "good" things. My pain is a bad thing to me, a horrible experience, a burden, but it's why I'm the person that my people know and (hopefully) love. My missteps in friendships, my love of reality television, my detachment from wanting a family, my chronically online existence: These parts of who I am are not "bad" when considered within the whole. They're just as much a part of me as the "good," like my undying support for my friends and family, my thoughtfulness in my comedy, my sympathy and understanding for those in pain, my always having snacks on hand in case someone stops by. They are all just me.

ACKNOWLEDGMENTS

Oh my god I can't believe I have to keep writing, I thought I was done! What the hell? I'm kidding, this is the part I was the most excited to get to. There aren't enough pages in the world to honor all the people I would like to thank.

I have to start with my brilliant, thoughtful, funny editor, Clio Seraphim. I knew you were the right person for the job when we spent an entire meeting talking about designer jeans from 2009. There is no way this book would be one one-thousandth as good without you and your incredible guidance. Thank you also to Whitney and Leila and the entire Dial and PRH teams for supporting this book from the beginning. A special thank-you to everyone at Random House who is still here from when I was an assistant (Hi, Ruth!).

Of course, a huge thank-you to my excellent literary agent at UTA, Meredith Miller, whose perspective and expertise helped take this from some random ideas to a complete proposal to a book that is now out in the real world. I've been so lucky to have the help and encouragement of my manager, Katie Newman, at 3 Arts, who has had to hear me be like "Is THIS a television show?" about so many of the essays. And thank you, Chris Burns, my manager when I sold this book. I'd probably still be writing the table of contents for the proposal today if you hadn't kept nudging me to just fucking finish.

I must also mention my friend and assistant-in-arms from so long ago at Random House, Annie Chagnot, who originally bought this book and even planted the seed that now is the time for it, after coming to my show. Speaking of the show, I'd like to thank Mike Lavoie and Carlee Briglia and the whole team who worked on *Oh God, A Show About Abortion*, which is undoubtedly the reason this book exists today.

I know this book is dedicated to them and I mention them a lot in it, but thank you to my parents for both the support and also knowing how to only ask, "So how's the book going?" every couple of phone calls instead of constantly for the last two years.

Thank you, Dr. Peeler, Dr. Hofmann, and the team at Johns Hopkins. You saved my life.

Okay, friend time! So many people deserve thanks. Natasha, you're my stern pair partner for life, and we've been working on our books (your second!!!) in tandem for the last few years in a way that has made this so much easier and more fun (and made me grateful that I just had to write some stories and not . . . everything you do). Alyssa, without our first two ebooks that we wrote on your couch late at night while drinking wine and eating Hershey's Kisses, I would never have known how to actually finish this. Halle, thank you forever for your unending patience while I did this while also doing our podcast. Josh and Maris, you're my friends, neighbors, expert complainers, but most important, fellow authors, who showed me there is a light at the end of the writing tunnel (and it's usually at Brooklyn Inn).

My other friends who have been a true support system through this entire process, from being a sounding board for ideas and jokes to just listening to me go on and on about it while we hang out: Divya, Kris, Andrea, Ilana, Taylor, Liza, Julia, The Nice Gals (Kara, Megan, and Erin, aka the TC's), Sarah, Jared, Team Frankenbaby (Joyelle, Tyrone, Jordan, Donwill, Sam, Josh), Siobhan, Justin and Gabrus (The Beach Charter), Kristen, Audrey and Jimmy, Emmy and Nick, and everyone else my brain is too mushy to name. I could go on and on about the unending support of my friends in this and in every corner of my life, but I've been writing long enough and probably need to wrap this up. If I know you and you're reading this, thank you.

Not to be all "corporations are people," but I do want to thank a few organizations and institutions here, as well. Without the Cornell University English Department, I would not be the writer I am today. And without the New York comedy open-mic and alt-show scene, I wouldn't be the funny writer I am today. Additionally, thank you to every editor and showrunner I have worked with. Thank you to NEW YORK CITY, the greatest city on earth, for being my forever home. Thank you to The RealReal for providing my breaks from writing so I could browse vintage YSL bags when my brain got overworked. And thank you, Diet Coke.

How could I forget my fifteen-pound fuzzy best friend, Rizz? You are the greatest cat on earth. You can have as many bags as you want in the living room!

ABOUT THE AUTHOR

Alison Leiby is a two-time WGA Award–nominated writer and comedian in Brooklyn, New York. She most recently wrote for season 2 of *Life & Beth*. Previously she wrote and was an executive producer for Ilana Glazer's *Comedy on Earth* for Comedy Central. She has also written for *The Marvelous Mrs. Maisel*, *Teenage Euthanasia, The President Show, The Opposition,* and many others. Alison wrote and performed her critically acclaimed solo show *Oh God, A Show About Abortion* at the Cherry Lane Theatre in New York with two extensions. It was named Best Political Comedy of 2021 by *The New York Times*. Alison's freelance writing has appeared in *The New York Times, New York* magazine, *McSweeney's, Vice, The Onion, Cosmopolitan, Marie Claire,* and many others. Her podcast *Ruined* has been named one of *Time* magazine's top ten podcasts of the year.

Instagram: @alisonleiby

ABOUT THE TYPE

■ ■ ■

This book was set in Apollo, a typeface designed by Adrian Frutiger in 1962 for the founders Deberny & Peignot. Born in Interlaken, Switzerland, in 1928, Frutiger became one of the most important type designers in the years after World War II. Between 1948 and 1951, he attended the School of Fine Arts in Zurich, where he studied calligraphy. He received the Gutenberg Prize in 1986 for technical and aesthetic achievement in type.

Books Driven by the Heart

Sign up for our newsletter
and find more you'll love:

thedialpress.com